Making Big Money in 1600

Middle East Studies Beyond Dominant Paradigms
Peter Gran, *Series Editor*

Making Big Money in 1600

The Life and Times
of Isma'il Abu Taqiyya,
Egyptian Merchant

Nelly Hanna

 Syracuse University Press

Library of Congress Cataloging-in-Publication Data
Hanna, Nelly.
    Making big money in 1600 : the life and times of Isma'il Abu
Taqiyya, Egyptian merchant / Nelly Hanna. — 1st ed.
        p.   cm. — (Middle East studies beyond dominant paradigms)
    Includes bibliographical references (p.   ) and index.
    ISBN 0-8156-2749-1 (cloth : alk. paper).—ISBN 0-8156-2763-7 (pbk. : alk. paper)
    1. Abu Taqiyya, Isma'il, d. 1625?   2. Merchants—Egypt—Biography.
3. Family—Egypt—History.   4. Egypt—Commerce—History.   I. Title.
II. Series.
    HC830.A539H36   1998
    380.1'092
    [B]—DC21   97-5469

Contents

Maps / vii

Foreword / ix

Acknowledgments / xiii

Introduction: Sources and Method / xv

1. Perspectives on the Period / 1

2. Merchants and Merchant Families / 15

3. The Structures of Trade / 43

4. Shifting Patterns in Trade / 70

5. Social Structures / 100

6. Shaping the Urban Geography / 119

7. Family Life in the Abu Taqiyya Household / 138

8. Conclusion / 165

Appendix / 177

Notes / 179

Glossary / 191

Bibliography / 197

Index / 205

Maps

1. The Eastern Mediterranean / 3
2. Abu Taqiyya's network of trade routes / 23
3. The northern section of Cairo / 49
4. Cairo / 134

Nelly Hanna is an associate professor of Arabic studies at the American University in Cairo. She is the author of *An Urban History of Bulaq in the Mamluk and Ottoman Periods* and the editor of *The State and Its Servants: Administration in Egypt from Ottoman Times to the Present.*

Foreword
Peter Gran

In this work by Professor Nelly Hanna, seventeenth-century Cairo turns out to be a sophisticated trade and production center, its leading lights well aware of the wider world. As would be the case in Europe (and indeed in any classic European novel), Cairo's men and women were bound to, and torn apart from, each other by property. This picture does not conform to the one we have come to expect: a backwater province in a bygone era. The Ottoman presence in this century turns out to be quite limited. Nor is an image presented that we might apprehend from the Egypt of the Bible with its Oriental despot or Pharaoh. Through Hanna's study, we discover that, although a land system is present, the economy is mercantile, artisanal, and tribal as well. Contrary to our expectations, the urban middle strata are very powerful. Cairo is culturally diverse and in our terms, multinational.

Although the specialist will appreciate this work for the new information it provides—and the information *is* quite new—the general reader will find much that is fascinating in this book as well. The world presented here eludes a sophisticated application of the dominant paradigm, such as is found in world systems research.

Defying established assumptions concerning early modern history about Egypt's undeveloped society, Hanna overwhelms us with a modernity we don't expect to find. In so doing, she uses Cairo to challenge and test these assumptions and, consequently, the paradigm which historians often call the "Rise of the West." For this reason, Hanna's book should be widely read.

• • •

In proposing the series "Beyond Dominant Paradigms," I was thinking about how our age is blessed or cursed by a recognition that its way of conceiving its own past is inadequate and must give way to something more comprehensive. What that comprehensive "something" is is not yet apparent. What interests me is how should Middle East studies attempt to contribute to this new, more comprehensive picture of world culture.

The paradigm followed by most contemporary historians studying the past five hundred years can still be described as the "Rise of the West" paradigm, a phrase taken from the well-known book by William McNeill. These scholars perceived northwest Europe to have been responsible for changing the world and moving it forward. This paradigm and its supporters emphasize the role of Europe from the Italian Renaissance onward, incorporating into the process the German Reformation and the economic development occurring first in Holland, then in France, and finally in England. What much of the new generation of historians (Nelly Hanna among them) is reacting to is a sense of dissatisfaction with the "Rise of the West" paradigm. Even if a particular study highlights something else altogether, it is made to conform to the contours of the history of northwest Europe.

To its critics then, this paradigm has enjoyed a rather illegitimate prestige that has allowed it to ride roughshod over areas where its flawed premises help obscure reality. One such area is the Mediterranean. For some years, the theory of sudden stagnation, i.e., the Baroque period, invented to explain the collapse of a mighty Spain, has troubled scholars. For some years, Italian historians have complained about the Italian Renaissance as well. Italian history and culture do not benefit from being periodized this way. More recently, questions have been raised about 1798 and the "Coming of the West" to Egypt and to the Middle East. Egyptian history is not so stagnant that it needs to be stirred up by a Napoleon. Indeed, as one progresses further and further away from the privileged terrain of northwest Europe, the defects of the paradigm become clearer and clearer.

If sugar, slaves, and other commodities in the Atlantic bring a higher revenue than textiles and spices in the Mediterranean, does the Mediterranean really become a backwater, irrelevant to the conceptualization of the modern world? Does bigger mean more modern? Does what is more modern displace what is more traditional? Have we abandoned vassalage, tax-farming, mercantilism, etc., or do these conditions live on under different names?

A number of assumptions of the dominant paradigm are brought into question in *Making Big Money in 1600*. Reading Professor Hanna's book, any thoughtful reader is forced to rethink what he or she understands to be the origins of the modern world.

Acknowledgments

In the course of the many years this project has taken to come to fruition, I have incurred numerous debts to friends and colleagues who gave me support at its different stages, from the time the idea of writing about Isma'il Abu Taqiyya was conceived until the moment it appeared in print. Amir Sonbol encouraged me from the start to develop my ideas into a book. We had many long discussions about Abu Taqiyya and his times, and her help was always forthcoming. With Raouf Abbas, who read the manuscript at various stages, I had an ongoing dialogue on the specifics of the text as well as on its fundamental issues. He generously shared with me the breadth of his historical knowledge. Jack Guiragossian's criticism of the text reflected the reaction of a lay reader and helped clarify the obscurities that may have been comprehensible only to historians. His many insightful remarks of the text were very important to me as I was writing. André Raymond, Afaf Marsot, and Peter Gran read the manuscript and made comments and suggestions for changes, clarifications, and elaborations. My thanks also go to Guilaine Alleaume in the CEDEJ, Cairo, for many discussions we had and for her help in making the maps included in the volume. The practical assistance I received from Amina Elbendary was of great help in the last stages of the book.

I also acknowledge the assistance I had from the American University in Cairo in the form of a grant for release time to help me write this book; and from the Ministry of Justice, which is in charge of the court records of Cairo (housed, at the time I consulted them, in the Registry Department, *shahr 'aqari*).

Introduction
Sources and Method

This book analyzes the activities of Isma'il Abu Taqiyya, a prominent merchant active in Cairo between roughly 1580 and 1625, and through this analysis it examines the social and economic background of the period. Although the study focuses on merchants and their activities, these are examined in the light of the general social, economic, legal, and cultural context. Accordingly, we can put commercial and economic changes in a social, legal, and cultural context, rather than considering economy as an abstract matter removed from any context. The conditions of the period were interlinked, and the life records of Abu Taqiyya can be used to illustrate the way that some of these links came about.

This approach allows us to find explanations for various questions that would not be raised in a study of commercial and economic matters alone. It suggests, for instance, why a merchant invested time and effort in activities that were not directly related to commerce: in large construction schemes, such as the two monumental *wikalas* (commercial warehouses) that Abu Taqiyya built in the heart of the city; in loans he granted, often to people who were close to power; in owning a large house filled with slaves, servants, and employees, that is, indulging in conspicuous consumption. Frequently, an act was motivated by cultural reasons, and these can be identified when we observe all the dimensions of a person's life. Abu Taqiyya's successful commercial ventures were the result of his commercial as well as his social skills and his ability to make and maintain good contacts. Life in the household in many ways reflected his social position outside the house, and, conversely, his own social position as a prominent merchant was enhanced by the kind of household that he headed and the house he lived in.

The study of Abu Taqiyya's life, although interesting in itself, is fur-

xv

ther revealing because it is also an analysis of the group to which he belonged. Merchants appear in a particularly important light during these years, emerging from the anonymity that seems to have characterized their existence in the earlier part of the sixteenth century. The extent and variety of their business dealings—as well as their economic prosperity—at a time when the trade of Egypt is thought to have been in decline is a phenomenon that needs explanation. By looking at the experiences of an individual merchant, we can reach certain conclusions about broader issues involving the roles played by merchants in the changes going on and the ways they adjusted their activities to cope with new conditions. Much of what Abu Taqiyya did was part of the pattern that the other prominent merchants of his generation were following. In the archival sources are recorded the activities of other merchants, such as the Ruwi'i family, the Shuja'i family, the 'Asis, and the Ibn Yaghmurs, who were involved, like him, in the Red Sea trade—their business, their partners, their loans, their investments, and so on—that thus provide comparative material for many aspects of Isma'il Abu Taqiyya's life and his commerce. By studying Abu Taqiyya's life records, we can study an important sector of the merchant community in Cairo during these decades, analyzing his individual conduct in terms of what other merchants of his generation were doing in order to see in which respects his conduct was typical.

In addition, through the study of one particular individual, we can observe the patterns of behavior of elite merchants during this period of flux. Abu Taqiyya was living when troop revolts were taking place in Egypt and other regions of the Ottoman Empire at the end of the sixteenth century. He was also a contemporary to changes in power relations, as a decentralizing process affected the center of power in Istanbul, gradually shifting it toward the provinces. He also witnessed the beginning of a similar process taking place in Egypt as power started shifting from the pasha, representative of Ottoman authority, to local elites. The study analyzes these transformations from the viewpoint of merchants, providing an angle through which to read the history of the period. At the same time, it defines the role played by merchants in bringing such changes about. The fact that merchants had large sums of money gave them a significant weight in shifting the power balance from the center to the periphery. They were not only a focal point around which certain conditions were changing but also significant actors in the adjustments occurring at the time.

Merchants in Cairo were thus playing a role in some of the major events of the time, a role that few sources have elaborated upon, and which has so far remained quite obscure. When major transformations take place in history, they are likely to affect many aspects of life and many layers of society. Often we content ourselves with writing about the top layers—those that are the most visible—mainly because the sources provide us with the most data about them. Historians have uncovered the way that these changes in power structure at the turn of the sixteenth and seventeenth centuries affected the sultan, the pasha governing Egypt, and the local military elites. However, none of the works covering Ottoman Egypt during this period has considered the activities of merchants and their relation to what was going on.[1]

If Abu Taqiyya, rather than any of his colleagues or contemporaries, was chosen to be the central figure here, the reasons are mainly practical ones. For one thing, he went to court very regularly, more often than any other of his colleagues. Court records are the main source for this study, and the data about him are abundant—more so than for any of his contemporaries in his profession, like Ahmad al-Ruwi'i, 'Ali al-Ruwi'i and Nur al-Din al-Shuja'i, 'Uthman and Muhammad Ibn Yaghmur, 'Abdul-Qawi and 'Abdul-Ra'uf al-'Asi, whom he knew and was in touch with, and who were involved in similar kinds of activity as he was. For another, the deeds he recorded in the court registers concern many subjects and elucidate a number of aspects of his dealings—partnerships, loans, and lawsuits, for example—as well as matters regarding his wives and family. At one level then, the life of Isma'il Abu Taqiyya can be taken to be typical of a certain kind of merchant during the period he lived in, the merchant in international trade or in the Red Sea trade, which was a major domain for his activity. At another level, we are dealing with an individual human being, with his own personality and his own idiosyncrasies. In that sense, his life will always remain unique. However, because the court records afford comparative material regarding his peers and his social milieu, it is possible to distinguish between what is typical and what is not.

The merchants included here—Isma'il Abu Taqiyya and many of his colleagues, such as the Ruwi'is, Shuja'is, Al-Dhahabi, the Yaghmurs, the 'Asis, and the Burdaynis—no doubt constituted the top strata of the merchant community in Cairo, who traded long distance and were involved in the Red Sea trade, the most profitable sector. Their business was extensive, both geographically and in terms of its volume. Even though they were only a few merchants from a much larger merchant community working in Cairo at the time, their acts were in some important ways representative of the dominant trends of the period. The very status of these merchants and the amounts of money that they were investing are an indication of a trend. More than once, Abu Taqiyya raised close to one million *nisfs* (the smallest unit of silver currency in use during the Otto-man period) for a particular trading venture, and al-Shuja'i was able to raise close to two million within his immediate family circle. These were no trifling sums, but such investments were also of importance in setting patterns for others to follow on a smaller scale. Furthermore, the com-modities they dealt in—most notably, spices, coffee, textiles, and sugar—were the major items in demand in Istanbul and many other regions of the Empire as well as in Europe. Their activity was thus very much in the mainstream of the trade of this period.

On the methodological level, because such a study emphasizes the concrete aspects of a person's life and the daily matters confronting that particular individual, it is a way of approaching history from the inside out. The kind of data it emphasizes and builds upon is the daily and the commonplace. One can, through such a microstudy, read the history of the period through people, not states, and through the daily functions of life, not state decisions and policies. It is on the basis of the microstudy that the conceptions are formulated, rather than the other way round, as is often done, by looking at data in relation to a model that was developed with regard to another period, or another culture, and explaining history by seeing where the model fits or where it does not fit. Histories of the Middle East have often relied too heavily on models from other regions and their elaboration and have not always paid the necessary attention to the documentary evidence, which is abundant for most parts of the Otto-man Empire starting with the sixteenth century. Biography shows another picture of the same reality and thus helps us to read history from below.

The study of Abu Taqiyya shows the intertwining of his individual life with the contemporary social and economic processes. It thus combines two levels of reality. On one level are the particular details of this mer-chant's daily dealings—the people he did business with, the merchandise he bought or sold, the agents and partners who helped him build his network. It shows how he witnessed, participated in, influenced, and was affected by some of the transformations taking place in commerce, in society, in the city, and in his own family. The second level has to do with more general considerations affecting the economy and society during the period at the end of the sixteenth century and the beginning of the seventeenth. The life story of that merchant is, in fact, used to write a history of the period he lived in. In the course of the four decades or so that the court records allow us to follow Isma'il Abu Taqiyya—from the time he was a young man; to his rise to become *shahbandar al-tujjar,* head of the Cairo merchants' guild; to his death, a somewhat disappointed man—we live, through his experience, some of the important economic, social, and political currents and trends in Egypt in those critical decades.

Court Records as a Source for Socioeconomic History

The period covered here is one of the most obscure in the history of Ottoman Egypt. One reason for this is related to sources, since very few chronicles or histories cover it. The little that historians have written is often either based on European sources or sources from other regions of the Ottoman Empire and applied by extension.

Material on individual lives is often not available for the premodern period. We do not have, in Middle Eastern history, the diaries or private correspondence that form the basis for many biographies. What we do have for certain periods is chronicles, of which the most important are al-Jabarti's. His obituary notices sometimes provide invaluable information about a particular person. Unfortunately, such information is rarely sufficient to allow a reconstruction of anyone's life. The obituaries tend to focus on political acts, the deeds of the ruling class, and on violent manifestations of conflict that often occurred in the city. And if the main professional or political events and achievements are mentioned, the lesser events, the more personal features, such as the family, rarely appear. Moreover, al-Jabarti's obituaries deal mainly with specific social groups, notably emirs and religious scholars, *'ulama'.* Other groups are neglected. Only occasionally is a merchant like Qasim al-Sharaybi or Mahmud Muharram mentioned, and other ordinary people have no existence at all.

Moreover, such obituaries of merchants emphasize those events in their lives that stand out, that are unusual—the actions that make people talk about them, those for which they are remembered. The chronicler is hardly concerned with the everyday life and the normal business that a merchant carried out, or with that aspect of his life that did not attract attention because it had to do with the ordinary. Chronicles, in other words, are concerned about a certain dimension in people's lives and almost totally neglect other dimensions. We may therefore confuse the habitual with the exceptional and the ordinary with the unusual. Writing history on the basis of chronicles can easily lead us to assumptions that are quite different from those we reach by using archival material.

And yet in spite of such shortcomings, al-Jabarti's obituaries are an indispensable source of information on the social history of the eighteenth century. Nothing comparable is available for the period before, except for the lives of holy men, by authors like the Sufi writer al-Sha'rani. For the sixteenth and seventeenth centuries the chronicles give us only very meager information about individuals, and usually only in relation to some important event. In general, next to nothing has been written about the social history of Egypt in the seventeenth century, especially the early part. And of the little that has been written about this period, much is simply applied by extension from later periods or earlier ones.

The name of Isma'il Abu Taqiyya does not appear in any contemporary history or chronicle, even though he was a high-ranking merchant who was renowned in his own lifetime. To reconstruct his life, his professional activities, and his place in society, we must therefore look elsewhere for information. Court records have been recognized as a valuable source of material on life in the city. A number of studies have appeared in the last few years showing how these archives can be used for social and economic histories. Social life, relationships between merchants and the ruling military elite in eighteenth-century Cairo and between religious communities in sixteenth-century Jerusalem, and the position of women in seventeenth-century Bursa, are among the subjects that historians have explored through the study of court archives.[2] This book is, nevertheless, the first time that these archives have been used to reconstruct an individual life history.

The archival material used here, the court records of Cairo, is alive with daily life—the problems that people encountered with business partners, with family, and with neighbors and the alternatives that were offered as solutions. This material is mainly about ordinary people—artisans, workers, traders. When it deals with people like Isma'il Abu Taqiyya, who was obviously more than an ordinary person, it is in connection with the routine matters he dealt with daily, rather than with any particular event he was associated with, for which he would go down in history. These records show us another level of reality: We see how various institutions functioned and what their relationship was to ordinary people.

A number of factors encouraged people to use the courts extensively. Justice was simple and quick. People who were not highly educated or sophisticated could have immediate access to justice. It was not necessary to have a lawyer to act as intermediary between the claimant and the judge, nor did people have to wait for months to have a judgment on a case. As a matter of practicality, numerous courtrooms were set up in the various districts of the city and were thus accessible for almost all its inhabitants. Every court, moreover, had representatives from the four legal schools of Islam (Hanafi, Shafi'i, Maliki, Hanbali), and a claimant had the right to choose whichever he or she liked. The same person could go to a Hanbali *qadi* (judge) when he or she was buying or renting a house and to a Hanafi *qadi* to get married; there was no obligation to stick to a particular *madhhab* (school of law). A more important factor that encouraged people to take their disputes to court perhaps, was that the *qadi*s took into consideration, when applying the law, the *'urf* (habits and traditions) of people. A matter about which the *shari'a* contained no specific provisions was decided according to the *'urf*. Consequently, in questions related to guilds, or to urban regulations, for instance, *'urf* was often taken into consideration. For these reasons, courtrooms were usually full of people, as the numerous daily entries in the registers testify.

The Ottoman administration was partly responsible for the extension in the competencies of the courts. Once the Ottoman armies had conquered a region, the control of the region was to a large extent left to administrative structures rather than to military ones. The courts, notably, in addition to their duties in the application of the *shari'a* (Islamic Law) were also partly responsible for the announcement to the public and eventual application of administrative decrees or decisions. The orders issued by the sultan in Istanbul were occasionally recorded in the registers of the courts of Cairo so that they could be referred to. Moreover, problems and disputes related to customs duties, or to the imposition of taxes, were dealt with by the *qadi*s. In these respects the courts were a significant part of the administrative system.

My study of Isma'il Abu Taqiyya is based entirely on the court records —several hundred court cases in which he appears as a claimant or a partner in a business venture or a witness. Of the fifteen courtrooms in Cairo, located in the various parts of the city, Abu Taqiyya had a preference for one in particular, the court of Bab'Ali. This was the main court (*al-mahkama al-kubra*) of the capital, in the city center.[3] It was located a few hundred meters from his house and within a short walking distance from the business area where he worked. But it was also the most prestigious court of Cairo, because it was presided upon by the Qadi al-Qudat, the head of the judiciary system in Egypt, sent from Istanbul. He occasionally used other courthouses, such as the court of al-Salihiyya al-Najmiyya and that of the Qisma 'Askariyya, but to a lesser extent. The details of Abu Taqiyya's life can be pieced together by the hundreds of court cases—mainly from the registers of Bab 'Ali court—in which he was involved over a period of nearly forty years.

The cases throw light on a number of aspects of life in this period. For one thing, we get a clear picture of how trade was conducted. This is particularly important in view of the fact that historians have so often stated that Middle Eastern merchants have not left us with any commercial papers. The documents in these archives are not only very detailed but also very varied, providing us with information about different kinds of dealings and transactions—sales on credit, loans, and partnerships, for example—as well as different ways these could be carried out, according to the stature and wealth of the merchants making a deal or according to the *madhhab* to which they had recourse. Through these documents we can piece together the trading patterns and commercial techniques of this period, and, crucial for a period undergoing transformations, the adaptability of these patterns and techniques to changing conditions. The documents therefore offer the historian invaluable material about the way that business was actually carried out, in contrast to, and as a complement to, studies like that of Abraham Udovitch, which concentrated on what works on jurisprudence had to say about the various forms of business dealings.[4]

Consequently, this body of archival material allows the historian to write a history of the region by using the indigenous contemporary sources. So much of the commercial history of the Middle East has been written on the basis of European sources—consular reports, company correspondence, and travelers' accounts—that certain biases, such as an overemphasis of the importance of trading relations with Europe during this period, cannot be avoided.[5] The court records, with all the rich details they contain on trade, can help the historian to approach the subject from the inside rather than from the outside.

Another significant feature of this body of archival material is related to the way that structures and institutions are portrayed. Rather than being seen as the embodiment of principles or ideologies—ideal systems unrelated to the realities of life around them—institutions such as the court system, for instance, appear in a dynamic relationship with the people who dealt with them or came into contact with them. Court records show how justice was actually practiced on a daily basis. The fact that the court system was supposed to embody the ideal of justice in no way lessened its impact on people's daily lives and activities. The ideal that the system represented did not prevent people from finding ways to further their ends.[6]

Court archives also can help us to better understand one of the least known aspects of premodern society—that of private, personal, and family life. Much of the work done on this subject has been based on religious works and legal literature, such as *hadith* (compilations of the traditions of the Prophet) and *fiqh* (the jurisprudence of the *shari‘a*). *Fiqh,* which provides elaborate legal opinions on matters of personal status, can be very significant in showing how these opinions evolved. But as far as practice is concerned, the daily problems brought to the *qadi* (judge or magistrate) and the solutions that were elaborated with regard to conjugal problems and family disputes are an indispensable source for the history of the family. The archival material available touches on other personal and private aspects of life that have escaped historians entirely—for example, the place of minors and children in the family, the relationships between brothers and sisters, and the place of friendship in people's lives. The archival material is particularly important because heretofore we have known nothing about such aspects of life during this period. The emphasis that has been placed on the position of women in the family, vital as it is, has tended to obscure other relationships, sometimes just as important, between different family members. The hints about these matters that we find in court cases are therefore very valuable for the light they shed on a domain that is still very obscure.

The study of Abu Taqiyya illuminates the role of the courts in family life. It is very significant that this body, closely involved in all aspects of personal status, functioned as an intermediary in family disputes. Various family members, including wives and children, had recourse to the courts to redress wrongs done to them. When the Abu Taqiyya children reached their majority, for instance, it was to the court that they addressed themselves to accuse their legal guardian of trying to prolong his guardianship. And when Umm al-Hana Abu Taqiyya's husband violated the clauses in their marriage contract, it was to the court that she made her accusation against him. In fact, people addressed family problems to the *qadi* even in cases when their family disputes could have been solved within the family circle. Our concept of the patriarchal structure of the family in the premodern period must therefore take into consideration the existence of these courts and the way that family members had recourse to them.[7]

The court cases about Isma'il Abu Taqiyya and his family show him not only in the context of his marriages to four different women, but also in the context of other relationships: with Yasin Abu Taqiyya, his brother, a relationship that went through different stages; with his sister Laila, a relationship that was tumultuous at times; and with his friend and colleague 'Abdul-Qadir al-Damiri, a long and stable relationship that lasted nearly forty years. Relationships like the one between Abu Taqiyya and Damiri are very revealing because the line between friendship and family is not as clear-cut as one might think; one could argue that this relationship is part of the private sphere of life that is associated with family only. Rather than applying models that may or may not fit the situation, the study takes the analysis of the situations as a starting point. This opens new perspectives, not only on how family was structured, but on how different members had a role to play in defining this structure, especially those members who may not have been visible to an outsider's eyes. Seen from this perspective, the family structure of the Abu Taqiyya household can be understood in terms of a number of different sets of relationships. Rather than portraying the family in terms of the flat patriarchal structure with which historians have often contented themselves, this approach not only reveals other dimensions within the structure but also shows that these dimensions are all interrelated.

Court records are also a very useful source for the analysis and understanding of particular social groups, whether a particular professional group such as merchants, or a cultural or ethnic group such as Syrians or Turks. In the case of the Abu Taqiyyas, because the family came from Hums and maintained close relationships of various kinds with persons of the same background who had settled in Cairo, we can observe some of the patterns of behavior of Syrians in Cairo and see how the Abu Taqiyya family fit into that community. It was fairly easy for a merchant family from a Syrian town to move to Cairo, and such a relocation did not entail any social marginalization upon their arrival. The Abu Taqiyyas, like several other merchants families of Syrian origin who moved to Cairo around the same time, were integrated into the merchant community and did not undergo any serious loss of status upon coming to Cairo. Their patterns for choosing business partners, spouses, and neighbors can indicate the degree of integration of this group into the society of Cairo. The development of this process of integration becomes evident by a comparison of patterns between one generation and the other.

The court records provide us also with important insights on urban history. We know next to nothing about the history of Cairo during this period—the kind of development it may have experienced, or why. The data regarding Abu Taqiyya and the merchants of his generation reveal not only the shape and the direction of urban development but also, more significantly perhaps, the role of merchants in this development. During this period merchants were playing a role that in earlier periods had often belonged to the rulers, the sultans and their emirs. Their public buildings and their development of new quarters in the city brought them a visibility on the urban scene that few merchants had had before.

In spite of the fact that one of the court's major functions was to mitigate cases of litigation, the archives contain much more than disputes between individuals. People willingly took cases to court that went far beyond such disputes. The result is that in many ways these records are a mirror of people's daily lives, much in the same way as the Geniza documents (found in an old synagogue in Cairo and studied by S. D. Goitein) mirrored the lives of the members of the Jewish Community in this city during the thirteenth and fourteenth centuries. (This is true for a large city like Cairo but may not necessarily be the case in smaller towns or in provincial areas where other less formal bodies may have played more important roles in people's lives.)

With all the important data that court records can offer historians, yet they too have their weaknesses in some domains. Court archives do not show us what was the image that society or that his contemporaries had of Abu Taqiyya. The kind of impression a chronicler like al-Jabarti or al-Damardashi was likely to record about a person is entirely absent here, so that this aspect of a public figure escapes us entirely when we deal with this type of source. We do not known what his contemporaries said of him or thought of him, if the acts he undertook were socially acceptable, praised or blamable. We do not know what people thought of his links to those in power.

Moreover, another aspect of life that remains fairly obscure is the

spiritual and religious. For obvious reasons, Abu Taqiyya's religious attitudes, important as they may have been, are not perceptible through these
records. Except for the hints we get from knowing that he reconstructed
a mosque in al-Azbakiyya or that the *wikala* (commercial warehouse) he
constructed contained a *masjid* (small mosque), we know next to nothing
about his religious life. He seems to have had some links to the growing
Sufi movement, notably the Sadat al-Wafa'iyya Sufi order whom he included among the beneficiaries of his *waqf* (religious endowments). In all
likelihood, his family maintained these links when he was gone, since his
granddaughter, Karima b. Zakariyya, was married to the *shaykh al-sijada*
of the Wafa'iyya.[8] This very prestigious title was given to the heads of a
few Sufi orders (like the Wafa'iyya and the Bakriyya), who claimed descent
from a companion of the prophet—'Ali b. Abi Talib for the Wafa'iyya,
and Abu Bakr for the Bakriyya. However, our sources are silent on the
nature of this relationship. On these matters, the biography of Abu Taqiyya must be incomplete.

Chapter Division

Each of the chapters deals with a particular aspect of Abu Taqiyya's life:
his commercial activity, his relations to those in power, his prominence in
the urban scene, and his family. At the same time, each chapter (except
for chapter 2, which presents his life chronologically) covers a stage in his
life, first as a young merchant, in his twenties or so, learning the ins and
outs of his profession; then as a successful merchant, in his thirties or
forties bringing adjustments to his trading patterns. In his forties or fifties,
he enjoys some of the social side-benefits that prominent merchants could
attain, and in the last decade of his life we see how his successful commercial ventures were reflected in his household and family structure.

Chapter 1 provides a conceptual framework that helps to put the half
century during which Isma'il Abu Taqiyya lived in the broader perspective
of Middle Eastern history and of more general seventeenth-century
history.

Chapter 2, which covers his life chronologically, points out some of
his associations, either formal or informal—with family, with partners,
with the Syrian community, and with the merchant community.

Chapter 3 is more specifically concerned with the structures and institutions for trading through which commercial ventures were funded and

organized. Abu Taqiyya would have had to familiarize himself with these at the beginning of his career, around the 1580s.

Chapter 4 analyzes the major changes that affected the economic conditions of merchants, with their emancipation from bureaucratic control and their increased Red Sea trade. It also traces Abu Taqiyya's involvement in sugar production. This stage in his career came after he had made large enough sums of money from trade to be able to invest in agriculture and production, in the late 1590s onwards.

Chapter 5, which covers the first decade or so of the seventeenth century, analyzes the social repercussions of these changes. Rather than becoming agents of the state or ruling bureaucracy, merchants became a group to be taken into consideration, sharing interests sometimes, and rivalries at other times, with those in the power structure. The social position of Abu Taqiyya was enhanced by his wealth. His involvement in agriculture, moreover, put him in close contact with the military groups that were rural *multazim*s (holders of a tax concession, tax farmers).

Chapter 6 reflects one of the major consequences of the emergence of merchants: their contribution to the urban scene, the buildings and quarters that bear their names. Merchants of the period started playing a role which in the past had been dominated by the ruling class. Towards the end of his life, Abu Taqiyya became involved in major construction projects that left landmarks in the city.

Chapter 7 turns to the inside of the home, analyzing family and private life. We see how life in the house of a merchant was conducted and observe the effects of the development of socio-economic conditions on family structure and on relationships between members of the family. This chapter covers the last years of Abu Taqiyya's life, once he had reached the peak of his career, and follows the family for a while after his death.

Chapter 8, the conclusion, places the findings of the book in the general context of the history of Egypt and emphasizes their significance for understanding the region as a whole during this crucial period.

Making Big Money in 1600

I

Perspectives on the Period

This study of Isma'il Abu Taqiyya's life records is also a study of merchants and commercial activity during the last decades of the sixteenth century and the first decades of the seventeenth. Because this period is one of the more obscure in the history of Egypt, on which research has been very limited, we have not been able to ascertain precisely its relationship to the periods before and after it. As a result, we have missed seeing how different periods were linked together and processes of change developed. One of my objectives here is to take a step in this direction. Through studying the life of one particular merchant who lived during this period, we can perhaps find a better way of understanding the half century between the end of the sixteenth century and the beginning of the seventeenth and putting it in a broader historical context.

During this half century, the region was being transformed. Various interpretations have been put forward to understand these changes. Until recently, the period following the death of Sultan Sulayman was considered the beginning of the decline of the Ottoman Empire, and the history of the centuries from then until the dissolution of the Empire in 1914 was viewed in terms of the decline.[1] A number of prominent historians, such as Bernard Lewis and Stanford Shaw, have emphasized military defeats and losses of territory as a measure of decline. Although the concept of attributing major changes to wars has been largely discarded by scholars studying European history, it continues to be applied to the Ottoman world. Historians employing this concept consider that decline and stagnation were arrested as the Ottomans realized, in the eighteenth and nineteenth centuries, that to keep apace with the expanding European powers they had to import models from Europe to renovate their administration and their military establishment as well as their educational and cultural institutions.[2]

There has been a similar approach to the economic history of the Ottoman lands. The economy is considered to have been stagnant until the nineteenth-century reforms of production, agriculture, and communication, usually based on European models or implemented on European initiatives, regenerated the region. Even Fernand Braudel's monumental work on the Mediterranean in the sixteenth century tends to downplay the eastern part of the Mediterranean, while emphasizing the dynamism of its northern borders on the European side.[3] Another approach to economic history emphasizes that the Islamic Mediterranean world lost its importance in the commercial currents of this period and became a backwater as a result of the new Atlantic trade routes and the direct routes to Asia, which bypassed these lands. Such views, however, were formulated before historians began to seriously study what was taking place in this region during the period and examine its voluminous archival sources.

Other reasons have been suggested to explain the stagnation of trade. Some of the internal factors were related to the weak position of merchants within the Ottoman state. By confiscating the merchants' surpluses, the government discouraged them from undertaking major money-making ventures. In addition, greedy customs officials took another portion of the merchants' gains, making it very hard for them to accumulate any significant capital. Other explanations, for the stagnation in trade are related to the merchants' trading techniques, which had become stagnant and had not been adapted to the challenges of a modern economy. Only with the introduction of western-style reforms in the nineteenth century was the situation reversed.

At the present time, more and more historians are finding these views that emphasize stagnation unsatisfactory. They challenge the approach that analyzes the region essentially in terms of its Westernization, using a chronology and concepts proper to European history, stressing the Western impact on traditional society as the main impetus for change and treating the history of the period prior to this impact as static or in decline, with inadequate and antiquated institutions and structures that were too rigid to be adaptable to new conditions and capable of change only as a result of external stimuli. Rather, these historians consider change from within to be particularly worthy of attention.

Reacting to the decline framework, historians like Rifa'at 'Ali Abou-El-Haj have attempted to understand the history of the Ottoman Empire between the sixteenth and eighteenth centuries in terms of a wider context

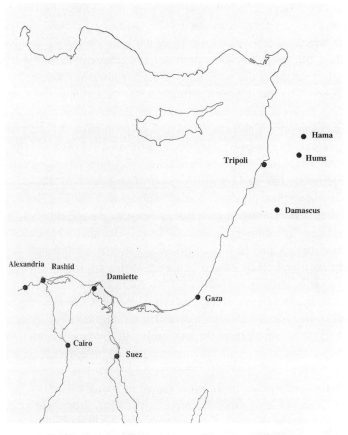

1. The Eastern Mediterranean. Courtesy of CEDEJ.

that includes the trends apparent in early modern Europe. In *The Formation of the Modern State: The Ottoman Empire, Sixteenth to Eighteenth Centuries,* Abou-El-Haj proposes to drop the notion of the uniqueness of Ottoman history and the emphasis on what is odd or unique (such as the royal cage where the sultan's rivals for power were put) and instead to see it as comparable to other histories—that is, to attempt to understand the broader social and economic processes that were taking place.[4] Thus, rather than consider the weakening of the sultanate in Istanbul as a sign of general decline, this approach would analyze it in terms of a power shift that allowed other groups to emerge and play a greater social and economic role.

A number of other scholars have applied the theory of incorporation into European capitalist economy to the Ottoman Empire. The process through which incorporation took place has been elaborated in a number of studies, but with different emphases and different dates for it. Huri Islamoglu-Inan dates the beginning of the peripheralization of the Ottoman economy to the sixteenth century, when the central administration, which had controlled the main aspects of the economy, such as the pricing of main commodities and the restriction or prohibition of the export of basic goods in short supply, started losing this control. Because the Ottoman state maintained tariffs on a number of commodities, especially on basic foodstuffs like grain and on raw materials such as those used by textile workers, their price was considerably lower than in Europe, which at the time was experiencing a price increase in a large number of basic commodities. Accordingly, merchants in the Ottoman Empire exported these raw materials to European markets, often as contraband. Both Islamoglu-Inan and Resat Kasaba believe that this contraband trade was a major factor in starting the process of incorporation.[5]

My book shares some of the views developed in these new approaches. I consider that the local, regional, and international developments occurring in the second half of the sixteenth and the seventeenth centuries were indeed vital in terms of the currents of trade, of routes, of commodities, of supply and demand. These transformations were important enough to have worldwide reverberations, affecting different regions in different ways. One of these regions was the Ottoman world in general and Egypt in particular. The changes that occurred in trading patterns and networks in these regions were an important aspect of the global changes, but one that is still little known. Although we have considerable knowledge about how these transformations affected markets and merchants in Europe, we know much less about the way that markets and merchants in the Middle East were affected and how they adapted their networks and patterns to such changes. This book concentrates on the way that merchants, Abu Taqiyya and his contemporaries, dealt with some of them. Thus, rather than considering the changes in internal or external conditions as ushering in decline to Middle Eastern and Mediterranean trade, or understanding this trade in terms of European impact, my study of Abu Taqiyya explores the way merchants were affected by the conditions of the time and brought certain adjustments to their businesses. It thus suggests understanding the economic and commercial history of Egypt in terms of its reactions in the face of new conditions, some of which were obviously negative, but others more positive, such as the increase in demand for certain commodities that merchants in Cairo were able to provide. In spite of European expansion along trading routes that had traditionally been dominated by Muslim merchants, some of the merchants still found ways to maintain extended networks. Even though Atlantic trade routes carried a much greater amount of merchandise, the Mediterranean trade did not necessarily lose its dynamism. A complex picture thus emerges of the trading world of Cairo as its actors were confronted both by new challenges to their livelihood and new possibilities for gain.

In a number of points, however, I do not concur with views formulated within the incorporation framework. In the first place, many historians adhering to this view were concerned primarily with the elaboration of a model. Their concern for documentary evidence was secondary. One consequence of this approach is the absence of specificity about place and the presumption that the world outside of the capitalist core could be treated as one undifferentiated mass. The implications are that the conditions described could apply to Anatolia in the same way as to the Balkans or to the Arab lands—unlikely, given the size of the Ottoman Empire and the condition of transport and communication in the premodern period. So little attention is given to the differences between one region and another, and to the historical developments taking place there, it is as if these had no effect on the way incorporation occurred or was applied. My study of Abu Taqiyya traces some of the main economic and social trends of his generation and shows how they may have influenced later developments. We can neither suppose that the kind of state control over the economy was the same everywhere, in distant parts of the Empire as in the central lands, nor presume that the processes bringing about incorporation took the same form. We know that the Ottoman state was eager to maintain the existing structures of the new lands it conquered, thus allowing for much regional diversity. Only after detailed regional studies have been undertaken will historians be able to know how far any model can be applied geographically.

A second problem related to the incorporation framework has to do with the chronology of this process—that is, the date at which a change occurred in the economic patterns, both of trading and of production, whereby importation of finished products curtailed local industries, and whereby the Ottoman Empire became part of the European capitalist economy. This is still a subject of debate.[6] Islamoglu-Inan dates this process to the sixteenth century, Kasaba to the eighteenth. For both, however, it immediately followed the period when the central state was less able to control the economy. The economy passed directly from control by the state to control by the capitalist economies of Europe. It is necessary to conclude from such an argument that at no time was there really an economy moved by its own impetus; instead, it was controlled by an outer force, whether the Ottoman administration or the European traders. This is a very debatable concept, which the voluminous documentary evidence of the period does not support.

If we were to date this process from the time that raw materials were sucked out of the Ottoman Empire and some local industries were negatively affected by the increasing volume of imports, there is no evidence of this becoming a dominant trend in Egypt before the middle of the eighteenth century. Until then, Egypt had had an extensive textile industry, with large-scale exports to North Africa, Syria, Africa, Europe, and various regions within the Ottoman state. In the course of the eighteenth century, observers noted large quantities of European textiles in the market, a trend that was detrimental to the local textile industry.[7] The same comments can be made about the sugar industry, which flourished in the seventeenth century and made the fortune of many merchants who exported this product to foreign markets. The situation changed drastically during the eighteenth century, when the refineries of Marseilles, Trieste, and Fiume started exporting their sugar to a number of centers in the Ottoman Empire, thus depriving the Egyptian sugar industry of some of its major outlets.[8] This reduction in demand for finished products may well have been behind the conversion of large tracts of agricultural land to cash crops destined for export as raw material. The increasing volume of exports of grain to France in the late eighteenth century illustrates this trend,[9] which was intensified greatly with the expansion of cotton plantations in the nineteenth century to produce raw material for the growing textile factories in Europe. The ground was thus laid for the creation of a dependent economy. Because the beginning of the seventeenth century preceded incorporation by some two centuries, the life records of Abu Taqiyya give us a chance to scrutinize commercial activity prior to incorporation—more importantly, during a time many have considered a period of decline.

A third matter of debate related to the concept of incorporation has to do with the relationship between the economy and the state. The study of merchants and commercial activity challenges the view that the economy went to pieces and crumbled when the central authorities, for various reasons, were unable to maintain their control over it, or that a well-run economy had to be politically controlled.[10] I thus concur with the approach developed by Abou-El-Haj insofar as it suggests that a significant factor in the reemergence of merchants in Cairo was that the state was less involved in their business than in earlier times, thus allowing them greater possibilities for gain. This study, consequently, challenges the view that a high level of efficiency occurred only when the economy was controlled by outside forces, either by the state-run system of Muhammad 'Ali or by a European capitalist system, and the view that economic forces became operable only with modernization in the nineteenth century.

On another level, the internal functioning of the economy and society is also a matter of debate among scholars. According to one view, before the modern period outdated structures, ossified for centuries, were a barrier to innovation. This static view of Ottoman society as a passive and immovable mass implies that social groups and the institutions or structures available to them were unable to react to change, much less bring it about. This view has been adopted by scholars who adhere to the concept of decline as well as those who favor the theory of incorporation. Scholars taking an approach centered on the capitalist world system, for example, have tended to consider peripheries as only passive recipients for the active forces coming from external stimulus. Historians like Huri Islamoglu-Inan and Resat Kasaba concur on this point with the views of Hamilton Gibb and Harold Bowen, whose study of the eighteenth century emphasized this passivity. Gibb and Bowen applied this concept to all aspects of life, not just the economy. They indicated that powerful controls were exercised over individual activity—both by traditions that dictated a person's conduct and by family, professional, and other structures—to the extent that initiative was not only stifled but, in their view, nonexistent. Rigid rules set by families, by guilds, by the state, or by religious law controlled conduct.[11] A concept underlying these opinions is that the social and economic structures functioned as a result of controls from above. Without such controls the structures fell apart and had to be replaced by more viable ones. This approach, emphasizing change from above, gives little or no importance to the possibility of change from below or organic change.

It is precisely these matters that this book addresses. From the life records of Abu Taqiyya, we can see how merchants made significant structural adjustments to their trading patterns, their initiatives occurring in an attempt to adjust to the changing conditions. They did this independently of the expansion of the European capitalist economy and of the incorporation of Ottoman lands; consequently, we see an indigenous system at work. The associations that merchants had, both formal and informal, and the ways that merchants used legal and commercial institutions involved in trade (most notably, the courts and the *wikalas*) to fulfill their needs show that these structures were not rigid or stagnant, as they have often been called, but quite the contrary—pliable and easy to maneuver. Many of the tools of trade and the trading patterns used by merchants had long been known, but during Abu Taqiyya's lifetime merchants were using them to various ends and adapting them to the particular conditions of the period.

New Trends in Egyptian Trade

The adjustments in commercial activity during this period conform to certain patterns. Their features are significant enough to have repercussions not only on commerce but on production and agriculture, and to leave their mark on social structures. There was even a development in the legal system at about the same time. This is not to say that the economic patterns shaped the way that justice was run, but instead that the transformations taking place were part of a broader picture, going beyond the commercial success of a handful of people, and that the role of the courts was a significant factor in the development of the trade of this period. We can see some similarities between this situation and that in Europe, which was experiencing what has been called the seventeenth-century crisis, a time of revolt and unrest everywhere; numerous explanation have been offered, among them that this turbulent period marked the transition from a feudal to a capitalist society,[12] and that it marked a change in the relation between state and society.[13] With regard to the Ottoman Empire, Abou-El-Haj suggests that the violence and unrest occurring at the end of the sixteenth century and the beginning of the seventeenth, in which the troops played an important role, was the visible sign of more profound economic and social transformations taking place as well as of the changing character of the state.[14]

Although research on the economic history of this region is still in its infancy, we can nevertheless identify important new elements that were being introduced into the economic life of Egypt during a period that is roughly the lifetime of Abu Taqiyya. (This trend may well have had the parallels in other parts of the Ottoman Empire that future research may identify.) During this period Egypt still formed part of the Ottoman world market but as yet had not been incorporated into the European capitalist market; that is, Egypt's economy had not yet been peripheralized and the region transformed into a producer of raw materials for the powerful core nations in Europe and a market for their finished products. This trend began during the second half of the sixteenth century and continued throughout the seventeenth and part of the eighteenth. The life records of Abu Taqiyya help define the main features of the period and to identify the major players.

The period is characterized by a reemergence of merchants to the fore, in terms of the wealth they accumulated, the social power they gained, and the influence they had on the political scene, directly or indirectly. The trend towards reemergence can be linked to two points. The first is the vitality of international trade. In other Mediterranean and European regions, the increased demand for international goods made the fortune of many merchants. Abu Taqiyya, al-Ruwi'i or Ibn Yaghmur, who made their money from international trade, were roughly the contemporaries of the great European merchant houses such as the Fuggers and Welsers, who emerged at a time when every sector of trade was expanding.[15] The second point is that merchants were less politically controlled, or more autonomous from the state, than they had been half a century or a century earlier.

It is very likely that at that time the title *shahbandar*, gained the prestige that remained attached to it till the early nineteenth century. Although this word was known at an earlier period, it was not until the sixteenth century that it became commonplace in Egypt and that the holder of this title commonly recognized as a person of high status. In studying the life of Abu Taqiyya, we find that this new status was manifested by a high visibility for merchants, partly because of their own efforts. Their large-scale construction projects, often in the choice areas of Cairo, were an announcement of their new position in society. Not only individual buildings for business, religious institutions, and charities but whole quarters now bore the names of prominent merchants. This vitality of construction contrasts with the silence in the chronicles with regard to merchants. It also contradicts the view, presumably based on the chronicles, that merchants tended to remain anonymous.

Moreover, by studying the private life of Abu Taqiyya, we can see how the marriage patterns, family structures and households of merchants were influenced by their growing wealth and prestige. Not only were merchants marrying into elite circles by the early seventeenth century, but a close examination of Abu Taqiyya's family and private life shows how these marriage patterns were adapted in accordance to his position in society. The phenomenon occurring in the end of the sixteenth century and the beginning of the seventeenth touched on numerous aspects of merchants' lives, both public and private. We can better understand the one in terms of the other. Thus, in viewing these interconnected layers of experience, we find that the study of commercial history becomes more than the analysis of a theoretical construct.

Some aspects of the legal system have some relevance to the way commercial activities were run. The life records of Abu Taqiyya shed light on the role of the legal structures in merchant activity and, more specifically, in the commercial revival that was taking place. They suggest that the retraction of the bureaucracy and administration allowed different structures to widen their functions and scope of activity; some of the functions that the state no longer undertook passed on to other bodies.

The system for carrying out justice in Ottoman Egypt was not a novel one. Justice was one of the major functions of the Islamic state, as can easily be observed under the Mamluk dynasty, which ruled Egypt, Syria, and part of the Arabian peninsula between 1250 and 1517, when the Ottoman army destroyed it. Nevertheless, the way the judiciary functioned and its insertion into the social system differed in time and place. A comparison between Mamluk and Ottoman courts is not possible yet, because although the Mamluk state had a very elaborate and sophisticated bureaucracy, we know little about the way that Mamluk courts functioned.[16] But what the evidence shows beyond any doubt is that the courts in Cairo grew in importance between the beginning and the end of the sixteenth century. Not only do the daily entries in the registers of all the courts in the city multiply many times over between, for instance, the 1530s or 1540s and the last decade or so of the century, but the kind of complaint taken to court encompasses a greater variety of matters and the social strata of the plaintiffs include a wider range of people. By the early seventeenth century, the courts of Cairo were involved in the commercial, economic, social, urban, administrative, and personal aspects of people's lives.

In essence, the justice system of the seventeenth century, like that of the preceding periods, had as its primary objective the implementation of the *shariʿa*. Yet at the same time, there is some connection between these changes in the system and the fluctuating social and economic conditions of the period. It is perhaps possible to make a general comparison with the European experience. Marc Bloch, notably, has shown that between the late Middle Ages and the French Revolution there was a significant change in the judiciary system in France, as seignorial jurisdiction, developed in the context of serfdom, gave way to public justice dispensed by courts.[17] Of course, the comparison would not be valid in its details, because neither did seignorial jurisdiction have a parallel in Islamic societies nor did the application of the *shariʿa* have a parallel in European ones. Yet the fact that the early modern period experienced changes that touched the way that justice was applied might itself be regarded as significant.

A business as extensive as that of Abu Taqiyya, al-Ruwiʿi, or al-Shujaʿi could not be run without solid legal and commercial structures. In studying the life of Abu Taqiyya, we can observe the role played by the court institution in different situations that merchants confronted in their daily work. The courts were involved in many public and private aspects of daily life. Ismaʿil Abu Taqiyya went to court when he bought a house and when he built his *wikala* or commercial warehouses. He went there to record his business dealings, to endow or to run a charitable foundation, or to be a guarantor to a debt. At his death, part of the settlement for his inheritance took place in court, including claims for goods and merchandise, debts that were to be settled, capital set up in partnerships that had to be settled, and so on. The frequency with which he involved the court in a variety of matters is in itself a testimony to the expectations he had about this institution. During certain periods he appears to have been present at court two to three times a week. As far as commerce is concerned, the activities of merchants show what a vital role the courts played in trade, providing legal guarantees to the merchants' deals and ventures, providing them with legal documents they could use in other regions, and sanctioning the various transactions and partnerships they undertook. Abu Taqiyya, for instance, registered in court his partnerships with other merchants, his transactions, and the loans he granted. Merchants seem to have relied on this institution when they undertook complex business dealings on a large scale.

Trade at the end of the sixteenth century had characteristic features. First, although trading in luxury goods, such as gold, coral or precious stones, remained an important feature, we can also observe an active international trade in bulk items such as indigo, a basic item in linen production, and certain textiles. Second, we can observe two currents of trade, one of which was the transit trade whereby merchants in Cairo imported goods for reshipment to further destinations—notably spices, coffee, and Indian textiles coming across the Red Sea and destined for European and Ottoman markets, or wood and metals coming from Mediterranean ports and reshipped to other centers. The other significant current relates to the export of local commodities. Of these, some were raw materials, like rice or grain shipped to Anatolia and the Holy Cities of Mecca and Medina. Others were finished products, like sugar and linen, which were in demand both in the Ottoman lands and in Europe.

I challenge the view formulated by Robert Brenner and other economic historians that prior to industrialization, no significant changes occurred in the economy, and that these remained stagnant or at subsistence level until the industrial revolution.[18] The biography of Abu Taqiyya does not uphold the view that the agriculture of Egypt remained at subsistence level until the nineteenth century. The fact that local commodities —like rice, grain, linen, textiles, and sugar—were regularly exported in considerable quantities indicates that large enough tracts of land were planted with these products to cover local consumption and have enough left over for export. Even though no figures exist for this period to allow us to determine the scale of commercial agriculture, the indications are that it was relatively widespread, at least in certain regions of Egypt. A good example of an agricultural product planted on a commercial scale is sugarcane, which we can follow in some detail through the study of Abu Taqiyya and other contemporary merchants. Thus there is abundant evidence for the existence of cash crops long before the nineteenth century.

Although we have no figures regarding the volume of trade between Egypt and its various trading partners before the nineteenth century, we may discern certain trends. Much of the trading of the period took place within the Ottoman world market, notably, with Anatolia and Syria. Moreover, the Red Sea trade remained extremely active, with spices and coffee dominating this sector. Yet during this period there was also active trading with Europe, in spite of Europe's penetration of Asian markets. We can, in fact, discern a significant demand for certain products—due to factors such as not only the general rise in population but also the increase in spending ability that was a result of the wealth coming in from the New World. Thus during this stage of commercial history, trade with Europe was neither confined to transit goods like coffee or spices, vital as these were, no dominated by the export of raw materials, a pattern that was to dominate commercial relations between Egypt and its European trading partners only at a later date.

The period before incorporation was also characterized by another feature that historians who have studied the history of eighteenth- and nineteenth-century Egypt think was introduced much later. This feature, the link between agriculture and trading needs, is usually associated with the policy established in the nineteenth century of the expansion of cotton agriculture to fulfill the demand coming from textile factories in England. Peter Gran, however, has shown that at the end of the eighteenth century, this phenomenon was already taking place. Mamluk emirs, who by then had become deeply involved in trade, were in fact converting agricultural lands in the Delta in order to meet the grain needs of France.[19] In examining the life records of Abu Taqiyya, we find a similar trend taking place about two centuries earlier, under entirely different circumstances. The fact that merchants like Abu Taqiyya or al-Ruwi'i, involved in international trade, played an important role in financing agriculture indicates the existence of this link.

My study of the life and times of Abu Taqiyya defines some of the features of production during this period—the locations, both urban and rural, and the role merchants played in financing it—using the sugar industry, which was so important at the time, as an example. The growth of the sugar industry is particularly significant because it was linked to demand and financed by the merchants who eventually exported sugar to other parts of the Ottoman Empire. It was probably their financial support that helped the industry come out of the deep crisis it had experienced in the fifteenth century.

We can, consequently, ask whether the industrialization process of the early nineteenth century was in any way linked to what had been happening before. The same question has been debated with regard to the industrial "revolution" in England, scholars asking the extent to which it was a *revolution* or an *evolution*. T. S. Ashton, for instance, in his book on the Industrial Revolution includes a chapter viewing earlier forms of industry in the eighteenth century as predecessors of later developments.[20] One would similarly argue that industrialization under Muhammad 'Ali was the culmination of a process that started earlier, on a more restricted scale and with more limited technical means.

One of the vital features of the period—and the one that distinguishes it very clearly from the period of incorporation in the nineteenth century —is the fact that commercial agriculture and the linking of agriculture to production and trade was undertaken not to benefit the textile factories of Manchester but the indigenous merchants who partially financed these operations. My study of Abu Taqiyya shows the beginnings of this important trend. I hope that future studies can elaborate on it in order to examine how this trend subsequently spread or retracted.

In spite of a number of adverse conditions, such as European penetration in Asian markets and their development of new international trade routes along the Atlantic, this was a period of commercial prosperity in Egypt—one in which important adjustments were taking place. The revival of the economy at the end of the sixteenth and beginning of the seventeenth century is a clear indication that the three centuries from that time to the dissolution of the Ottoman Empire should not be viewed as one long line of unrelentless decline. Such an approach can only blur the complex realities of the period.

Without understanding this period of Ottoman history, we cannot understand the subsequent changes occurring in the region. Some of the vital social and economic structures we usually associate with modern developments in the nineteenth century were, in fact, taking shape much earlier—before the French Expedition, before Muhammad 'Ali, and before the penetration of European models of trade—by means of indigenous tools and methods. Using different sources and exploring a different period, I nevertheless concur with the view expressed by Peter Gran that significant commercial changes occurred prior to the period of massive importation of European models that started with the Napoleonic invasion of 1798, and as the result of an internal dynamic.[21] The earlier period during which Abu Taqiyya lived is thus a very important stage in the economic and social history of Egypt. Because it is at the base of many developments that came later, it is vital to our understanding of the eighteenth and nineteenth centuries.

2

Merchants and Merchant Families

An examination of the activities of Abu Taqiyya and other elite merchants of his generation helps elucidate a number of matters about the society of his time. It has generally been thought that, prior to the nineteenth century, rigid rules of conduct prescribed many if not most aspects of people's lives. For example, social mobility, whether vertically, up the social scale, or horizontally, from one social group to another, was restricted. However, because such views have often been formulated on the basis of theoretical models from other societies or other periods rather than on the documentary evidence of the period it is significant to ask how far they are supported by concrete archival data in relation to a specific society. There is general agreement among scholars that families, guilds, ethnic communities, and legal institutions placed restrictions on people's behavior and that many of their actions had to conform to rules set up by these bodies. But there is disagreement about exactly how strict these rules and regulations were during any particular period.

Abu Taqiyya, like most of the inhabitants of Cairo, moved among a number of different groupings. For him, the most important were his own family, the merchant community, and the Syrian community in Cairo. In addition to family and professional guild, other Cairenes might have had membership in one of the numerous Sufi orders that people turned to for religious guidance or belonged to a residential quarter (hara), which grouped the inhabitants of a particular location. By adulthood a person thus would likely have been associated with several of these different bodies that involved his professional, his religious, and his family life.

This multiplicity of associations might give the impression that a person's life was entirely dominated by various groups, each of which imposed certain obligations, leaving him little room for his own initiatives. It seems quite plausible to maintain that in a period of flux, as this one was, these limits and restrictions must have been much looser than in more stable periods. In studying the life of Abu Taqiyya, we find that even though the grouping a person belonged to—whether family, professional guild, or another kind of association—necessarily imposed certain restrictions on individual behavior, we can nevertheless observe that there were many ways in which people's lives were not dominated by restrictions. Channels existed through which a private initiative could find expression, particularly in times of change. Otherwise it would be difficult to understand how the transformations in this family's professional activities took place. Isma'il Abu Taqiyya by his association with his family and ethnic community worked his way up the merchant hierarchy from within the system. The Abu Taqiyya family experienced not only geographical mobility, in the family's move from Hums to Cairo, but eventually social mobility as well, for his descendants moved from one social stratum to another, in rising from the merchant group to the ruling elite.

This study of Abu Taqiyya shows his links to these different groupings in a dynamic rather than a static way, emphasizing the way that he dealt with them. In other words, we can observe how at different periods of his life he maneuvered his way between one and another, relying more on the one or the other according to the circumstances he faced at any particular moment. At certain times, for example, he was in close contact with the members of the Syrian merchant community; at other times he did business with an Egyptian partner. Likewise, within the family, his contacts with his brother were very close at first; then they stopped doing business together. We can observe a certain fluidity in the way he formed relationships with the members of these different groups, strengthening his ties at some periods in his life, loosening them at others.

One of these groupings was the family. Isma'il Abu Taqiyya did not, so to speak, choose his profession, since most males in his family were merchants for at least three generations back. Not only Ahmad, Isma'il's father, Isma'il himself, and his son Zakariyya were merchants, but also Ahmad's brother, 'Abdul-Raziq, and his son, as well as Yasin, Isma'il's brother. In this respect, the Abu Taqiyyas were like many other families in which one particular profession dominated: A father taught his son the profession that he himself practiced, and the son trained his own children in it, and so on. The family group, in such cases, was in charge of a number of functions. Training of young men, for instance, took place within the family. At certain times, business was also carried out within the family, either in formal partnerships or in informal arrangements. When need arose, a merchant could borrow money within his family group. Certain marriages, moreover, were also conducted within the family circle. The family must also have helped its members in other ways when necessary, standing at their side in troubled times or providing moral support.

A second group within which the Abu Taqiyyas moved, either individually or as a family, was the Syrian community in Cairo. From the many names that indicate an origin, we know that Syrians living in Cairo were numerous: al-Shami, al-Halabi, al-Safadi, al-Hamawi, al-Humsi, al-Baʿlbaki, al-Nabulsi, al-Qudsi, and many others. Some were merchants, others were craftsmen, especially in the textile industry, and more specifically, in the silk, industry. Many of them came as students in the Azhar, the oldest, and the most prominent, college in Cairo, where religious sciences were taught. As a matter of fact, since the time of the Mamluk Sultan Qaytbay (d. 1496), the Azhar had a *riwaq* (lodging for students) al-Shawam for students from Bilad al-Sham. They seem to have been quite a large community. However, we have no evidence for the existence of a Syrian *taʾifa,* that is, a formal structure for the Syrian community, recognized as such by the state, with its own leader or spokesman as a liaison between the community members and the state. The Ottomans had a policy of formally recognizing such communities in their different territories and, when necessary, using them to control their members. This policy allowed subject populations to maintain their traditions and way of life as long as it did not disturb Ottoman interests. Cities like Cairo, Aleppo, and Jerusalem might have Turkish, Armenian, North African, Jewish, and Greek populations, each of which maintained their cultural, religious, or linguistic identities. The absence of a Syrian *taʾifa* in Cairo was probably due to the fact that its members were more integrated into the majority population of the city than any of the other groups that were structured into a *taʾifa,* both because they were very numerous and because they had long-standing historical links with Egypt. It is therefore quite interesting to be able to follow a family of Syrian origin to trace the degree and the pattern of integration into the society of Cairo. In the case of the Abu Taqiyyas, we can observe the way they merged into the merchant community, which was made up mostly of Egyptian merchants.

The Abu Taqiyyas' links to the Syrian community were complex. For many years, long after they had settled in Cairo and integrated their lives into its fabric of life, their connection to their Syrian origin remained alive. Syrians helped them to settle in their new surroundings when they first came to Cairo. Likewise, when Isma'il Abu Taqiyya became *shahbandar,* the Syrians living in Cairo certainly expected some support from him. Abu Taqiyya quite often chose Syrians to be his business partners. In addition, marriages within the Syrian community were frequent, and many of the Abu Taqiyyas chose spouses from among its members. For decades, we can trace different kinds of links between members of the Abu Taqiyya family and various individuals of Syrian origin, at the same time observing the family becoming more and more integrated into the top layers of the social structure.

A third group within which the Abu Taqiyyas moved was that of merchants. Again, this was a multifaceted relationship—professional, social, and structural, since merchants were grouped in guilds. Merchants had to work together in order to get their business done, as partners, as agents to other merchants, or in other capacities. The larger a venture was, the more merchants it involved. There were significant differences in level between members of the merchant community, some of them maintaining their trading within a limited scope, others functioning on a wide scale with extensive networks at their disposal. The titles that merchants were given are a significant indication of this social mobility within the merchant community. When Ahmad Abu Taqiyya first appeared on the scene, he was mentioned as *khawaja* or *tajir khawaja, tajir* referring to the profession and *khawaja* being the title with which merchants were addressed, sometimes with a qualification like *tajir fil harir* (silk merchant) or *tajir fil sabun* (soap merchant) to indicate the commercial specialization. Within the category of *tajir khawaja* some carried the honorific title of *fakhr al-tujjar* (literally, the pride of merchants) or *min a'yan al-tujjar* (the notable merchant), or sometimes even *'ayn a'yan al-tujjar* (the most notable among notable merchants). Some of these *tujjar* had a position as *shaykh* of a particular *suq* or market (*shaykh* of Suq Khan al-Khalili) or commercial warehouse, such as *shaykh al-tujjar bi wikala al-sabun* (head of guild of merchants of the soap *wikala)* or Suq al-Fahhamin. These would have been at the upper level of this category of merchants. Ahmad Abu Taqiyya in his early days had been a *tajir saffar* (traveling merchant), fairly low in the trading hierarchy. He could work either for himself or for other merchants, buying and transporting goods from one region to sell in another one, which at one time he was doing, between Egypt and Syria. Higher up in the hierarchy of titles was that of *khawajaki,* a title for a large-scale long-distance merchant, which was already commonly used in the fifteenth century; the *khawajakis* were, by comparison to the ordinary *tujjar,* few in number, but carried great economic weight. Isma'il Abu Taqiyya attained this title in the early 1600s, once he had reached prominence and become a large-scale merchant with extensive trading networks. The highest position a merchant could attain was that of *shahbandar,* head of the merchants' guild. Although this term of Persian origin was occasionally used in the fifteenth century, it did not become commonplace until the Ottoman period.[1] Isma'il Abu Taqiyya attained the position of *shahbandar,* head of the merchants' guild of Cairo, in 1022/1613 and kept it (except for a few months when he was ill in 1031/1621) till his death. Implying wealth and social power among the trading community of Cairo, it was also one of the most prestigious titles within the social structure of the city—perhaps the highest nonpolitical position that members of the indigenous population could reach, with close links to the authorities.

Numerous guilds grouped together the merchants of Cairo. Sometimes they were organized on the basis of the location where they practiced their trade; the merchants of Suq Marjush, for instance, were in one guild. Other guilds were made up of merchants selling the same goods. The position of *shahbandar* was given to the person heading the guild of Red Sea merchants, because this guild included the most prominent merchants of Cairo. Like heads of other guilds, the *shahbandar* was a liaison between the merchants and the authorities and had numerous expectations to fulfill toward his fellow merchants, such as mediating among merchants when disputes arose.

Unfortunately, of all the guilds functioning in Cairo, the one we know the least about was the merchants' guild. For some reason, the merchants' guild did not find it necessary to bring their guild matters to court, certainly not as often as many other guilds did. Although the court records are full of cases involving artisans' the tradesmen's guilds, such as the house painters' guild, the tanners' guild, and the water carriers' guild, and provide information about the election of their *shaykhs,* the rules governing the guilds and the behavior of guild members, the quality of the products they produced, the way they obtained raw materials and divided them among members, and many other matters of concern to the members of a certain craft, this is not true for the merchants' guild. We therefore know very little about the kind of support or of restrictions that the merchants' guild imposed on its members. Historians seem to agree that there were much fewer constraints upon merchants, than upon artisans. In the case of the archival sources, the only time the merchants' guild is mentioned with regard to Abu Taqiyya is when he became its head.

By and large, much of the activity of merchants was based along entirely informal lines, and the most important ventures were undertaken almost independently of the guild structure. That was only to be expected of a guild that was composed of merchants in international trade; unlike the artisanal guilds, the merchants were not faced with such problems as getting access to raw material, distributing it among artisans, or controlling the quality of goods produced.

Merchants were thus left on their own to find their way in the world of long-distance trading. Isma'il Abu Taqiyya's partners in his trading ventures were often either family members, like his father or brother, or other merchants who, like him, had a shop in Suq al-Warraqin, where they would have become acquainted with each other. Occasionally they were Syrians—from Hums, Damascus, Tripoli, or Safad—whose common origin was a factor in bringing them closer. Exactly how the guild was used by the merchants to further their interests is as yet a matter for conjecture.

On a more personal level, the daily dealings of merchants in the marketplace sometimes led to close ties that could last a lifetime. Such was the case in Isma'il's relationship with 'Abdul-Qadir al-Damiri, a merchant he met at the silk market as a young man. At other times these daily dealings of merchants led to marriage alliances, as we see with Isma'il himself, his sisters, and his daughters, especially those who got married during his own lifetime.

These three groups in Abu Taqiyya's professional and personal life often overlapped, sometimes one dominating a certain period in his life and sometimes another. But all three were present with him throughout. One can conveniently divide the decades covered by this study into three stages of family history. The first covers the move from Syria to Egypt and the early years of Isma'il and his brother Yasin. The second deals with Isma'il as he reaches maturity and forms a partnership with his father and brother for important trading ventures. The third treats Isma'il Abu Taqiyya's work outside the sphere of family partnerships. Although it was during this stage that he reached the peak of his career and attained the position of *shahbandar* his last years were disappointing on the personal and family level.

From Syria to Egypt

The first stage takes us from Ahmad Abu Taqiyya to Isma'il Abu Taqiyya's early years. The *Humsi* connection that Isma'il Abu Taqiyya maintained in his commercial, social, and family relationships was formed by what took place during this stage. On a broader level, it shows the kind and extent of exchange between Egypt and Syria—commercial, cultural, and social.

This phase of the family history is the one that is the least documented. No date for the birth of Isma'il Abu Taqiyya or any other members of his family is available. This is only to be expected, because dates of birth were not normally reported. Chronicles, for instance, do not provide this kind of data either. Nor do we know exactly when the family moved from Hums to Cairo, or at whose initiative the decision to leave Bilad al-Sham was made, although we do know that they were living in Cairo by the 1580s. It may well have been Ahmad Abu Taqiyya, Isma'il's father, who first settled in: Of the three generations of Abu Taqiyyas traceable in the archives, Ahmad Abu Taqiyya is the one who kept the identification *al-Humsi* appended to his name until he died in 1005/1596; Isma'il and Yasin were calling themselves al-Humsi regularly only until the early 1600s, then tended to drop it. By the time that Isma'il's son, Zakariyya, reached maturity, the term was no longer used with his name. Moreover, it was *khawaja* Ahmad Abu Taqiyya who maintained links with Bilad al-Sham, traveling to and fro between it and Egypt. By the time that his young boys had reached maturity and started to stand on their own feet, sometime in the 1580s, the family seems to have been well settled in Cairo.

One question that we can ask is why Ahmad Abu Taqiyya decided to move from a moderate-sized city like Hums to Cairo, the second-largest city of the Ottoman Empire after Istanbul—especially as Aleppo, a major commercial center, was much closer. Bruce Masters has noted that in the second half of the sixteenth century, the trade of Aleppo was gradually being transformed; pepper was being replaced by raw silk from Iran as the main trade item of the city, as the demand for Persian silks increased.[2] It is very likely that this pepper trade was being channeled through the Red Sea via Cairo, because demand for this product was generally on the increase. Great population growth in the urban centers of the Ottoman Empire and in Europe had created new levels of demand. This must have made Cairo a particularly attractive place to go to for merchants from other centers during those years. The Abu Taqiyyas' move can therefore be placed in the context of the economic attraction of Cairo at the time.

The desire to rise in the merchant hierarchy must have been a major motivation for this decision. Ahmad Abu Taqiyya was a merchant and belonged to a merchant family: His father before him and his brother 'Abdul-Raziq also bore the title *khawaja,* which put them on a certain social scale in society. Merchants were usually better off than members of most other professions (artisans and tradesmen, for example), whether in Syrian cities or Egyptian ones. The hope of earning a better living in a larger city than what Hums could offer may well have motivated Ahmad Abu Taqiyya to come and live in Egypt. After all, Cairo was a great commercial metropolis. It as at the center of a number of major international trade routes, notably the Red Sea route, through which the merchandise of India and other parts of Asia traveled via Suez to Cairo and from Cairo to further destinations. The spices and textiles coming through this route, in great demand in both the Ottoman Empire and Europe, brought great profits to the merchants who handled the trade. Another important route linked Cairo to North Africa, a region that traded heavily with Egypt. Still another route, through which gold and slaves traveled, linked Cairo to Black Africa (Bilad al-Sudan and Bilad al-Takrur). The city was also linked to Mediterranean ports, both in the Ottoman Empire and in Europe, notably Venice. The possibilities for trading were consequently very rich and very diverse.

Ahmad Abu Taqiyya was certainly aware of the possibilities awaiting a merchant who did business in Cairo. Nevertheless, there were difficulties of various kinds that he had to put up with. Any long-distance travel had its dangers, even for a traveling merchant familiar with the discomforts of such journeys between one commercial center and another. In his travels between Cairo and Bilad al-Sham, Abu Taqiyya could have used either the sea route or the overland route. A merchant, however, would probably not choose to take the overland route unless a relatively large number of people were traveling together, for he could travel by sea, and that route took less time.[3] The Sinai route linking Cairo to Bilad al-Sham, in spite of its dangers and discomforts, was nevertheless used by many travelers.[4] In addition to the heat and the possible shortages of water and food, travelers were also open to attacks by brigands or bedouins after their money or

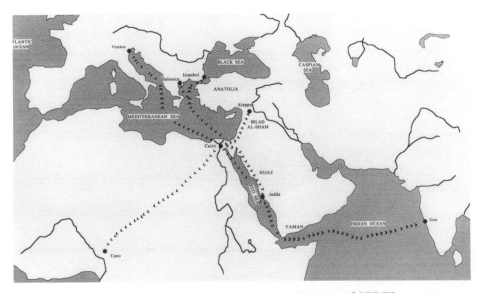

2. Abu Taqiyya's network of trade routes. Courtesy of CEDEJ.

their goods. And yet, security on these major routes was relatively well maintained during those years.

The safety of these roads depended largely on how strong the state was and how able it was to exert its presence. If Ahmad Abu Taqiyya was taking the trip in the 1560s or the 1570s, Ottoman state power was still centralized and the sultans in Istanbul were extending their authority over the provinces. Certainly, they considered the maintenance of security along trade routes one of their vital responsibilities, and the Ottoman authorities made great efforts to ensure the safety of travelers. The sultans in Istanbul ordered the building of armed fortresses at the stopping points; during the second half of the sixteenth century, no less than eight such fortresses between Egypt and Syria were either built, rebuilt, or restored.[5] Sultan Sulayman, who died in 1566, constructed a number of khans linking the major cities of Syria. Likewise, Sinan Pasha, the Ottoman governor of Egypt, had constructed khans for travelers along Egypt's major routes.[6] Because of these policies, roads were made safer and easier to travel on, whether for pilgrims or for merchants. This factor must have helped consolidate the links between the different regions of the Ottoman state in general, and between Egypt and Syria in particular.

Ahmad Abu Taqiyya must have faced other kinds of difficulties once he had arrived in Cairo. Not only were there cultural differences between the inhabitants of Syria and those of Egypt, but Hums was a comparatively small city of secondary importance, while Cairo was a very large city, crowded and cosmopolitan. Competition in such a large metropolis must have been hard for a newcomer. Moreover, because travel was slow and difficult, and news from home was not always forthcoming, separation from one's family, even if only the extended family, must have been a painful experience. People who moved from one city to another obviously wished to have with them close family members. Ahmad Abu Taqiyya was lucky in that his brother, 'Abdul-Raziq, also a merchant, found his way to Cairo and settled there permanently. Eventually, his daughter Rumia would marry Ahmad's son Isma'il, and his son Ahmad would marry his brother's daughter Laila.

For Ahmad Abu Taqiyya, the migration from Hums to Cairo was less abrupt than it might have been for someone else. The reason was that he was a traveling merchant. In all likelihood, before coming to settle permanently in Cairo, Ahmad Abu Taqiyya had carried out business in that city, coming as a traveling merchant *(tajir saffar)* to sell the goods he brought with him from Syria and taking back with him Egyptian merchandise in demand there.[7]

He was of course not the only one to do this: It is a pattern that we find among contemporary merchants of Syrian origin, who first came to Egypt as traveling merchants before settling down in Cairo permanently. The geographic proximity and historic links between Egypt and Bilad al-Sham were such that at any time there was movement between the two regions. During certain periods, however, there was more actual migration, with people coming and settling. This is what seems to have been taking place in those last decades of the sixteenth century, at least among merchants, to judge from archival sources. Among the acquaintances of the Abu Taqiyyas, there were a few other such families originally from Hums or from Aleppo who followed this pattern. The Ibn Yaghmurs, one of whose members, 'Uthman, also became *shahbandar al-tujjar,* had originally come from Aleppo as traveling merchants: In a document dated 993/1585 Muhammad Ibn Yaghmur is referred to as a *tajir saffar.* The family soon settled in Cairo permanently. The Ibn 'Ariqats, or simply 'Ariqats, as they eventually were called, a family originally from Hums who were close friends of the Abu Taqiyyas throughout Isma'il's lifetime, followed a similar pattern, traveling between Egypt and Syria, then settling permanently in Cairo.[8] This pattern had obvious advantages: By the time that the merchant decided to settle down with his family, he was familiar with the new surroundings, had probably formed some kind of network in the market, and knew more or less where he wanted to live.

Another factor facilitated Ahmad Abu Taqiyya's move from Hums to Cairo. A person traveling from one region of the Ottoman Empire to another could expect to find certain similarities between different regions under Ottoman rule. On coming to Cairo, someone like Ahmad Abu Taqiyya could expect to find a social structure not too different from the one he had left in Hums. He could continue to be a merchant without any fundamental change in either professional or socioeconomic level. It was, in other words, easy to become integrated socially at a level quite similar to the one he had been used to; he did not have to be marginalized upon his arrival in Cairo. This was also true for people in other professions. Scholars, for instance, were noted for being a mobile lot, moving from one educational center to another. The sixteenth-century biographies of al-Ghazzi,[9] for instance, are full of examples of *ulama*' moving between the various cities, settling temporarily or permanently in one of them, either to join an educational or a judiciary institution, and maintaining a similar social status regardless of where they were. Thus, although long-distance travel was always uncomfortable and sometimes dangerous, there was, at another level, great fluidity of movement between diverse regions of the Ottoman Empire.

This fluidity of movement clearly indicates that the political events of the time did not necessarily affect such matters as migration or trade. The migration to Cairo of merchant families like the Abu Taqiyyas and the Ibn 'Ariqats from Hums, the Yaghmurs from Aleppo, and others, indicates a continuity of commercial and economic ties between Egypt and Syria in spite of the fact that the Ottoman conquests of 1516 and 1517 had separated the two lands previously under the centralized rule of the Mamluk dynasty.

Ahmad Abu Taqiyya maintained his ties with Bilad al-Sham after he had settled in Cairo, traveling to and fro, selling Egyptian goods and products there, and bringing Syrian goods for the Cairene market. He seems, in fact, to be the only Abu Taqiyya for whom traveling to Syria can be documented. Certainly there is no evidence that Isma'il ever went to Bilad al-Sham, but many of the people that Isma'il Abu Taqiyya did business with were Syrian. Cairo did not have a *hara* for Syrians, like the Hara al-Maghariba in the north of the city, or Hara al-Afranj, where Europeans lived, where the Abu Taqiyyas could have settled. Nevertheless, some places of work—the silk market, for instance, or the soap warehouse (Wikala al-Sabun)—had a high proportion of Syrians, and the Abu Taqiyyas naturally had their dealings in a silk market with a high proportion of Syrian merchants. The family members, moreover, often chose marriage partners from members of the Syrian if not the *Humsi* community in Cairo. And yet changes occurred between the early years after the migration to Cairo and later on when the family fortune grew and the Abu Taqiyyas developed closer links to the ruling class.

Growing Up in Cairo

The second phase in the family history includes the early years and education of Isma'il and his brother Yasin and their introduction into the trading world. During this time the Abu Taqiyyas, father and sons, worked in close collaboration. First, the sons were trained by their father; then, as mature men, they formed a family trading partnership. Throughout this stage of their lives, much of their activity revolved around two closed groups, the family and, the members of the Syrian merchant community in Cairo.

There are no documents that cover the period of Abu Taqiyya's childhood and youth. That is only to be expected, given the nature of the court records. It is only by looking at hundreds of documents carrying references to children that it is possible to form a clear idea of what his youth may have been like. We can assume, however, that the two brothers, Isma'il and Yasin, followed the established patterns of education for boys of their age and social strata in that urban society, in terms of both learning and professional training.

The education of a young man from the trading and commercial sector started with learning to read and write. Isma'il and his brother were certainly literate. That Isma'il constantly recorded everything in writing and owned books is sufficient evidence. In Cairo the level of literacy was relatively high; Chabrol in 1798 estimated that between a third and a quarter of the male population was literate.[10] Because the poor, who were numerous, would not have been among those who benefited from an elementary education, Chabrol's estimates must apply to the middle and upper strata of the population. Elementary education could be obtained in two ways, either through institutions set up for that purpose or through private tutoring, the latter preferred by wealthier families. For the majority, the spread of elementary schools all over the city (some three hundred at the time of the French Expedition of 1798) made them accessible to the majority of the population and provided large numbers of young boys with the opportunity to learn reading, writing, and basic arithmetic. These elementary schools, called *maktabs* or *kuttabs*, were very often financed by charitable foundations and were thus free of charge for the children who attended. Isma'il may have attended a public elementary school or was perhaps taught at home by a *faqih* (teacher), like the boys from more prosperous families.[11]

The other aspect of education was initiation into a profession. This was usually done through the father's teaching and training, beginning when the boys were quite young. By the time they had reached physical maturity at fifteen or sixteen, they were actually sometimes conducting business on their own. Archival documents do not provide the numerical age of children (or anyone else, for that matter), but instead use terminology based on physical descriptions of various stages of human life. The first was the *radi'*, or feeding infant, and next the *qasir*, or minor (that is, child), who was legally not considered a full person. Then came the *shabb baligh*, or young man, major in the legal sense (that is, his testimony could be taken, he could handle his own money, and so on), but not having reached manhood. Manhood was usually defined by physical maturity rather than by a specific age, (that is, when a beard appeared; hence *rajul*, man, or *al-rajul al-kamil*, literally, fully a man, that is, a man having reached manhood, or maturity). Yasin Abu Taqiyya, Isma'il's brother, while still a young man *(shabb baligh)* was dealing in large sums, loaning money and selling coffee for 1200 golden dinars.[12] Although these dealings were perhaps undertaken partly under his father's guidance, they were nonetheless in his own name, and the money was his. By that time therefore, although he may have been only fourteen or fifteen years old, he had already acquired some experience in the marketplace. The same must certainly have been true for his elder brother Isma'il. Other young men of their age among their acquaintances were doing the same. When *khawaja* Abul Nasr al-Tarabulsi, a colleague of Isma'il Abu Taqiyya's, died, his son Husam al-Din, had just turned major *(baligh)* but was still quite young *(shabb)*. This did not prevent him from taking over his father's commerce, continuing the partnerships his father had founded, and consequently being called *khawaja*. He had to deal in large sums and take care of all the business that was unfinished at his father's death.

Isma'il Abu Taqiyya in the early 1580s was being prepared for his career by being trained in the ins and outs of trading. As a young man, Isma'il had his first experience in the circles where Syrian merchants in Cairo were active and in the markets where Syrian goods were sold. The Abu Taqiyyas—Ahmad and his two sons, Isma'il and Yasin—seem to be closely linked during those years to Suq al-Harir, a silk market situated in Suq al-Warraqin, where many textile merchants had their shops, close to the busy commercial quarter called Ghuriyya. This market in the center of the city had a number of Syrian merchants, and although it was by no means a Syrian market, it probably sold the silk brought from the cities of Bilad al-Sham. A small deal Isma'il made in 995/1586 is indicative of a pattern: His partner, 'Abdul Qadir al-Damiri, was an Egyptian silk merchant in Suq al-Harir; his client, a certain Nasir al-Din Ibrahim 'Abdul-Raziq, was a *Humsi;* and the goods exchanged were raw silk and silk textiles.[13] In the years when he was being trained, Isma'il was therefore also being exposed to influences that would define and shape his career.

The Family Partnership

We can observe the Abu Taqiyyas moving from being a family of merchants to becoming a merchant family. They had been a family of merchants since Ahmad Abu Taqiyya's father and his grandfather, perhaps even before that. The family members actually engaged in trade and carrying the titles of *khawaja* or of *khawajaki* were Isma'il's father, Ahmad; his uncle 'Abdul-Raziq; his grandfather, Yahya; his brother Yasin; and eventually his son Zakariyya. But there is no evidence that this was a merchant family—a family that worked together in the business, pooled its money, and sent its members to the places where goods were bought and sold.

A shift took place in the Abu Taqiyyas' relationship to each other, probably towards the late 1580s or early 1590s. As Isma'il and Yasin reached maturity and were able to conduct business independently, they and their father attempted to form a family business, that is, a partnership in which each one of them invested part of the capital and shared the profits. At this stage they were becoming a merchant family instead of just a family of merchants. The phenomenon of merchant families in long-distance trade was well known. The Karimis, a very prominent and wealthy group of merchants who had in the fourteenth and part of the fifteenth centuries monopolized the spice trade in Egypt, were often organized into family corporations. Not only the profession was passed down from father to son, but also the networks that they developed—in Asia, along the Red Sea coastline, and in Africa. However, merchant families and families of merchants were not two mutually exclusive forms. Merchant families did not employ family members exclusively; there must have been outsiders to do a multitude of jobs that were essential to running the business smoothly. Likewise, for merchants who essentially organized their trading activities with other merchant colleagues, the occasional participation of a family member in the business was quite possible. But certain organizational differences nevertheless characterized each form; for instance, recording and documenting transactions or agreements was more important among trading partners who were not related to each other.

The immediate reason for the Abu Taqiyya family's shift in pattern probably had to do with the Red Sea trade. That was the trade in which elite merchants were involved, because that was where the highest profits were to be made. What André Raymond describes with regard to eighteenth-century merchants was already true in the late sixteenth century: The wealthiest merchants in Cairo were those who handled the Red Sea trade. The shift from Syrian trade to Red Sea trade therefore represented a stage higher in the hierarchy of trading. The fact that the Abu Taqiyya family was able to penetrate the circle of Red Sea merchants at that particular time—that is, about a century after the Portuguese had settled in India—is an indication of the intensity of trading activity. Even at the end of the sixteenth century, this sector of trade, which included the Cairene merchant aristocracy, could still absorb newcomers like the Abu Taqiyyas and Ibn Yaghmurs, freshly arrived from Syria. For them, admission into this circle implied a new level of integration into the merchant community of Cairo.

Trading in the Red Sea implied traveling to Mecca and Jedda, which were the major entrepôts for goods coming from India. This was a journey that could be made either by land, notably during the pilgrimage, or by sea, depending on the season, the Red Sea being navigable only during certain months of the year. Because the trip required larger sums of money and longer absences in Mecca and Jedda as well as a network of people to organize the purchase, handling, and shipment of merchandise, the Abu Taqiyyas found it necessary to pool their money and efforts in such an undertaking.

The Abu Taqiyya family was encouraged by the fact that a number of their merchant colleagues were organized as merchant families. For example, the Ruwi'is, whom the Abu Taqiyyas knew very well, employed the different family members up to three generations apart, not only brothers and sons, but nephews and cousins. Evidently not everyone involved in the family business shared equally in the profits: Some were direct beneficiaries, sharing in the risks and the benefits; others were paid a fixed salary. The family enterprise had a head, who was in charge of running the business; at one time, it was Ahmad al-Ruwi'i who presided over the family enterprise; later it was his nephew 'Ali al-Ruwi'i, who was *shahbandar al-tujjar*. At the time that Ahmad al-Ruwi'i was in charge, one of his brothers, Muhammad al-Ruwi'i, was in al-Hijaz; the other brother, 'Isa, was in Mukha in Yemen; and his nephew Muhammad al-Rashidi, son of his sister Fatma, was sent to pick up merchandise from both of them and cash a number of debts for unpaid merchandise—for which he received a fixed salary of 150 dinars a year.[14] The existence of such a family enterprise implied that a number of its members pooled their capital together (though probably in unequal parts) to carry on the commercial activities. Sometimes each member had specific functions to fulfill—traveling, taking delivery of goods in a specific port, and so on. It was along similar patterns, but with fewer family members, that the Abu Taqiyyas undertook their commercial ventures.

The Abu Taqiyyas must have been doing business together for some time, when in Shawwal 1004/1595 Ahmad Abu Taqiyya, an experienced traveling merchant, set off on a long trip with his younger son, Yasin, to Jedda and Mecca with the yearly pilgrimage. In addition to fulfilling an important religious and spiritual function, the pilgrimage offered merchants a number of important advantages. Traveling in a group was safer than traveling alone. Moreover, the state offered protection along the long and risky route, the pilgrims being guarded by troops accompanying them. Mecca during the pilgrimage was a meeting point for merchants from all over the Muslim world—from Asia in the east to North Africa in the west, and from Anatolia and the Balkans to Bilad al-Sudan—bringing with them diverse goods for exchange. As a center, it thus offered great opportunities. Another important advantage accrued to merchants traveling with the pilgrimage. Their merchandise was exempt from customs duties.

During that fateful year when Ahmad Abu Taqiyya went on pilgrimage, Isma'il was left in Cairo to see to the family's business there. Yasin empowered him to take care of all his own private financial affairs while he was gone, to buy and sell on his behalf, and to collect his debts.[15] It was a momentous trip, from which Ahmad did not come back; while in Mecca, he died, leaving his grieving son Yasin to take the return trip to Cairo alone. This was the last time that the Abu Taqiyyas worked together as a merchant family; Ahmad's death brought to an end Abu Taqiyyas' family enterprise so recently begun.

New Patterns

The third phase of the family history may be dated from the time of Ahmad Abu Taqiyya's death, which shifted the patterns that Isma'il was to follow. He was to leave behind him the family enterprise and conduct his commercial ventures with partners outside the family network. To a certain extent, there were practical considerations for this decision. A merchant family of three people was a bare minimum for the kind of network that international trade required; with only two of them left the family enterprise did not seem practicable. But there were also personal considerations. Practically speaking, Isma'il could have expanded the family network by including his Abu Taqiyya cousins or some of his in-laws, among whom were some experienced merchants. In that sense it was a deliberate choice on his part—and one that to a certain extent was made at the expense of family loyalties. During this phase, Isma'il Abu Taqiyya reached the peak of his professional career, extending his trading networks further than ever before and attaining the position of *shahbandar al-tujjar*. These achievements were on the basis of his individual enterprise and with partners largely outside of the family circle.

One of the factors behind this new shift could have been the underlying tensions between him and his brother Yasin. In a society where family disputes were most often settled within the family circle, the fact that disputes of the Abu Taqiyyas were sometimes taken to court is indicative of a deep underlying tension; perhaps his brother and sisters were jealous of Isma'il's apparently more dominant and outgoing personality. Both his young brother Yasin and, sometime later, his sisters took him to court for money matters. Yasin's grievance involved money owed him by Isma'il's wife (by 1000/1591, Isma'il was married to Badra b. 'Abdul-Rahman Ibn 'Ariqat). After their father's death in Mecca in 1005/1596, three of Isma'il's sisters, Laila, Budur, and Sayidat al-Kull, had the impression that he had cheated them out of their inheritance by claiming that the goods and merchandise stored in Cairo were his. He was able to provide documents showing that he had sole ownership of the goods in question,[16] thus proving his innocence, yet it would seem somewhat unlikely that his sisters would have hurled accusations and taken him to court unless some wrongdoing had really taken place. These incidents no doubt created bad feelings that were not easily forgotten and surged up periodically.

It is most probable that the death of Isma'il's father, Ahmad Abu Taqiyya, was what pushed him to change his patterns of trading and establish himself independent of family networks. Certainly, he was encouraged to do so by the relationship he established with 'Abdul-Qadir al-Damiri. They had met, probably sometime in the mid-1580s, in Suq al-Warraqin and Suq al-Harir, where silk merchants sold their goods. It was in Suq al-Harir that *khawaja* 'Abdul-Qadir al-Damiri, an Egyptian silk merchant, had the shop where he carried on his business. Starting at first to do business together on a small scale, the two young men formed a working relationship that was to help them embark on the difficult road of international dealings. Together they undertook a number of ventures —sometimes just the two of them; sometimes with 'Abdul-Qadir's relative, Abu Bakr al-Damiri; sometimes with other merchants. In the course of these ventures, which were to make them successful in their business dealings, they developed a strong friendship.

This relationship between the two men is particularly interesting to analyze. Although some data is available regarding the way relationships worked within a particular social body (such as the family, the guild, or the ethnic community), it is quite rare to find a relationship that developed independently of (or beyond the strict scope of) a social grouping and responded to its own rules of behavior, defined by the two men concerned, rather than those of others.

It started off as a business partnership but in time developed a number of other dimensions. For Abu Taqiyya, this was perhaps his most stable and solid relationship. Their friendship was in fact lifelong, surviving all the storms and trials that a joint business could bring. Although there were no blood ties between the two men, or even ties by marriage, in some ways, their friendship bore resemblances to a family relationship, but one that came by their own choice rather than being dictated by family obligations. They not only shared their business ventures but also owned property jointly, endowed their property jointly, and shared shops in Suq al-Warraqin. Joint ownership of urban property was common, because any inherited property was likely to be owned by several people. In this case, however, the ownership was between Abu Taqiyya and al-Damiri because they decided that was the way they wanted to channel their funds jointly, not because of any social or legal constraint imposed on them. Toward the end of Isma'il Abu Taqiyya's life, the two of them together undertook their largest construction project, building two monumental commercial structures, *wikalas*, that they subsequently jointly endowed into *waqf*, with part of the revenues going toward charitable institutions. The remains of these buildings can still be seen in the street in Cairo called Shara' Khan Abu Taqiyya.

Moreover, another aspect of their ties to each other can be observed in their residential patterns. For many years they lived close to each in the same neighborhood, 'Abdul-Qadir al-Damiri renting a house in Khatt al-Amshatiyyin, near Darb al-Shabrawi, the alley where Isma'il Abu Taqiyya lived. Thus an easy flow existed between the houses, with family visits and all the implications of being neighbors. It was only in 1029/1619, when the first of the two *wikalas* was built, that 'Abdul-Qadir rented out this house to Isma'il, and himself moved to the house *(makan)* adjacent to the *wikala* so that he could go to and fro easily between the two.[17] A case in the court registers dating from the weeks that followed Isma'il's death in 1034/1624 is indicative of the closeness of 'Abdul-Qadir to the Abu Taqiyya family. At the news of the death, he immediately came and offered his services to the bereaved family. The offer was taken up by Isma'il Abu Taqiyya's widow, 'Atiyat al-Rahman, and by her two daughters, Jami'a and Um al-Hana, who mandated him to represent them in court for the division of the inheritance and other matters that came up. Because the relationship with al-Damiri was so old and so solid, he was apparently permitted to participate in the family affairs, as his dealings with Isma'il's widow indicate.

In terms of Abu Taqiyya's professional life, his relationship with al-Damiri marked the new kind of trading pattern that he was in the process of creating, leaving behind him both his Syrian connection and his family's business. That does not mean that he did not deal with Syrian merchants. As a matter of fact, quite often, the records show a partner of his with the surname of al-Tarabulsi, that is, the family was originally from Tripoli; or al-Safadi, from Safad; or al-Shami, from Damascus; or, more often, al-Humsi—all major towns in Bilad al-Sham. He never broke his link with merchants of Syrian origin, but henceforth they were no longer in the fore. They were neither his only nor his most frequent partners. Nor did he stop trading with Bilad al-Sham, but it was neither his primary interest to do so, nor where he made the largest investments. The same is true of his links to his family. Although he was never again to let the pattern of family partnership dominate his business, once in a while Yasin was in-cluded in a venture of his, and later Isma'il's son-in-law, Ahmad 'Ariqat, was also involved in some deals. Henceforth, his business ventures were marked by more formality than was usually followed within merchant family groups. This is manifested by the official *shirka*s or contracts of partnerships that there one in writing and recorded in the court. The court registers record over twenty of these partnerships Abu Taqiyya en-tered into between 996/1587 and 1025/1616. His special relationship with al-Damiri becomes apparent from these contracts, because he was a partner in no less than fifteen of them.

From the early 1590s, Isma'il Abu Taqiyya's career as long-distance merchant developed in many directions. In geographical terms, the Red Sea route remained the major sector of his activity, but he eventually came to extend it eastward—to Mukha in the Yemen and to India. Like other merchants of the period, the network that he formed included partners and agents, either traveling directly from Cairo to India, or traveling to Mecca and Jedda, where they mandated a partner or agent there to travel to India on their behalf. Some merchants had a resident partner or agent in India. This was the farthest point in the East to which the merchants of Cairo had direct access during this period. Moreover, direct trading links to India remained restricted to a small number of merchants, the other Red Sea merchants buying Indian and other Asian goods from Mukha, Mecca, or Jedda. The Egypt-India network is an important indication of how far some of the merchant networks were still extending during the early years of the seventeenth century, more than a century after the first Portuguese settlements in India, and shortly after the formation of the Dutch and the English trading companies.

The trading towns around the Red Sea, such as Mukha and Jedda, were important centers, and judging from a contemporary description of

Mukha, the merchandise that arrived there during the trading season of 1616 came from various parts of India and South East Asia: Diu, Surat, Sumatra, Malabar, Calicut, Dabhol, Shaul, Atchi; and from many more sources.[18] These markets were therefore rich in the variety of goods they offered. Nevertheless, those who were able to penetrate the Indian market directly, like Abu Taqiyya and a few others, had an advantage over merchants who purchased Indian goods in Jedda or Mukha because they eliminated the profits of the intermediaries.

Abu Taqiyya also developed a network along the Mediterranean cities to Istanbul, Salonica, and Venice. A significant portion of the Red Sea merchandise he handled was destined for further shipment via the ports of Alexandria, Rashid, and Dumyat, whence it was shipped to other Mediterranean ports in the Ottoman Empire and Europe. In Africa, the source of gold, feathers, ivory, and black slaves, he had an agent reaching as far as Cano. This sector, studied by Terence Walz, was to a large extent in the hands of Upper Egyptians and North Africans, because the routes to Bilad al-Sudan and Bilad al-Takrur passed through Upper Egypt and up the Nile to Cairo, or across the Saharan desert to the Nile Valley.[19] Although it remained a secondary concern of Abu Taqiyya, his involvement in the African trade is significant. That he was neither Upper Egyptian nor North African—nor a specialist in this sector—indicates that the upper strata of merchants were less specialized in the goods they handled and the regions they covered than the more modest merchants.

Not least of all, Isma'il Abu Taqiyya also interested himself in local trade, especially in the Delta area. A great diversity of merchandise passed through his hands, both very luxurious goods, like precious stones, rubies (*yaqut*) from Ceylon, and the gold that he was buying in Cano, and commonplace items. By the end of the sixteenth century, spices (or at least pepper) seem to have become a bulk item rather than a luxury, and coffee was probably somewhere in between. This same was true of sugar, which Abu Taqiyya was exporting in increasing quantities at the beginning of the seventeenth century. He also dealt extensively in textiles, both local products he exported and imported textiles. During his lifetime the shift from spices to coffee as a major item of the Red Sea trade was taking place, a trend to which he contributed. In other words, he and his agents and partners were handling a wide variety of merchandise—luxury goods and bulk items; foreign goods like wood, metal, and corals, and local products like sugar, rice, and textiles; goods passing through Cairo in transit, like the spice and coffee in demand in many commercial centers, and goods for local consumption, like the indigo that was used as a dye for textile manufacture.

Starting from around the first decade of the seventeenth century, Abu Taqiyya was also developing a network within Egypt itself that extended to the rural areas in the Delta, especially the sugar-producing provinces of al-Munufiyya and al-Gharbiyya, and investing in sugar plantations and the refining process. In this venture Abu Taqiyya's investments were done individually; it was one of the few ventures that he did not share with al-Damiri, even though it meant large capital investments. Perhaps the reason was that al-Damiri spent much time taking care of the business in Mecca and Jedda. Abu Taqiyya was taking advantage of being in Cairo, which enabled him to have the kind of social contacts that eventually opened up the possibility of conducting a successful sugar business. But regardless of the reasons he may have had for undertaking this venture individually, what it shows us is a certain versatility in the associations he made—working at certain times within the family group, at other times with a partner, and at still other times alone. This versatility—in his associations, in establishing his networks, and in the commodities he dealt in—helped him significantly because he could introduce modifications to his business patterns and adapt to changing market conditions more rapidly than other merchants.

Isma'il Abu Taqiyya's career was crowned when in 1022/1613 he took the position of *shahbandar al-tujjar,* head of the merchants' guild, replacing his old friend and colleague, *khawaja* 'Ali al-Ruwi'i. The guild he headed was notable for including the merchants involved in the long-distance trade with the East, that is, the most prosperous merchants of Cairo. This was a very prestigious position, a clear indication that he was among the most prosperous merchants of his time. It is a position he kept till his death in 1034/1624 (except for a brief interruption in 1621 when he was ill and was temporarily replaced by *khawaja* 'Uthman Ibn Yaghmur for a few months).

Little is known about the way that a *shahbandar* in Cairo was elected or appointed. Although the court records contain material on the *shaykhs* (heads) of other guilds—whether merchant guilds, like the soap merchants (those of Suq Marjush, for instance); artisans' guilds, such as those involved in textile production or in building activities like stonecutting or painting; or the numerous workers' guilds, which included water carriers, mule and donkey owners, and numerous other unskilled jobs—no information has so far been found about how the post of *shahbandar* was reached. What we do know is that the post was not hereditary at the beginning of the seventeenth century, nor did it run in families. Nor were *shahbandar*s from any particular origin. They could be Egyptian, Syrian, or North African. For example, *khawaja* ʿAbdul-Qawi al-ʿAsi was a merchant from Bulaq; al-Ruwiʿi, Abu Taqiyya's immediate predecessor, was from a family from Rashid; Jamal al-Din al-Dhahabi from Cairo; and Ibn Yaghmur from Aleppo. Moreover, the post was not necessarily a lifetime one; although Ismaʿil Abu Taqiyya died while in the position, many of his predecessors kept it for a few years, until someone was appointed to replace them. In other words, the post at this period was a fairly mobile one, open to those who were the most successful or the most meritorious among the merchants. This situation, which characterizes the post of *shahbandar* in the early seventeenth century, seems to have been modified by the eighteenth; the work of André Raymond suggests that the position tended to remain within some families, like the Shara'ibis and, later, the Mahruqis.[20] The same procedures were probably followed for the appointment or election of a *shahbandar* as those followed for other guilds; that is, a person was chosen by a consensus of the other guild members and then confirmed by the court. Given the importance of this position the authorities would certainly have had to confirm his appointment.

Like other guild *shaykhs*, the *shahbandar* had numerous responsibilities. He would, generally speaking, be called upon to mediate in conflicts between merchants, or between merchants and the authorities. Although the position implied close contact with the authorities, the degree of closeness must certainly have varied considerably between one period and another, the links tightened at times when the state was centralized and loosened when it was less so. It is very unlikely, for instance, that Ismaʿil Abu Taqiyya in the early 1600s had the same kind of link with the state that Sayyid Muhammad al-Mahruqi, *shahbandar al-tujjar* under Muhammad ʿAli, did some two centuries later. This personage, according to al-Jabarti's narration of the events of 1232/1816, managed Muhammad ʿAli's business dealings and partnerships and was charged with the dispatch of troops and supplies for Muhammad ʿAli's expedition to the Hijaz. In addition to mediating between merchants, Mahruqi seems to have had some responsibility for settling disputes among craftsmen and vendors in Cairo, punishing the wrongdoers among them. We have no evidence at all that the *shahbandar*s of the seventeenth century had any such responsibilities to tradesmen and artisans.[21] The cases of artisans brought to court, on the contrary, suggest that they were dealt with by the head of their own guild, and although Abu Taqiyya's position gave him immense social power, there is no evidence that he had any responsibility with regard to artisans' guilds.

Isma'il Abu Taqiyya took his duties as *shahbandar* very seriously, intervening in matters where merchants were concerned. Isma'il Abu Taqiyya was a witness in court cases where merchants were involved in a dispute, for example, in 1028/1618 the case in which *khawaja* Karim al-Din al-Burdayni, a Red Sea merchant, was accused of not returning a loan he had taken.[22] Sometimes before traveling to a distant land, a merchant left an expensive item in his keeping *(amana)* until his return—in one instance a golden sword inlaid with emeralds, rubies, and diamonds.[23] He was most likely also expected to assist them personally in times of crisis. Isma'il Abu Taqiyya was present when the inheritance of a deceased merchant was divided if the deceased died in a distant land. Likewise, he was present when a merchant made his deathbed wishes, perhaps because the merchant's son was away. His very presence was important on such occasions, even private or family matters, such as when he witnessed a marriage or a divorce case. The kind of assistance he could offer merchants was varied, often depending on how much he was willing to give in terms of time and effort.

Syrians living in Cairo, and *Humsi*s in particular, were well aware of the prestige that Abu Taqiyya's *shahbandariyya* bestowed on them, and Isma'il tried not to disappoint them, especially in matters where his mere presence gave weight to the occasion. As *shahbandar*, he was approached by a *Humsi* or a *Shami* more often than ever before to stand by and mediate between a divorcing couple or be present at the division of an inheritance. Perhaps because the Syrians of Cairo were not an organized community, when a Syrian reached an important post like that of *shahbandar*, the other Syrians of Cairo would tend to regard him as a leader in their community.

The prestige of the *shahbandariyya*, however, went beyond these restricted circles. The social position of a *shahbandar* in the large urban community is clearly indicated for example, in a tale of *The Thousand and One Nights*. On the basis of internal evidence, some of the tales have been dated to the Ottoman period—and more specifically, to Cairo. In one of these, the merchant Shams al-Din is described as being "the best and most veracious of all the merchants, and was the possessor of servants and other dependents, black male slaves and female slaves, and mamluks, and of great wealth and he was *shahbandar* of the merchants of Cairo." A mother tells her son, "thy father. . . . is *shahbandar* of the merchants in the land of Egypt and Sultan of the sons of the Arabs," meaning that he had the highest position among the indigenous population. It is informative to see how the *shahbandar* was received when he appeared every morning in the market to attend to his business: "It was customary when the *shahbanddar* came from his house in the morning and sat in his shop, for the *naqib* [holder of a position in a professional guild] of the market to approach and the merchants to recite the *fatiha* [opening chapter of the Quran] to them, whereupon they arose and came with him to the *shahbandar* and recited the *fatiha* to him, wished him good morning, then each departed to his shop." [24] The tale shows the degree of esteem that the holder of this post held in society. It is likely that Isma'il Abu Taqiyya was honored daily by this kind of ritual as he started his day at the market, and his lifestyle during the last decade of his life must certainly have resembled that of the *shahbandar* described above.

Conclusion

Isma'il Abu Taqiyya had developed a successful commercial enterprise, first within the family, then independently of the family, with different partners and with complex networks. But to keep the trading profession in the family, as it had been for some generations, it was essential to have sons and grandsons who would take up where he had left off. In this effort Isma'il was not successful, and his monumental enterprise, put together over many years did not survive him for long. There were, of course partly personal and family reasons for the demise of the Abu Taqiyyas' family business. Historically speaking, however, merchant families—whether Karimi families like the Kharrubis or the Ibn Kuwayks of the fourteenth and fifteenth century, or those who were contemporaries of Abu Taqiyya, like the Ruwi'is or the Shuja'is—did not generally survive more than two or three generations. Accordingly, we need to look into cultural and legal reasons in order to explain the phenomenon.

Among the personal reasons was the absence of mature male heirs. Abu Taqiyya had many children, but with one exception, Zakariyya, those who survived were girls. Years later, the same thing happened to Zakariy-ya, who also was survived only by daughters. If he had had any male children, they had died in infancy or childhood. Zakariyya was therefore the last of the male line of Abu Taqiyyas. Moreover, because Zakariyya was still a minor at the time of his father's death, Isma'il did not have the advantage of easily passing on his profession to his male descendants, as many of his colleagues did.

On reaching maturity, Zakariyya might have carried on the business had he been able to rely on his father's close partners. Capable men like al-Damiri or Ahmad 'Ariqat were familiar with much of Isma'il's activity and for a while helped Zakariyya. But it soon became obvious that Ahmad 'Ariqat, on whom Isma'il had placed much trust, did not quite measure up. Rather than play the role of elder brother to his numerous cousins, he must have given the family the uncomfortable feeling that he was instead pursuing his own interests, above all else. Later, in fact, there were occasions when his acts cast serious doubts upon his loyalty and even his honesty—such occasions were particularly disappointing because Isma'il was fond of him.

Another reason that the family business did not survive was related to the personal abilities of Isma'il's son, Zakariyya. Zakariyya, who reached his majority shortly after his father's death, certainly did not have his father's ability or personality. From his appearances in court records in the years that follow Isma'il's death, we have indications of the direction he was taking. He seemed to possess little, if any, of his father's ability to gather people around him and gain their respect, cementing relationships with all types of people. One of Isma'il Abu Taqiyya's outstanding personal qualities was his ability to make and maintain relationships. Until the end of his life, he had close relationships with the Syrians and Humsis he had known as a young man. With his merchant colleagues, with al-Damiri, and with family members, he was on cordial terms throughout. That was precisely the quality that Zakariyya did not have. Too often, rather than the formation of a partnership or the sale of merchandise, his court appearances, alas, involve his bickering over the rent of one of the shops of the *wikala* or one of its living units. When al-Damiri died, some seven or eight years after Isma'il, Zakariyya did not keep a cordial relationship with al-Damiri's widow, and the income of the joint Damiri–Abu Taqiyya *waqf* provoked conflicts that were settled, in the widow's favor, in court. This—a court appearance in which the *qadi* ruled against him—

had never happened to Isma'il Abu Taqiyya; he went to court only when he was confident of his position. His success in his various ventures was not based simply on his being a clever merchant but involved many other qualities as well. Unfortunately, Zakariyya did not possess these.

Inheritance law also played a role in the fragmentation of the Abu Taqiyya fortune. Given the large number of heirs Isma'il left behind him —three wives, who were entitled to one-fourth of his fortune, and eleven children, of whom Zakariyya was the only male—whatever Zakariyya inherited could not have been an enormous fortune. His share came to a bit more than a tenth of what his father had left. Even so, he remained a man of wealth, between the inheritance, the part of the income from some of his father's pious endowments, and his mother's private fortune; but his fortune, no matter how great, could not equal his father's. Here again, whereas other merchant families of his generation found solutions for this problem, his family did not. The Ibn Yaghmur brothers, for example, at their father's death pooled assets with the female heirs, recombining what had been divided by inheritance, and we find the sister, Mu'mina, sharing in her brothers' trading ventures. Isma'il's children do not seem to have followed this course.

Another reason that the family business did not survive him was institutional. Isma'il Abu Taqiyya's enterprise, large and complex as it was, did not have a legal identity independent of his person, one that could continue to exist regardless of his own presence. Nor did it have a budget independent of the private funds of the partners who participated in individual ventures. An independent legal identity and an independent budget would have facilitated the survival of the enterprise for longer than the two to three generations we generally find among merchant families. In the meantime, the Abu Taqiyyas were shifting away from trade and closer to the ruling elites. Zakariyya was occasionally involved in trade; shortly after he attained his majority, he had acquired the title *khawaja,* and then *khawajaki,* an indication that for a while he continued his father's business. But this did not last long, and soon all references to his commercial activities come to a stop.

If Zakariyya's interest in trade was restricted, he nevertheless managed to maintain good relationships with those in power. Isma'il's rise to economic and social power had opened up new avenues for mobility that his children made use of. By maintaining links with the military elites who were in the process of establishing themselves, Zakariyya managed to insert himself in the hierarchy through the Mutafarriqa military corps that he had joined. During this period of social mobility, when the military began to emerge, the family fortunes thus moved in a different direction from the one Isma'il Abu Taqiyya had established.

Isma'il Abu Taqiyya brought a family of merchants to the peak of achievement for any merchant of his time. Yet none of his offspring or descendants, so far as they can be traced in the archives, came anywhere near his own fame and accomplishments, the family fading back into the relative obscurity of his father and grandfather. The trading patterns in which he had been involved and the increasing dealings in commodities that had become popular during his generation—notably coffee and sugar —continued to dominate the commercial scene in Cairo for another century or so. But the great profits to be made thereof passed on to other merchants rather than to his own offspring.

3

The Structures of Trade

When Isma'il Abu Taqiyya was introduced into the trading world at the beginning of his career as a merchant, not only would he have had to familiarize himself with the tools and techniques that merchants needed, but he would also have had to be introduced to the various structures and institutions related to trade. Like other merchants, he would quite early have come into contact with the structures that a major trading center like Cairo offered and learned how to make use of them. The first archival references related to Abu Taqiyya's links to these various structures date from the 1580s and 1590s, when he was launching his commercial career. The structures and institutions themselves, however, were much older.

The analysis of these trading structures used by the merchants of Abu Taqiyya's generation is important for our understanding of the period during which merchants brought new approaches to their trading patterns. Isma'il Abu Taqiyya's active years were a century or a century and a half before Egypt's incorporation into the European capitalist economy.[1] Thus, by observing the way that merchants of his time carried out their commercial activity, we can discern the structures and the institutions available to them and the way that they made use of them long before European merchants and their agents came to dominate the commercial scene. The tools and techniques that merchants were using were much the same as those used by earlier generations; continuity with earlier periods is easy to discern. It was with these traditional structures that novel trading patterns were eventually developed, manipulated by powerful merchants like Abu Taqiyya to fit their interests.

Commercial history of the region has very often been written on the basis of European sources, such as travel literature and consular reports. These sources reflect the bias of their writers. In the best of cases, they concentrate on trade with Europe, which was the sector of trade that they were interested in. But this was not the only sector, nor was it even the most important one. Moreover, travelers, especially those interested in trade, described what they could see—the kinds of goods available, their prices, and who was buying them, for instance. They were rarely interested in the processes or the procedures that indigenous merchants followed in order to bring these goods to the markets of Cairo or Alexandria. They could easily miss seeing how conditions changed or what merchants did to adapt to different situations, such as times of crisis.

Some historians have concentrated on the period immediately prior to European domination and focused on the factors that enabled Europeans to displace indigenous forms. There is a wide range of explanations, but what many of these studies have in common is their emphasis on the incapacities of the indigenous systems.[2] The weakness or absence of specialized commercial institutions like those that existed in the West—banks, exchanges, western-style merchants' guilds—is for the proponents of this view, among the reasons for the failure of the Ottoman trading system in competing with its European counterpart.

The absence of specialized skills among the merchants themselves is one explanation offered for why European merchants found it easy to penetrate trade in the Ottoman Empire. One formulation of this view can be found in Niels Steensgaard's model of the peddler, a type that he took to be the typical Middle Eastern merchant. He based his formulation on the Armenian merchant Hovhannes, whose travels of 1682–1693 were minutely recorded in his diary. Hovhannes wandered from town to town with no apparent plan. He took with him only as much merchandise as he could handle personally, presumably because there were no specialized institutions in the markets he frequented. In every town he went, it was to the Armenian community that he addressed himself, probably because it was the only group that might provide him with assistance. Furthermore, Hovhannes himself was not a specialist in terms of either the areas he frequented or the commodities he dealt in.[3] Bruce Master's view of Aleppo merchants is modeled along similar lines. He argues that there was broad participation of the population of Aleppo in commercial activity. His findings, based on archival sources, indicate that anyone with sufficient funds could become involved in trading for a limited period.[4] Of course, the fact that such persons were involved in occasional trading did not necessarily mean that merchants were not specialized as a profession. A second explanation for why merchants were unable to cope with change, to confront the superior organization of the Dutch merchants and trading companies, or to compete with the European merchants who traded in cities like Aleppo is that the institutions necessary for carrying out trading activities and banking were nonexistent.

In examining Isma'il Abu Taqiyya's life records for data about commercial structures and institutions, we are not attempting to find out why European-style forms and structures did not exist in the Middle East. Rather, we are seeking to understand the dynamics of a particular society, in its own terms, by closely observing how merchants carried on their trade and identifying those structures available to them to see how they used them to their own benefits for different purposes, such as funding their ventures, organizing their trade, and marketing their goods. We can thus see the shortcomings as well as the accomplishments of the system.

The trading structures were available to all merchants, but it was merchants at the top of the merchant hierarchy who used them most extensively. Their activities were broader, extended further, and were consequently more complex than those of more modest merchants. The big merchants were the ones who were most likely to need support from whatever structures were available in an important commercial center like Cairo. They were also in a better position to take advantage of the system.

In terms of socioeconomic status, the merchant community included a diverse set of people, ranging from those with modest resources to exceedingly wealthy ones. There were small-scale peddlers and short-term merchants, but there were certainly also large-scale, full-time, and lifelong merchants. They were the ones referred to as *tajir* or *khawaja,* these titles not being used for a person with another profession, such as a *qadi,* for instance, or a bey, who invested part of his capital in trading. The circumstances and conditions under which people like Isma'il Abu Taqiyya carried out their trade are quite different from the haphazard activities of Hovhannes. The general features of trade, and the way Abu Taqiyya's own activity inserted itself within the commercial framework of Cairo, indicate a certain level of complexity that seems absent in these models. This is not to say that all the merchants working at that time were equally involved in complex networks, but simply that because the model offered by Steensgaard is applicable to only one type of merchant, and one who would be in the lower echelons of the merchant hierarchy, it provides only a small part of a much larger picture.[5]

This complexity manifests itself at several levels. The geographical extension of Isma'il Abu Taqiyya's commerce, like that of a number of other merchants operating in Cairo was very wide. To the east Abu Taqiyya traded with the cities of Syria, the Hijaz in the Arabian Peninsula, Yemen, and as far as the western coast of India. In Africa his agents were traveling as far as Cano in Nigeria. Along the Mediterranean he was doing business with Istanbul, Salonica, and Venice. His network is therefore in some ways comparable to that of the great merchant dynasties, such as the Karimi merchants, dealing in the Red Sea spice trade, who were active during the Mamluk period, and the Jewish Geniza merchants of the eleventh and twelfth centuries, whose travels took them from North Africa to India. The Karimis, whose wealth was proverbial, had extended their travels much further east, reaching Samarqand, Herat, and China, points that the merchants from Egypt had long since dropped from their itinerary. And yet in the 1600s, Abu Taqiyya's Mediterranean network was probably more developed than theirs.

Closer to home, the network that Isma'il Abu Taqiyya operated also extended to other parts of Egypt, both rural and urban. Because a good portion of the eastern goods he imported was intended for reshipment to European and Ottoman ports, the port towns of Alexandria, Rashid (Rosetta), and Dumyat (Damietta) formed an important link in the network. The traveler Christopher Harant mentions the numerous *funduqs* (commercial houses) that the Europeans—the French, Venetians, Genoese, Florentines, and Austrians—had in Alexandria in 1598.[6] Another contemporary traveler, Aquilante Roccheta, found Alexandria to be the most important port in Egypt, where an infinite amount of merchandise was sold to merchants coming from all over the world.[7] For ships whose destinations were the eastern Mediterranean, however, Dumyat was the major port. Merchandise destined for Istanbul was also handled there. It was, moreover, close to the regions where rice, an important export crop, was grown. Abu Taqiyya had to establish some sort of mechanism in these port towns in order to deal with such matters as the packaging, delivery, and handling of merchandise; the payment of customs; and the shipping of merchandise back to Cairo. Likewise, his search for products brought him in touch with rural land holders, especially in the Delta area.

Abu Taqiyya operated this network without apparently ever himself leaving Cairo, either to travel abroad or, as far as the documentation suggests, to go to other parts of Egypt. This could not have been a simple matter. Nor can it be explained by the fact that his function was simply to finance other people's commerce. It implies a degree of complexity in trading patterns and in organization that goes far beyond the simple patterns that some historians indicate. Abu Taqiyya was, of course, financing trading ventures, but he was also closely involved in running the commercial network.

As with other merchants who ran large long-distance trading businesses, the network implied making use of the services of partners, agents, and employees—whether family members or not—who either made journeys to other commercial centers to accompany the merchandise or settled in cities like Mecca, Jedda, or Istanbul, where business was intensive, on a short-term or long-term basis. Merchants sometimes asked a colleague who traveled on business of his own to act on their behalf in one of the commercial centers. Depending on the kind of arrangement between the two, the merchant could be asked to sell or buy merchandise on behalf of another merchant, to pay for goods, to cash debts, and to pay customs and handling charges, while tending to his own business. Some merchants had a permanent representative in an important center like Jedda, whose sole business was to handle their merchandise and represent their interests. Others went back and forth, returning to Cairo after the trading season was over. Often slaves were employed to travel, accompanying goods or arranging for their shipment to other destinations. The commercial centers of the Ottoman Empire and the Mediterranean, as well as the Indian Ocean ports attest to the presence of important trading communities. Large-scale merchants like the Abu Taqiyyas and the Ruwi'is had access to many categories of people undertaking multiple activities in the different commercial centers to help them carry out their business.

Because of the breadth of his dealings and the width of his geographic extension, with all the complexities involved therein, Abu Taqiyya had to rely quite heavily on the structures and the institutions that were available to merchants during this period in order to operate his network. It is possible that some merchants made more use of these institutions than others. The larger the ventures, the more a merchant would need the support of institutions; the more complex his dealings, the more he would have to turn to institutions for help in running his business. Merchants whose businesses were family organizations had less reason to utilize institutions than those whose businesses were more broadly based. Also, merchants who dealt with many distant regions were able to use these institutions more effectively in those regions where there were similar institutions. To identify what these institutions were, what they offered merchants involved in long-distance trade, and how Abu Taqiyya adapted them to his particular needs is essential for our understanding of the way merchants of the time carried out their business—funding their ventures, organizing their trade, and forming their networks. From Abu Taqiyya's experiences we can also identify the problems posed by the workings of this indigenous commercial system.

Role of the Courts in Trade

The geographical radius within which Abu Taqiyya moved in the course of his daily routine did not exceed about one kilometer. From his house near Suq Amir al-Juyush in the north of the city, his daily itinerary took him along the main route, past the Fatimid mosque of al-Aqmar and the Mamluk complex of al-Mansur Qalawun in the heart of the city, to one of his shops (*hanuts*) in the market of Suq al-Warraqin or storerooms (*hasils*) in Wikala al-Hamzawi, and eventually to al-Wikala al-Kubra and al-Wikala al-Sughra, behind the Qalawun complex. These monumental structures housed multiple and intricate functions, not only for merchants residing in Cairo like Isma'il, but also for merchants who were in transit.

These were the locations where he carried out his business. Closely tied to this routine were his frequent visits to the courts, where the deals he negotiated in the market or in the *wikala* were put on paper and registered in the court books. Thus with the commercial institutions and the legal institutions within walking distance of each other, Isma'il Abu Taqiyya was able to operate a trading network covering three continents.

His trade, both in Egypt and abroad, required legal tools with a certain degree of sophistication. The numerous deeds that Abu Taqiyya contracted in court in the course of his long career as a merchant provide a wealth of details for students of commercial history. The documents are all the more interesting because until quite recently scholars believed that no commercial papers existed in the Middle East before the modern period. This documentation sheds light on the way Abu Taqiyya personally conducted his business; thus we can follow one individual merchant as he undertakes commercial ventures of varying scopes and learn about some of the difficulties inherent in this kind of trade. On a broader level, this documentation shows how some of the provisions of Islamic *fiqh* regard-

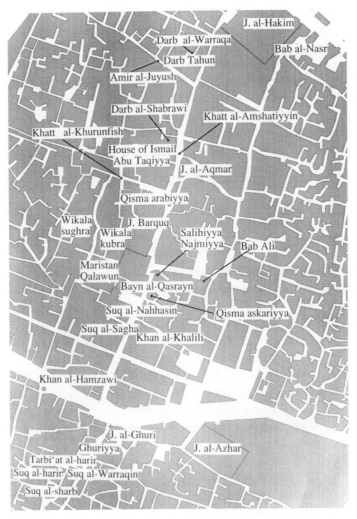

Darb al-Warraqa
J. al-Hakim
Bab al-Nasr
Darb Tahun
Amir al-Juyush
Darb al-Shabrawi
Khatt al-Amshatiyyin
Khatt al-Khurunfish
House of Ismail
Abu Taqiyya
J. al-Aqmar
Qisma arabiyya
Wikala sughra
J. Barquq
Wikala kubra
Salihiyya Najmiyya
Bab Ali
Maristan Qalawun
Bayn al-Qasrayn
Suq al-Nahhasin
Qisma askariyya
Suq al-Sagha
Khan al-Khalili
Khan al-Hamzawi
J. al-Ghuri
Ghuriyya
J. al-Azhar
Tarbi'at al-harir
Suq al-harir
Suq al-Warraqin
Suq al-sharb

3. The northern section of Cairo. Courtesy of CEDEJ.

ing business ventures were implemented in seventeenth-century Cairo. The relationship between law or legal opinion and actual practice is still being debated. Most scholars now question the views of the earlier Orientalists who claimed that the law of business partnerships had no bearing on the way that business was practiced.[8] The work of historians like Ronald Jennings and Haim Gerber on Kayseri and Bursa have clearly indicated that the classical Islamic business laws were still being practiced in seventeenth-century Anatolia.[9] The archives of seventeenth-century Cairo provide further evidence to support the findings of both Jennings and Gerber.

The role of courts in the daily life of urban populations in various parts of the Ottoman state is by now well known. What is less well known is that this institution played a role in helping merchants to run their businesses. Going to court was a routine matter for Isma'il Abu Taqiyya. The courtroom closest to his house was that of Bab 'Ali; it was also the most prestigious court because it was presided over by Qadi al-Qudat. Abu Taqiyya sometimes used the court of Salihiyya Najmiyya. This court, very close to Bab 'Ali, was held in the Mausoleum of Sultan al-Salih Najm al-Din, the last Sultan of the Ayyubid dynasty (which ruled Egypt from 1171 to 1250), who died while fighting a crusader army. Abu Taqiyya's close relationship to the courts is graphically illustrated by the frequency of his court appearances, as a sample taken over a number of months in Bab 'Ali alone, while he was at the peak of his activity, shows very clearly: In 1026/1617, in the month of Rajab, the seventh Muslim month of the year, three times (12, 14, 24); in the following month, Sha'ban, three times (5, 6, 12); in Ramadan, the month of fast for Muslims, five times (4, 5, 10, 12, 13); and in Shawwal six times (8, 9, 15, 16, 19, and the last day of the month), averaging roughly one visit a week to that particular court. It is very likely that business was more active during Ramadan because many Muslims traveled to Mecca to spend the month of fast there and returned the following month, Shawwal. Another sample from the year 1028/1618 is equally impressive. During Rabi' I, the third month of the Muslim calendar, Isma'il was in the court of Bab 'Ali on 8, 20, 26, and 28; the following month, Rabi' II, on 9, 10, 12, 15, 18, 20, 23, and 24; the month after that, Jumada I, on 5, 15, and 24; and the following month, Jumada II, on 3 and 26; during the next month, Rajab, on 5, 9, and 26; during Sha'ban on 6; during Ramadan on 13, 14, and 15; during the next month, Shawwal, on 13 and 19. For him, the courts were part of the routine of doing business. For us, the documents in the court registers provide a wealth of data on the way that business was conducted and a view of the practical application of the business procedures that legal literature has outlined.

The courts of Cairo clearly played vital and multiple roles in commerce and for merchants, Abu Taqiyya included. The fact that deeds regarding loans, credit, partnerships, deposits, and transactions for goods

of various kinds were regularly recorded in court registers is of great
significance. This meant that a merchant had guarantees, especially if any
disputes arose. A merchant did not simply have to depend on the other
party's good faith, important as that was. Abu Taqiyya may have insisted
on recording his daily, routine deals on paper and having them registered
in court on a regular basis because he had so many business affairs and
such large sums of money were involved.

Another reason why Abu Taqiyya involved the court in his business
affairs was that this institution not only provided a variety of mechanisms
for facilitating business, but also—more significant for a merchant whose
activities could be quite complex—allowed him a high degree of maneu-
verability. The legal tools could, to a certain degree, be adjusted to his
individual needs. A merchant could choose to make a contract with a
partner or client according to one of four rites or *madhhabs*, the Hanafi,
Maliki, Shafi'i, or Hanbali, because each court provided four *qadis*. He
could decide to address himself to the *qadi* of one of the rites for a certain
type of deed, and to that of another rite for another type of deed, when it
was more advantageous for him.

Still another reason that Abu Taqiyya and other merchant colleagues
whose trade covered such long distances relied so much on courts was
that the court documents issued in one city were recognized in the other
cities. While in Cairo, a person could record a sale for a house he owned
in Damascus, Jerusalem, or Jedda. Or a merchant could issue a power of
attorney to a colleague or assistant to do business for him in Mukha or in
Istanbul. Likewise, the court could intervene to secure inheritance rights
for heirs of a merchant who died away from home—in Mecca, Jedda, or
Mukha, for example—and see that the heirs in Cairo got their rightful
share of the goods stored by him in Jedda. In one complicated affair in
the court of Bab 'Ali in Cairo that Abu Taqiyya was involved in, he, acting
as the agent *(wakil)* of the purchaser, bought a house in Jedda from the
owners in Cairo. He had to declare, as was always done in such contracts,
that the purchaser (in Jedda) had taken delivery of the house.[10] For merchants, the fact that the deeds of mandate or of partnership issued in
Cairo were recognized in Istanbul, Damascus, Aleppo, Mecca, Jedda, and
Mukha, was no doubt convenient. We can see that the legal system offered
merchants guarantees and facilities beyond the borders of its direct jurisdiction. In all these domains, the courts, though not essentially a commercial institution, were performing functions of vital importance to

commerce and merchants—notarizing documents, providing guarantees, and intervening in disputes.

The difficulties and complications that such a system could generate should not be minimized. People did come to Cairo and present deeds issued in Mukha, Aleppo, or Hums, which the *qadi* accepted. But matters could be greatly complicated if two parties in a dispute challenged the authenticity of each other's deeds. This kind of problem is evident in the case of *khawaja* Ahmad al-Sawwaf, a merchant who acted as an agent in Mecca for the Ruwi'i brothers. The Ruwi'i brother who was in Cairo had given him a mandate with restricted powers to represent the family interests; the other Ruwi'i brother, in Mecca (since dead) had given him a full mandate to take care of all the family interests. The *qadi* was left with the difficult decision of validating one of the two. First he asked each one to produce the document. Each one was able to do so, and in both cases it confirmed what each said. As no agreement between the two parties ensued, the next step for the *qadi* was to ask each one to produce the witnesses to the document. The Ruwi'i in Cairo was able to do so, while *khawaja* Ahmad al-Sawwaf, at an obvious disadvantage, was not able to bring the witnesses to his deed.[11]

A further reason for Isma'il Abu Taqiyya's frequent court appearances is the fact that his trading operations were with partners who were neither his relatives nor necessarily merchants of Syrian origin like him. Unlike the Jewish Geniza merchants of the eleventh and twelfth centuries that S. D. Goitein's work has brought to light, the Karimi merchants, or the Armenian merchants who monopolized the silk trade of Persia in the sixteenth century, he had a business that was neither a family enterprise nor based within an ethnic group. He dealt with family members occasionally, and with Syrians occasionally as well. But for the most part, his dealings were with partners whom he chose either because he trusted them, or because they had particular skills, or because they happened to be available at the right time. For any of these reasons, his need for legal guarantees was probably higher than other merchants.

Obviously, some merchants made more use of the courts than others, depending on the kind of network in which they were involved. They probably felt it less necessary to register ventures that were undertaken within a family enterprise, between brothers, or between a father and his son. That is not to say that merchant families did not make use of the legal facilities available, even when dealing within the family circle. A family enterprise like that of the Ruwiʿis, which included many members in the trading profession, may have not recorded their partnership contracts as regularly as Ismaʿil Abu Taqiyya, but did register other kinds of deeds. *Khawaja* Ahmad al-Ruwiʿi, for instance, empowered his nephew ʿAli al-Ruwiʿi to collect the merchandise and the debts owed to him by clients in Mecca. The document was registered because ʿAli might have to prove that he was representing his uncle.[12] Because the Ruwiʿi business was so important, their dealings were probably recorded in writing even when deeds were not actually registered in court. It is hard to imagine such a large-scale business involving so many people being carried out without some type of written record, even if only an informal one.

Likewise, the head of one of the great merchant families of Ismaʿil Abu Taqiyya's generation, *khawaja* Nur al-Din al-Shujaʿi, does not seem to have kept regular registers of the family business in the court, as Ismaʿil Abu Taqiyya did. But nevertheless, when Nur al-Din prepared a consignment for Mecca and Jedda, he recorded in the court registers that he had borrowed the sum of 45,000 *dinars* from his son ʿAlam al-din, his daughters Nazirin and Khatun, and his grandson Fakhr al-Din.[13] This transaction was probably registered in the court records because the sum was so enormous, and even within a family the lenders would want to have some kind of guarantee for the return of the money. This kind of case appears in the court records less often, however, with small amounts of money.

Fund Raising

In the course of any commercial venture a merchant passed through various stages that brought the venture to a successful—or not so successful—conclusion, as the case might be. At each of these stages—from fund raising, to organizing the venture, to the time the goods were redistributed—he could have recourse to the various legal tools and mechanisms and to the commercial structures available. The body of deeds available with regard to Abu Taqiyya's commerce show how merchants used legal documentation for different purposes and objectives (to raise funds, to divide risks, to organize the trade and divide responsibilities) and under different conditions (for larger or more restricted ventures, with one or several partners whose responsibilities could be defined in the deeds, for shorter or longer periods and so on). In other words, the practice of trade on a daily basis, with all the various circumstances that merchants could encounter, indicates the way that the system functioned. In a microanalysis of the system, we can see not only how complex it was, but, more significant for Abu Taqiyya, the various ways that he could make use of it to achieve his goals.

One aspect of trade in the Middle East that has often been emphasized is that there was no system to advance funds to merchants—that is, there was no equivalent to the European banking system on which European merchants were heavily dependent—and the lack of such a system supposedly handicapped merchants of the Middle East. That is perhaps so, but the functions of this institution were in part fulfilled through the legal system, which provided a legal framework for the advancing of funds by individuals to each other. This could take a number of forms, which Abu Taqiyya's activities illustrate amply—pooling of capital, loans, credit—forms that often fulfilled more than one function.

Of the numerous forms of fund raising sanctioned in courts, the form that Isma'il Abu Taqiyya preferred was the 'aqd shirka (partnership contract). This contract brought together two or more people who pooled their capital, shared the risks, and divided the profits between them according to set shares. The records of Bab 'Ali contain close to twenty references to such partnerships that Abu Taqiyya contracted in the course of his career, many of which were operating at the same time. He probably found the 'aqd shirka useful because it served not only to fund his projects but also to organize them. Yet their usefulness had its limitations. Judging from Abu Taqiyya's pattern of use for this kind of partnership, it is evident that it was particularly efficient for certain regions. Most of his shirkas were used for trading ventures in Mecca, Jedda, and to a lesser extent, India, and later Yemen; for other regions like Bilad al-Sham and Anatolia, there exist few records for his shirka agreements. Possibly, he made use of forms other than the shirka for these regions. Apparently, in the eighteenth century the shirka was still essentially a tool used for Red Sea trading.[14]

The shirka was a major form for Abu Taqiyya's trade, as we can see in tracing his efforts to enlarge his ventures and increase the capital he invested in them. He was using it as a tool for the reinvestment of his profits and as a method to expand the business, whereby profits were reinvested into the trade. This trend is particularly obvious in the first ten years of his career, from the late 1580s to the late 1590s. The three shirkas traced in the records for this period involved capital (ras mal) of 56,000 nisfs in

1587; 80,000 in 1592 and 920,000 in 1597, that is, a several-fold increase. The capital in subsequent *shirka*s was rarely as large as that in any particular venture. But the number and frequency of these ventures increased. This pattern could mean that the capital he disposed of was being divided among many smaller ventures.

The *'aqd shirka* probably suited Abu Taqiyya's particular needs more than the *commenda (mudaraba)* for two reasons. In the first place, the *mudaraba,* for which the term *commenda* was applied by the Italian merchants who had long-standing trading links with the Middle East, meant that one party contributed funds, the other party contributed the skills and then profits were divided. One of the two parties was the capitalist who funded the venture and the other the merchant who did the traveling. Abu Taqiyya, however, was more than the capitalist funding commercial ventures, because he was personally involved in the running of the business. In the second place, the *'aqd shirka* seems to have been the more flexible of the two types of agreements, in terms of both financing and organization. The *shirka* was a contractual agreement to which the partners could add the clauses they agreed upon. It was up to them to decide the amount of money to be put, the currency to be used, the way funds were to be used and by whom; thus it could be adapted to a one-time venture or to an ongoing one.

The partnership contract did not specify a set period for its validity. Most of them, in fact, indicated that the partners should make continuous and repeated shipments. The contracts used such phrases as *al-marra ba'd al-marra wal karra ba'd al-karra* or *waqt ba'd waqt wa hal ba'd hal* (one time after another) to indicate that the partnership was a continuous one or that one voyage after another was undertaken. The contract was probably terminated when the partners wished to share the profits. *Shirka*s of this kind varied in length three or four years for some, ten or eleven years for others. At any one moment, Isma'il Abu Taqiyya had several *shirka*s in operation, with different people and in different locations. Significantly enough, a *shirka* could be inherited if one of the partners died. It was included in the property that was to be shared by the heirs, and they received their shares in it as they would if it were a piece of property.[15] Such an arrangement evidently could be of help to a son who wished to continue his father's business, but he might have to face the problem of the fragmentation of the *shirka* among several heirs.

Partnerships were very variable with regard to the sums of money involved. Some merchants formed partnerships for fairly small sums. Of the contracts for trading in Bilad al-Sudan published by Terence Walz, one was for 175 *dinar*s, another for 180 *dinar*s, and a third one for 207 *dinar*s and seven jointly owned camels.[16] Such sums seem modest in comparison to the amounts that Abu Taqiyya's partnerships involved, but that difference could be a function of the region where these merchants traded and the capital that they could dispose of. The amounts of money that Abu Taqiyya pooled in the different *shirka*s in which he was involved varied considerably; some of the contracts were for very large sums of money, others were more modest. The higher investments were in the range of 920,000 *nisf*s,[17] and 22,000 *dinar*s (equivalent to 880,000 *nisf*s);[18] a lesser investment might be only a tenth of that (2,250 *dinar*s or 90,000 *nisf*s in 1016/1607).[19] Many of Isma'il Abu Taqiyya's *shirka*s were formed with sums of money in between these two extremes.

Like other merchants involved in large-scale ventures, Abu Taqiyya had to balance two concerns when undertaking a commercial venture: He had to make sure that he kept risks as low as possible while at the same time not missing a good opportunity for profit. Risks that merchants faced were varied. Sometimes a natural disaster hit, like the shipwrecks that occurred in the dangerous waters of the Red Sea, whose coral reefs were a constant threat. Sometimes the danger was brigandage; along the land routes peopled by bedouins merchants might lose all or part of their shipments of merchandise. There were also risks of loss from delays in the arrival of goods, which automatically meant delays in the profits, or from damage to goods because of faulty storage or humidity.

One way of dividing risks was to include more partners in the *shirka,* with three or sometimes four merchants sharing the investments and sharing the risks. This pattern, more frequent when large sums of money were involved, was one that Abu Taqiyya often used. He employed other methods as well, such as forming several *shirka*s, all at one time, with different people (although his partner 'Abdul-Qadir al-Damiri took part in most of them). We can see this happening at busy times of the year, such as the time of the departure of pilgrims going from Cairo to Mecca. In mid-Rabi' II, 1016/1607, for instance, as the season for the departure of the pilgrims approached, Isma'il Abu Taqiyya and his colleague 'Abdul-Qadir al-Damiri prepared for this event by forming three separate *shirka*s. The two of them were sole partners in one of them (capital invested 8,000 *dinar*s).[20] The other two *shirka*s they shared with a third person: With *khawaja* ʿUthman al-Sunbati, a silk merchant whom they knew because he, like them, had a shop in Suq al-Warraqin, they arranged a more modest *shirka* of 2,300 *dinar*s;[21] and, the same day, 14 Rabiʿ II, a third *shirka* with *khawaja* Abil Surur al-ʿAmriti, also a silk merchant in Suq al-Warraqin with whom they were acquainted, for even less, 1,550 *dinar*s.[22] In other words, rather than forming one *shirka* with all the money—that is, nearly 12,000 *dinar*s—Abu Taqiyya had three separate arrangements independent from each other, presumably so as to spread risk.

A merchant like Abu Taqiyya could find in the partnership contract sufficient leeway to manipulate its clauses to his advantage. His partnerships with al-Damiri, his lifelong colleague and friend, were on an equal footing, both sharing the venture capital and the profits equally; each partner had the freedom to use his judgment in deciding what to buy, what to sell, how and for how much. But when other merchants were included, especially some of the merchants of more modest scope, or merchants with whom he dealt with only occasionally for a particular venture, like al-Sunbati or al-ʿAmriti, this did not apply. Various mechanisms could be used to control their actions. One of them was for Abu Taqiyya to put more specific conditions in the contract. For instance, al-ʿAmriti was allowed to sell on credit only for a sum of up to 2,000 *nisf*s; Sunbati was not allowed to sell on credit at all. Moreover, they were not handling very large sums of money either—that was his way of controlling what could be poor judgment or bad intent on their part. They were all partners in the contract, but they were unequal partners, and the stronger party was the one who could impose his conditions on the others. In other words, this legal tool, the *ʿaqd shirka,* could be adapted to Abu Taqiyya's circumstances. With conditions of this kind included in the contract, it is certainly not accidental that most of Abu Taqiyya's *shirka*s were formed according to the Hanbali law and by the Hanbali *qadi,* not so much because of what Hanbali law said specifically about *shirka*s, as because it regarded any clause in a contract valid and binding as long as the signatories agreed to them.[23] We have here a good example of the way that Abu Taqiyya could maneuver the legal tools to fit his needs and maximize his profits, while at the same time functioning within the system.

The legal system provided another variation for the partnership contract, which gave the merchants involved a certain degree of flexibility in their dealings with partnership funds. This was the "sub-*shirka,*" or the *shirka* within a *shirka,* which Ismaʿil Abu Taqiyya and his partner ʿAbdul-

Qadir al-Damiri frequently made use of. This was simply a form whereby one of the partners to the contract, using part of the partnership funds, entered into a partnership contract with a third party. In Isma'il Abu Taqiyya's case, such an arrangement proved useful on two levels. First in terms of dividing the risks, it fulfilled the same function as having more than one partnership. From a *shirka* he shared with 'Abdul-Qadir al-Damiri, the sum of which is not indicated, his partner 'Abdul-Qadir took 2,000 *qirsh* (60,000 *nisfs*) from their common capital and formed another partnership with two other people who put up an equal sum of money.[24] Second, a sub-*shirka* allowed Abu Taqiyya to experiment with new commercial territories—notably, to trade directly with India, something he tried for the first time in 1006/1597. The original partnership Isma'il formed that year with *khawaja* 'Ali al-Wafa'i, was for 920,000 *nisfs*. The following year, this partner, once at Mecca, used 4,620 *dinars* from the original capital (207,900 *nisfs*) to form another *shirka* (or sub-*shirka*, to be more precise) with third parties who used it to carry out the trade from Mecca to Goa.[25] Thus, whatever increased risk Isma'il incurred from the greater distance was minimized by this method. A few years later, once his first experiment had brought fruit, Abu Taqiyya formed a partnership for a very large sum of money (22,000 *dinars* or 880,000 *nisfs)* which carried his network to India.[26] We can see here how Isma'il Abu Taqiyya used the *shirka* as a tool for breaking new ground in his commerce. This tool was one that he could adapt to different uses to serve his end.

In addition to the legal framework these *shirkas* gave to the business of trading, they also offered certain economic benefits to those concerned, because they could be used for reinvestment. Very likely, when a particular venture was successfully terminated, the merchandise sold profitably, and the profits divided among the partners, these profits were reinvested, in either the existing partnership or perhaps a new partnership contract that absorbed both the original capital and the profits the merchants had made. In the course of his long career, Abu Taqiyya had many occasions to do this. In 1015/1606, for instance, on the very day that he and his partner Abu Bakr al-Damiri annulled *(faskh)* a *shirka* for ten thousand *dinars* formed between them in 1010/1601, they reinvested the capital plus another 12,000 *dinars* in a new *shirka* formed then and there, bringing the total to 22,000 *dinars*.[27] We would, of course, suspect that the extra 12,000 *dinars* newly invested was the profit they had made from their venture, perhaps with some additional funds. In another instance, a large sum of money was injected into an existing partnership. Isma'il Abu Taqiyya had formed a *shirka* for 66,000 *nisf*s with 'Abdul-Qadir al-Damiri and two Sunbati brothers, Ibrahim and 'Uthman, in 1011/1602. A year later —perhaps with the profits accruing to them from this venture—the capital was brought up to 87,000*nisf*s, the new contract specifying that the other clauses *(ahkam)* of the partnership contract remained unchanged.[28]

The variety of purposes to which these partnership contracts were put to use is worthy of special attention, especially in view of the fact that so much has been written about the rigidity of Islamic law and its inability to adapt to various kinds of situations. The experience of seventeenth-century merchants, who carried out a significant portion of their trade within the framework of the judiciary system, gives an entirely different perspective on this matter. Rather than a rigid set of imposed laws that were supposed to have suffocated business, the commercial documents of Abu Taqiyya show a legal system that was adaptable to various kinds of situations. Certainly, the way he himself used such documents did not have to be identical to the way other merchants did, either in his choice of *madhhab*s or in his methods of controlling some of the activities of his partners. For Abu Taqiyya, the legal system was not a barrier to carrying out business, but quite the contrary, for he (and many others) could turn it into an asset.

Most of Abu Taqiyya's investments seem to have taken the form of partnerships. Occasionally, however, he utilized less formal agreements, notably with close family members. We find out, for example, about an informal arrangement of this kind when he was taken ill in 1031/1621 and thought he was going to die. A court employee was called to his bedside, to put into writing what had so far been a verbal agreement with Ahmad Ibn 'Ariqat, his nephew and son-in-law. To this court employee, Isma'il Abu Taqiyya declared that Ahmad had a right to one-fourth of the goods, merchandise, money, and debts with Fadli Pasha, Ottoman governor of Yemen, and Ahmad Pasha, Ottoman governor of Habash. Thus if Isma'il Abu Taqiyya died before these two had settled their accounts, Ahmad could guarantee the would get his share.[29]

Organizing the Network

The search by scholars for an association or institution that was devoted entirely to organizing trade has been fruitless. We have no evidence that such a thing existed. But this is not to say that merchants did not make use of the structures so as to allow efficient trading. In reality, rather than look for institutions that did not exist, we can instead identify the structures through which certain vital functions were accomplished. To a large extent, the organization of Abu Taqiyya's trade depended on a contractual agreement between two or more parties that specified which way to divide the trading activities among the parties and how to parcel out the geographical regions for which each was responsible. This was done as part of the ʿaqd shirka that pooled their capital. The same contract also defined the responsibilities of the respective partners. It was therefore an organizational tool as well as a financial one. This form seems to have been particularly useful for trade in the Red Sea, a major sector in the network, which was particularly heavy as a trading route.

The partnership contracts that Abu Taqiyya formed covered a number of routine matters related to trade, some more important than others. Rather than leave them to be decided on the spot, these merchants obviously thought it preferable to regulate matters in a more formal and binding way. Many of the responsibilities of each partner were thus defined by contract. However, the contracts in question mention no penalties if one of the partners did not fulfill his obligations. We must therefore conclude that in spite of the formal contractual links, merchants doing business together had to have a certain degree of mutual trust in order to minimize risks. Once the partners pooled their capital, the contract indicated what was to be done with the money. What usually happened was that one of the partners was charged with taking the money and using it to purchase products from the local market—Egyptian textiles (aqmisha misriyya), refined sugar, paper—that he could then accompany to Jedda or Mukha. A partner going to Damascus might also include in his purchases pepper and coffee.[30] The market of Cairo furnished these cities with both transit goods from the Red Sea trade and Egyptian products in demand in other commercial centers.

Occasionally, however, it was not merchandise but cash that was transported from Cairo by one of the partners, a project fraught with dangers, because the risk of theft and accident was compounded by the possibility of raiding bedouins attacking the convoy. In 1012/1603, for instance, when Ismaʿil Abu Taqiyya and ʿAbdul-Qadir al-Damiri entered a partnership with khawaja Abul Nasr al-Tarabulsi, the 12,000 qirsh (360,000 nisfs) that they had pooled was handed over to him to take to Mecca and

Jedda with the pilgrimage that year.[31] He therefore traveled carrying the money with him. The reason for taking this risk can only be guessed. It was not the absence of a form for the transfer of funds. The bill of exchange was known and could have been used. Debts were, in fact, often transferred on paper to a third person. These transactions were recognized in Islamic law, and had long been practiced in the region, as Goitein's study of medieval merchants in Egypt demonstrate.[32] The so-called *suftaja* (letter of credit, a word of Persian origin) was used specifically to avoid the risk of transport. The transport of cash was more likely to have been part of a current of transfer of precious metals from Europe to Asia, with which Europeans were paying for their purchases in the East because they were not in a position to provide Asian traders with products in demand in India or elsewhere.[33] André Raymond has noted this same phenomenon in the eighteenth century and has also explained it in terms of the export of precious metals from Europe to Asian markets.[34] Whatever the reasons, such an uncomfortable and risky way of transferring money was one of the serious problems that merchants in Cairo had to face.

Contracts always specified which of the partners was going to do the traveling and what his destination would be, sometimes even giving specific indications about his form of transport. Travelers from Cairo could reach Jedda by the overland route via 'Ajrud, Nakhl, 'Aqaba, Muwaylih, and Yanbu', a trip that lasted a little over a month.[35] The sea route—overland to Suez then by ship to Jedda—could take about two weeks to Jedda and a month from Jedda back to Suez because of the adverse winds.[36] It was more costly to transport merchandise by land, but sometimes it was the only usable route because seasonal winds over the Red Sea hampered sailing for about half the year. The partnership contracts frequently had a clause stating that the traveling party could send merchandise either by land or by sea, whichever he deemed more convenient. As for trade with Yemen, one ship a year made the trip between Suez and Mukha. A partnership contract between Abu Taqiyya, al-Damiri, and Mustafa al-Safadi specified that al-Safadi would take with him the sugar, paper, and Egyptian textiles purchased locally to Mukha, and indicated the type of ship he would use to travel along the Red Sea.[37]

One of the most interesting arrangements to be found laid out in the details of contracts is the occasional division of responsibilities on a regional basis. One such arrangement, made between Abu Bakr al-Damiri and Isma'il in 1015/1606, stipulated that Abu Bakr would travel to

Mecca with the products bought with the partnership funds. Once there, he was responsible for a number of things. It was up to him to sell this merchandise and to buy goods from the market there to reship to his partner Isma'il in Cairo. He was also expected to ship merchandise from Mecca to Yemen and to India. Abu Taqiyya's responsibility covered Cairo, Alexandria, and Rashid, the Mediterranean ports where he sent the goods he received from his colleague in Mecca. Each of the two was therefore responsible for a certain region. Abu Bakr's journey to Mecca was evidently expected to last some time. According to the stipulations of the partnership contract, each of them could make use of the agents and assistants to handle the merchandise, preparing it for shipment in bales or sacks and accompanying the goods during the voyage. In other words, each was going to have to deal with all the matters at his end, employing other people when necessary.[38] The way some of the business was handled is indicated in one of the court deeds shortly thereafter. Isma'il Abu Taqiyya, in fulfillment of his part of the deal, prepared a shipment of 24 loads (himls) of coral (morjan), sugar, and other goods, to be sent to Mecca (each himl costing 21 dinars), presumably by the overland route.[39] His partner in Mecca made similar arrangements in order to send merchandise to Cairo. A continuous process of mutual shipments thus traveled in the two directions.

Such court deeds clearly show that merchants like 'Abdul-Qadir al-Damiri or his cousin Abu Bakr, who often took the trip between Cairo and Mecca or Jedda, were very far from being simple peddlers or traveling merchants who sold their own or someone else's goods. The arrangement they had in Mecca or Jedda paralleled the one Abu Taqiyya had in Cairo, though perhaps on a smaller scale. They bought and sold goods; they arranged for the shipment to different destinations—to Cairo, and to Yemen and India; they employed people to do different jobs for them. They were, in other words, representing the interests of the partnership in Mecca, and their specific functions and duties were spelled out on paper.

Once the partnership was terminated, the profits were divided according to the share each one had assumed. This again was done in court, in the form of a termination of contract (faskh 'aqd) and fulfillment of its obligations. The equal sharing of the profits put the partner who had done the traveling at a disadvantage. Even though the expenses of the merchant who traveled could be charged to the shirka, he rarely seems to have been directly compensated for the inconveniences of traveling and its dangers, and leaving his home and family. When Abu Taqiyya formed a *shirka* with Abu Bakr al-Damiri, he twice gave him an important loan as he was getting ready to travel—1,000 *dinars* (40,000 *nisfs*) each time—and the profits Damiri made with that amount were to remain his.[40] But with Abu Taqiyya's other partner, 'Abdul-Qadir al-Damiri, who was a modest person, only once does such a loan take place, and for a more modest sum, 12,000 *nisfs*.[41]

This form of organization was not equally effective everywhere. The Cairo-Mecca-Jedda axis, sometimes including the towns of Bilad al-Sham on the way, was a major one, used very frequently. The commercial traffic on it was heavy, and the profits were high. It therefore made sense for someone like 'Abdul-Qadir al-Damiri or Abu Bakr al-Damiri to spend extended periods of time in Mecca and Jedda, and to make frequent trips. It also made sense for these merchants to set up their own network there, aided by assistants and agents. Also, there may well have been close similarities in structure between cities like Cairo, Mecca, and Jedda. Although information on the commercial structures of the Hijaz where Mecca and Jedda were located, in the Arabian peninsula, is scanty, the legal documents issued in the courts of Cairo were recognized there. With the partnership contract in his hand, Damiri could, while in Mecca or Jedda, act as representative of the partnership, make partnerships there with third persons, receive and ship goods as a representative of the partnership, and so on.

But the commerce of Abu Taqiyya extended to regions beyond the Ottoman state and beyond the world of Islam, where these legal structures were less meaningful and merchants might not find it as feasible to use the same tools and methods of trading. Some places, like Cano in Nigeria, for example, were of lesser importance to his trade. One is of course not equally well informed about each sector of the trade to be able to discern the patterns that were used for the different sectors.

Another legal tool used by long-distance merchants was the *tawkil*, the mandate or power of agency. This was a much looser tool than the partnership, and merchants could make use of it in many ways. A *tawkil* could specify a limited function that the person mandated was competent to carry out on behalf of the person who mandated him, which the deed clearly spelled out. Before a voyage to Mecca, for example, Yasin Abu Taqiyya mandated his brother Isma'il to cash the debts owed to him and to buy and sell goods on his behalf.[42] The *tawkil* could empower the person mandated simply to act on behalf of the person issuing the mandate. This *tawkil mutlaq,* as it was called, gave the person mandated full authority to act on behalf of the other.[43] A merchant traveling to another commercial center with this deed in hand could thus represent the interests of the other merchant once he got there, buying goods and shipping them, without any restrictions.

This power of agency could be issued to a skilled merchant, who, in addition to his own trading, agreed to act on behalf of another merchant while traveling. The Ruwi'is disputed a case in court that involved a *khawaja* Ahmad al-Sawwaf, stationed in Jedda, who claimed to have a *tawkil mutlaq* and who also claimed 5 percent of all the goods he dealt in for the Ruwi'is.[44] Or it could be an employee who worked with a merchant for a fee. As far as Isma'il was concerned, he does not seem to have used merchants to act on his behalf. It was probably more in keeping with the hierarchy he was running to make use of paid employees, whom he empowered to act on his behalf, or enfranchised slaves, whom he probably compensated somehow.

Isma'il Abu Taqiyya had agents *(wakils)* in different regions helping him in the business. The *wakil* who handled Abu Taqiyya's business in Cano was Haj Muhammad 'Izz al-Din Badir, about whom we know little. In Istanbul, Abu Taqiyya had an agent by the name of Haj Rajab al-Hamawi. The *wakil* representing him in Mukha was an enfranchised slave, a *ma'tuq.* At Isma'il Abu Taqiyya's death, his family and heirs empowered another agent, Haj Abu Bakr al-Jabalawi, to travel to Mukha to look into the goods and merchandise, as well as the debts in Isma'il Abu Taqiyya's name, a job for which he has going to be paid 10 percent of the value of what he was able to retrieve.[45] For his trading activities inside Egypt, Abu Taqiyya sent his *wakils* to the various places where he bought or sold goods. Through these agents, he spread his network within the country, both in towns and rural areas, especially in the Delta. The *wakil* thus offered another way of operating the network.

Isma'il Abu Taqiyya's dealings with Venice are of great interest because we know so little about the networks of Muslim merchants in Europe. It has generally been taken for granted that the transit trade between East and West was first carried out by Venetian merchants and subsequently by Dutch and French ones. We know very little about the role of Muslim merchants in this trade. And yet Braudel does mention that in the sixteenth century, "eastern" merchants had started forming colonies in Italian Adriatic ports; in Ancona, there was a *fondaco* (warehouse) for Turkish and other Muslim merchants; and by the end of the sixteenth century, Eastern merchants had communities in Venice, Ferrara, Ancona, Pesaro, and Naples.[46] The implication is that during this period Middle Eastern merchants expanded their trading networks to include Italian coastal centers. This is a phenomenon of great importance that calls for more research, because we do not have any hard evidence prior to the Ottoman period. The activities of Abu Taqiyya and of the other merchants of his generation can shed some light on this matter.

The trading structures he had with Venice were quite loose. Neither partnerships nor *wakils* seem to have been used. He placed his orders for goods from Venice with Jewish merchants traveling there, through the Jewish customs or *multazim,* and also shipped merchandise there through them. We find out about such transactions from the deeds between Abu Taqiyya and the customs tax farmer of Alexandria, *muʿallim* (master, teacher) Salamon b. Daʾud b. Salamon, who declared having received the duties on the merchandise Abu Taqiyya had arranged with the two brothers Naharon and Shuʿa.[47] The exact arrangements for buying from Venice and transporting to Alexandria are not clear, but once the venture was terminated, a court document was issued to say that each side had fulfilled its obligations to the other. Other merchants of his generation were mandating the Venetian merchants who came to Cairo to buy or sell goods for them in Venice.

If many aspects of the organization of the commercial network were institutionalized, a number of others were not. In addition to the contractual arrangements, many duties—some more important than others—were being handled outside of this framework. Numerous activities necessary for running a business involved no contracts. Like many other merchants, Abu Taqiyya engaged his enfranchised slaves in his trade, sometimes having them travel with goods, as in the case of Hajj Hamdun b. ʿAbdalla al-Habashi. We learn of these informal arrangements only when something goes wrong. Hamdun, for example, died while in Mukha, and his widow in Cairo came to court (or was made to come to court) to declare that all the goods in his charge in fact belonged to Abu Taqiyya and she had no claims on them.[48]

Exchange and Distribution of Merchandise

Much of Abu Taqiyya's working day was spent in the market, either in one of the *wikala*s where he had rented storerooms or in the shops he rented in Suq al-Warraqin, and later, more and more in his own *wikala*. That was where prospective clients coming from different parts of Cairo or of Egypt, or foreigners passing through Cairo, gathered to buy or sell merchandise. Because Cairo was a major distribution center, there was usually a high level of activity in a market or *wikala*.

These great complexes, many of which still adorn the major commercial thoroughfare of the old city, have long been used in Cairo as distribution centers for trade. Built around large courtyards, these buildings contained depots or rooms for storage, which were rented out to merchants who stored their goods there and eventually sold them from that location. Along the upper floors, living units (usually a room or two with commodities) were also rented out and could lodge merchants in transit. The activities inside these *wikala*s are described by an eyewitness, Johann Wild, who was a contemporary of Isma'il Abu Taqiyya, a German who, as a mercenary soldier in Hungary, became a prisoner of war and was sold into servitude, changing masters several times, until he ended up in Egypt. Johann Wild was able to give a vivid picture of commerce in the *wikala*s. According to his eyewitness account, once the word got around that merchants were starting to arrive with their goods, the intermediaries came to inspect the goods, going around the *wikala* from one storeroom to another, inquiring about what was available and asking everyone they could about the kind of merchandise he wished to buy. They then brought buyers and sellers together, taking prospective buyers to the appropriate storerooms to examine the goods. If a deal was concluded, they got a commission.[49]

*Wikala*s provided a number of basic services to merchants, both traveling and resident ones. A merchant coming to trade in Cairo for the first time, who was familiar with neither the city nor any persons there, could direct himself to one of these *wikala*s and find not only a space to store his merchandise but also a place to stay. In the daytime, the courtyard of the *wikala* was filled with people providing all kinds of commercial services. The brokers, *simsar* or *dallal*, brought together prospective buyers and sellers. *Sarraf*s (money changers) and *qabban*s (weighers of goods) became involved when a deal had been made between buyer and seller.

Once the deal had been concluded, arrangements were made for transporting the goods; human porters, mules, and camels could all be found in the courtyard of the *wikala*. In other words, even for a stranger, this institution offered services sufficient for him to complete his business without having to move around very much.

The same services were obviously also available—and essential—to resident merchants in Cairo. In addition, as a meeting place between people newly arriving from a journey and others preparing to undertake one, the *wikala* also served as a place for exchange of news and information, such as which goods were readily available and which were rare at that time of year.

To a certain degree, the intensity of commercial activity depended on seasonal factors, like the departure and the return of the pilgrims, as well as the sailing seasons in the Red Sea. The same applied to the trans-Saharan caravan that brought goods from Black Africa to Cairo. Merchants adapted their business to these periods of higher or lower trading activities. Isma'il Abu Taqiyya's was busiest before the pilgrimage or *hajj*, when goods were bought locally, stored temporarily, and then packed for the oncoming journey; and lists made of the merchandise that would be handed over to the traveling partner, who would accompany it to its destination. For all these odd jobs, there must have been many workers—some skilled, some unskilled—that merchants employed for these various preparations. Another peak in business accompanied the arrival of goods, when pilgrims returned from Mecca, for instance, or the arrival of a ship in Suez was announced.

Prices also fluctuated accordingly. If a large shipment of spices reached Suez, prices might go down, but if merchants came from Jedda announcing that spices were in short supply there, prices went up. As the merchandise, sometimes in large quantities, arrived in Cairo—charged on camel-back from Suez—a merchant could sell immediately or, if his finances were more solid and he could afford to do so, he could wait to sell later, when he estimated he could make a better profit. Only the wealthier merchants could afford to delay their sales. Those who needed capital to carry on their business sold their goods upon arrival.

Depending on circumstances, merchandise could be sold either for cash or on credit. Cash was the surer and quicker way to make a profit; credit was slower but presumably raised the price of the goods. Isma'il Abu Taqiyya carried out sales on credit quite frequently, and when he did so, he promptly accompanied the purchaser to the court of Bab 'Ali. These sales were registered in court records as a guarantee in case of nonpayment, especially because large sums of money were often involved, a thousand *dinars*, (40,000 *nisfs*) for instance, for 52 *qintars* (each *quintar* equaled about 44 kilos) of pepper he sold in 1014/1605;[50] or 1,500 *dinars* for a variety of spices and coffee he sold on credit to a traveling merchant, Hajj Muhammad al-Hinnawi.[51] The document was sometimes specific about the exact date that repayment was expected—or if installments were going to be made, and when. But even with such precautions, who could guarantee that he would get paid, or that he would get paid in time? A large-scale merchant like Abu Taqiyya probably found it profitable to sell a portion of a large shipment on credit. But there was always sure to be someone who occasionally did not pay up on time. The courts helped sometimes by having the debtor imprisoned, but for a merchant who wanted his money, this might not be the best solution. Or the court could see that some compensation was obtained. Instead of an unpaid debt of 300 *qirsh* from a certain *sayyid sharif* (descendent of the Prophet) named Hasan, Abu Taqiyya in 1025/1615 took this person's house, sold it for 400 *qirsh,* gave Hasan 100, and kept the rest.[52] And another time, he and 'Abdul-Qadir were compensated for an unpaid debt with a Bosnian slave woman.[53] But even with the most efficient court system, the best incentive a person had to pay back a debt was not the menace of a court case but the desire to stay in business. Because most of Abu Taqiyya's business was in wholesale, he was in touch with numerous other members of the merchant community, especially smaller-scale merchants who did not themselves have a long-distance network or whose capital was limited. They bought the goods that he offered and resold them, either in Cairo or in other Egyptian cities to which they traveled.

Working Within the System

We can draw more than one conclusion from the preceding statements. In the first place, there was probably not much new about the way that Isma'il Abu Taqiyya and his generation carried out their business. The tools and mechanisms that the court records mention—the partnership, the mandate, the sale on credit—seem to be similar to those that Goitein found in the Geniza documents of the twelfth and thirteenth centuries. This similarity testifies to a great continuity between these two periods in spite of the six centuries that separate them. Moreover, these partnerships and mandates seem, for the most part, to be well within the prescriptions of the *shariʿa*. The trading system of the period can thus be considered to be a traditional one. And yet this does not mean that conditions were stationary over the centuries. A comparison with the period Goitein covered, for instance, shows a significant difference in approach—notably, a growing formality of trading relations, which indicates the complexity of the commercial situation in the later period. Goitein stressed the importance of family relations and informal relationships between merchants; family members played important roles organizationally and consequently family members had to be on good terms with each other. He found innumerable references to merchants cooperating with each other informally, carrying out mutual favors, and doing business on the basis of trust and friendship.[54] For Ismaʿil Abu Taqiyya and his contemporaries, with the spread of the court system in Cairo, the tendency was to do things in writing and to record deals in court, even in the case of Ismaʿil's closest and most trusted friend and partner, ʿAbdul-Qadir al-Damiri.

In the second place, the longevity of the system within which Ismaʿil Abu Taqiyya and his generation were functioning can be explained in part by the fact that it was a fluid system, adaptable to different needs and situations. It provided them with both formal and informal mechanisms for organizing and carrying out their business as well as with a commercial and legal framework within which they could carry out their activities. Although this system was able to cope with the needs of small traders and traveling merchants—that is, merchants at the lower scales of the hierarchy—it evidently had a greater significance for fulfilling the more complex needs of the large-scale merchants who had widely spread international networks. Because the various mechanisms and legal tools could be used in different ways, people tried to adapt these to their needs and to their situation in the trade hierarchy. About 1600, therefore, merchants were making use of the commercial and legal institutions and functioning within an indigenous system, from within which they were going to have to confront the shifting patterns of trade that the coming decades would bring.

4

Shifting Patterns in Trade

The half century linking the last decades of the sixteenth century to the early ones in the seventeenth is one of those periods during which a number of political crises came to the fore in Egypt and in other parts of the Ottoman Empire. Historians writing about Egypt have tended to concentrate on these—troop revolts against the Ottoman pasha, for example, or the emergence of Mamluks as a power group and their challenge to Ottoman authority. A decline in commerce during this period has been assumed, though not studied. As a matter of fact, the region as a whole—Egypt, the Eastern Mediterranean, Anatolia—is often considered to have lost its earlier dynamism during this period as a result of major transformations in international trading routes. Both direct access of European merchants to Asian merchandise and the development of Atlantic routes are cited as major factors in the decline of the region's former importance. Such explanations, however, tend to blur a much more complex reality, which is impossible to understand by reading the region's history either through the optic of European history or from European sources only, as has often been done in the past. By observing merchant activity during this crucial period, we can put matters in a different perspective and identify some of its salient features. Even if the fortunes of Europe had taken a turn for the better, it does not follow that the Mediterranean region fell into a slumber, as some historians have claimed: firstly, because of the primary importance of trade within the Ottoman world; secondly, because of the nature of trade relations with Europe. Historians who object to the isolation of Ottoman history from world history could point to the parallels between the violence and unrest in the different parts of the Ottoman Empire and the seventeenth-century crisis in Europe, where similar phenomena of revolts and unrest are understood as being the outward signs of important social and economic transformations.[1] The same pattern might apply to Cairo.

By closely following the activities of merchants in international trade, we find a different picture of the period emerging than the one generally drawn. New commercial trends during this period were characterized by an extension in trading networks and by merchants' investments in agriculture and production of commodities in high demand for export, of which sugar was among the most important. It was also during these years that a new and important item, coffee, was introduced to the international market, and the merchants of Cairo managed to monopolize its trade. These developments were major factors behind the reemergence of merchants and their great prosperity. Abu Taqiyya's involvement in these developments can be dated to the first and second decades of the seventeenth century, after he had been in the trading business for a long while and become an experienced merchant with a complex set of networks.

Rather than the decline of trade and agriculture, we may, on the contrary, see a period of economic vitality that touched many aspects of the economy, including trade, agriculture, and some aspects of production. It is in the context of these economic changes that we should view the emergence of merchants to new levels of wealth and prominence. The lives of Abu Taqiyya and his colleagues mirrored many of these developments. The direction in which Abu Taqiyya's fortunes developed was in many ways a reflection of larger and more important changes taking place, both regionally and worldwide.

For a number of reasons, the condition of merchants underwent major transformations in the course of the sixteenth century. These changes had a bearing on their economic as well as their social situation. They were in the process of emerging as a group that was economically independent of the Ottoman bureaucracy, a process that probably took close to a century. In studying this process, we need to address two questions related to the link between the Ottoman administration and the economy. The first involves the degree of control the state had over trade. A number of studies on trade have emphasized the importance that the state played in regulating trade during the early period, when it was still very centralized. Some historians have closely linked the Ottoman state's ability to survive to its capacity to control and guide economic and commercial activity. As long as it was able to maintain its control, it could keep European capitalist penetration out. Peripheralization of the economy is seen as the result of the loss of this control.[2] This view, in other words, perceives that the economy passed from a stage when it was controlled by the state—that is, politically controlled—to one in which it was controlled by European capitalism. The implication is that initiatives always came from above, and that little space was left for forces moving up. Such a view plays down the importance of economic forces and the actors who concretized them. Halil Inalcik, for one, does not believe that this approach can be substantiated on the basis of documentary evidence. He believes that following a stage of a politically controlled economy, another stage emerged during which economic forces played a greater role.[3] My study of Abu Taqiyya supports Inalcik's views and maintains that the removal of state controls on international trade, which in Egypt occurred at a different period than other regions, resulted in the emergence of an active merchant group who revitalized commercial life. Their initiatives, which served to enhance their wealth and their social positions, also introduced new trading patterns into the commercial scene. The entire economy did not, in other words, suffer because of the absence of political controls.

The second question has to do with diversity within the different regions of the Ottoman state. Even presuming that the state exercised strong controls on economic activity, such as the restrictions on the export of grain and some raw materials, we can question whether this control was equal everywhere, given the mere size of the region and the quality of communications at that time. The technology necessary to control a multitude of economic activities over such vast areas had not yet made its appearance. As M. N. Pearson has argued, there was no way that a government could control economic activities in areas as far apart from each other as Southeast Europe, Aden, Basra, and the Maghreb.[4] Moreover, Egypt was in many ways a special case. No matter how strong state controls were, economic activities were unlikely to be as closely supervised as they had been during the Mamluk period. The Mamluk state had been very centralized, and this centralization could hardly be maintained at the same level once the center of the empire became distant. Thus, even during the period when Ottoman power was centralized, it was likely to be a less rigid kind of centralization than that of the Mamluk sultanate.

The individual and collective life records of Abu Taqiyya and his contemporaries of the late sixteenth and early seventeenth century suggest divergences and diversity rather than uniformity between different regions in the Ottoman empire. Although a number of historians have argued that incorporation into the European capitalist economy took place as early as the sixteenth century, it is evident that there were important variations between one region and another, and that even if we accept such statements with regard to Anatolia or the Balkans, they are far from true in Egypt, where incorporation took at least another hundred years to appear.

We can conveniently divide the period during which merchants re-emerge into two main stages, an earlier one during the last years of Mamluk rule and the first decades of Ottoman rule and a later one during the second half of the sixteenth century up to Abu Taqiyya's lifetime.

The concurrence of two factors dominated the early stage. First, with the integration of Egypt into the Ottoman Empire, a very important change occurred in the condition of merchants in Cairo: They were released from their close ties to the state that had been created in the early fifteenth century. In 1432 the Mamluk sultan Barsbay had introduced trade monopolies whereby the state became involved in the purchase and sale of some of the major commodities of the Red Sea trade, notably pepper and some other spices. From then on, no merchants were allowed to handle these commodities except when the royal warehouses had been emptied. This situation, of course, drastically changed the position of the Karimi merchants, who had held a monopoly on the Red Sea trade since the thirteenth century. Once the pepper trade was made a state prerogative, the Karimi merchants were reduced to becoming agents of the state, dealing in spices for the sultan's account, and selling their own pepper only when the royal spices had been sold. Their profits, moreover, were curtailed because pricing was determined by state policies, and to the state's benefit, not the merchants'. The Karimis' freedom to act was, as a result, restricted, as was their ability to make profits, and by the end of the fifteenth century, they eventually disappeared from the commercial scene and were not heard of again in Cairo. The system that Sultan Barsbay set up, which must have procured hefty revenues for the state, was continued by his successors.

The state monopolies on pepper and other Red Sea goods were discontinued as a result of the Ottoman invasion of Egypt in 1517. The Ottoman state had no particular interest in maintaining these monopolies, especially given the critical conditions emerging because of the early Portuguese settlements in India. This major change in the structure of trade was to affect the position of merchants in the decades that followed. The Ottoman state appeared to concern itself primarily with the customs duties that this trade brought to the state and with obtaining certain products, like rice and sugar, that were demanded for the imperial kitchen every year. The field was now left open to merchants, who henceforth once more reaped the profits of the Red Sea trade.

In the second stage, after the first shock that followed the Portuguese penetration of Asian spice markets, starting the middle of the sixteenth century, trade along the Red Sea route, for several reasons, resumed the levels it had reached before the appearance of the Portuguese. Frederic C. Lane even suggests that the volume of spices after the mid-sixteenth century exceeded the level prevailing before the Portuguese settled in India; he estimates, in fact, that at least as great a volume was passing by the Red Sea route as was shipped directly to Lisbon via the Cape of Good Hope. Fernand Braudel notes that as of approximately 1550, the Red Sea spice trade was revitalized and the Venetians, who controlled roughly half the spices sold at Alexandria, were buying phenomenal quantities. According to one consular report, in 1564 they purchased 12,000 quintals (roughly 50 kilos per quintal) of pepper, to the horror of their main competitors in the European market, the Portuguese.[5]

There are several explanations for Egypt's new success in the spice trade. One of them involves the way that the Portuguese conducted their commercial activities and their inability to set up effective controls on the spice trade. They tried to enforce a close guard over the sources of the spices but did not have the facilities to maintain it for long. Another explanation is that the Red Sea route was, more and more, providing the various regions of the Ottoman Empire with Eastern goods. The integration of Egypt into the Ottoman world, which opened up new markets for Egypt within the Ottoman Empire itself and with its trading partners, probably greatly increased the demand for the merchandise coming across the Red Sea via Egypt; the population increases of the sixteenth century, both in the urban centers of the Ottoman Empire and in Europe, must also have been a contributing factor. The profits merchants made during the second half of the sixteenth century were therefore excessively high, and in the last two or three decades, merchants were accumulating large sums of money from their trading activities in the Red Sea—certainly more than merchants had been making any other time since the beginning of the Ottoman period.

Among the beneficiaries of the revival of the Red Sea spice trade were centers like Cairo as well as Alexandria, the port handling much of this trade. The Venetians were also major beneficiaries because they could maintain their position as distributors of Eastern goods in Europe. Not least were the merchants in Cairo handling the Red Sea trade, whose rate of business dealings was allowing them to intensify their activity. In fact, it appears that by the middle of the sixteenth century, a new generation of merchants, who were not Karimi merchants, but who shared a number of features with the Karimis, was beginning to emerge. The disappearance of the Karimis, so often linked to the general commercial decline in the region, can be seen in a different light in view of these later developments.

The second stage of the period during which merchants reemerge coincides with Isma'il Abu Taqiyya's lifetime, and its changes were just as important as those of the first stage. Merchants of his generation made major modifications to their trading patterns. Because they had been accumulating enormous wealth in recent years, they were able to undertake various types of investment that gave them a measure of control over commodities in great demand. The micro analysis of the way Abu Taqiyya and other merchants of his generation carried out their business on a daily basis sheds light on some of the little-known dimensions of merchant activity during the period. Utilizing the mechanisms and institutions available at that time, they adjusted their trading patterns so as to include investments in commercial agriculture and productive activities, which thus enabled them to link the sources of production to the demands in the export market.

To put it another way, the adjustments that Abu Taqiyya and other merchants of his generation made in their economic activities and their trading patterns were neither initiated by political forces nor associated with European penetration of the trade of the region. These changes are precisely the ones that historians usually associate with the incorporation of Ottoman lands into the European capitalist world economy, which resulted in their eventual peripheralization. But in this case, the adjustments of the half century between the end of the sixteenth century and the beginning of the seventeenth were undertaken within the Ottoman world market and entirely unrelated to this process of peripheralization; they were not part of the process of creating a dependent economy, nor did they necessarily lead to this. Nevertheless, the very same phenomena that we know occurred at the start of European commercial penetration of the region were taking place—commercial agriculture, for instance, and links between agriculture, production, and demand in the market—but independent of European capitalism and about two centuries before peripheralization occurred.

Some of the immediate reasons for these changes may be inferred. On the one hand, if merchants made major investments in agriculture or production, they must have felt a certain level of security, in spite of the political troubles of the time (a merchant would need to have some confidence that his property would not be confiscated, for instance). Moreover, we must also assume that they were able to accumulate a certain amount of wealth—an assumption well borne out in Abu Taqiyya's case—enabling them to remove part of their capital temporarily from trade to invest it in activities that took a longer time to produce revenues.

On the other hand, changes in international markets were also influencing the way that trading took place. Merchants in Cairo may have had to adjust in order to face a reduction of their activities with regard to the Asian trade. The formation of the Dutch East India Company in 1600 and its merger with other companies in 1602 marked a new phase in the history of European penetration of Asian markets and of the Dutch trade empire in Asia. The company's clear-cut policies, particularly its use of armed trading, gave it much greater control of the sources of the spices than the Portuguese had ever had. The process of ousting the Portuguese evidently took some time; it may have been as late as the middle of the seventeenth century before it was completed.[6] A number of historians are suggesting, however, that the Dutch did not really ever fully monopolize the spices and the economies of Asia remained full of vitality.[7] Dutch penetration of the sources of spices certainly did not put an end to the spice trade in the Red Sea, for Egypt continued to furnish the Ottoman Empire and North Africa with Asian goods coming across the Red Sea. But it does mark the beginning of new conditions, notably, the loss or considerable shrinking of a market for merchants in Cairo when the Dutch came to dominate the spice markets of Europe, until then furnished in spices by the Venetian merchants who bought them in the ports of Alexandria and the Levant. Braudel gives 1630 as the year after which the spices and pepper bound for Europe—or Western Europe, anyway—seem to be diverted to the Atlantic route.[8]

Moreover, the growing prosperity in Europe, a result of its expansion, brought about a greater demand for certain commodities, with the result that Europe was consuming more and more goods coming from outside its borders. There was, in fact, an expansion in all sectors of trade during the sixteenth century. One manifestation is the growing competition among European nations for trade in the Mediterranean: The English, the Dutch, and the French competed with the Venetians for the opportunities this domain opened. These conditions provided a chance for indigenous merchants to find new outlets for their commercial activity. We can thus put the developments in Cairo in the context of the intensification of world trade.

Merchants in Cairo felt the repercussions of these changes in different ways. This becomes clear when we compare the scope of geographical extension of the Karimi merchants of Mamluk Egypt with the Ottoman merchants contemporary with Isma'il Abu Taqiyya. Karimi merchants who dominated the Red Sea transit trade for more than two centuries extended their commercial activities as far as China, Samarkand, and Herat. By the end of the sixteenth century, the furthest point that Abu Taqiyya or al-Ruwi'i reached was the western coast of India—centers like Dabhol and Goa. Some time later, the commercial activities of the merchants of Cairo became more and more restricted, until by the eighteenth century they did not trade any further east than Mecca and Jedda.

It is also likely that merchants faced difficulties in obtaining the quantities of merchandise they were looking for in markets like Jedda or Goa. Heavier European purchases in Asia, moreover, probably raised the price of spices, and such a situation was likely to cause problems in these markets. Pyrard de Laval quoted by Braudel, commented in 1610 that the spices the Portuguese had been buying a few years earlier for only one sou now cost the Dutch four or five.[9] Another problem was that the Venetians, who had been good clients in Cairo and Alexandria, were now buying less. Unable to sell to their traditional clients, the Venetians may have been coming less frequently, leaving people like Abu Taqiyya with merchandise that was not selling at the price he had wanted. Abu Taqiyya could see the goods—bales of pepper, perhaps—piled up in the storerooms of the *wikala* because the Venetians had not bought much during a particular season. Or he might be astute enough to sell his merchandise quickly enough at a competitive price, but then be left with more cash than he wished to have. Given the inflation of the early years of the seventeenth century, the best way to deal with cash was to spend it rapidly. All these situations could pose problems for merchants like Isma'il Abu

Taqiyya. Even though trade with Europe constituted only a portion of his global activity as a merchant, his trade empire was slowly having to change its contours and adapt to new and different conditions.

Behind the adjustments that merchants like Abu Taqiyya made in their trading patterns were changing tastes and growing demands for certain commodities. A clever merchant had to be sensitive to market conditions and had a much easier time because of the structures and networks available, in both Cairo and the other major urban centers that merchants dealt with. Abu Taqiyya was among the few most prominent merchants who had the means—accumulated capital, tools, structures, and personal insight—to adapt his commercial activity to the new conditions around him. From the various centers where he had partners or agents—Istanbul, Mecca, or Jedda—he was well placed to feel shifts in patterns of demand or changes in the price of merchandise and to reassess his own trading procedures accordingly. He could afford to delay making an immediate profit while a new pattern was being put into place. The *wikala*s, where he spent much of his time, must have given him a sense of market conditions. Especially when the word reached them that a caravan was expected, merchants from many different regions gathered there, to find out the kind of merchandise it was bringing in and to estimate the quantities. And as they waited, they exchanged information on the availability of supplies and the expectations of demands. The fact that Isma'il Abu Taqiyya was always in Cairo was particularly advantageous in bringing about this kind of coordination because it permitted him to receive information about supply and demand from his various agents and partners coming to Cairo from the various centers of trade with which he dealt.

New Trends

One way of tracing some of the significant commercial trends of the period is to follow the activity of some of the most prominent merchants: They were the ones who could make the largest investments in any particular project, and they could to a certain extent establish the direction in which change was to move. The way that merchants like Isma'il Abu Taqiyya, 'Ali al-Ruwi'i, and Jamal al-Din al-Dhahabi reacted to the shifts in world trading patterns during this period is therefore indicative of a trend.

The main changes in their patterns of trading involved two commodities, coffee and sugar, for which great increases in demand had become apparent. Yemeni coffee was becoming a very popular drink in Egypt and other regions in the Ottoman Empire. For most of the next two centuries, Egyptian merchants managed to monopolize the coffee trade. Most Yemeni coffee passed through their hands; it arrived directly in Egypt and from there was shipped to other destinations within the Ottoman Empire and to other lands. In the case of sugar, it was sugar produced in Egypt that was for another hundred years or so to play a major role in Egyptian trade. The merchants of Cairo dealing in this commodity had to provide competitive prices because sugarcane cultivation and sugar processing was expanding both in America and in Europe.[10] Sugar, moreover, involved basic changes in patterns of investing and trading for Abu Taqiyya and the other merchants; having taken an interest in this commodity, they were putting money into its agriculture and production. Merchants in Cairo who monopolized the coffee trade, on the other hand, did not attempt to control its production by pouring in capital for the expansion of coffee agriculture in Yemen so as to control production at the source. That Yemen was at a distance from Egypt is certainly part of the explanation, but important merchants had agents who traveled on their behalf. Specific conditions in Yemen, as yet to be studied, may perhaps offer explanations.

With sugar, which was grown closer to Cairo, the situation was different, and merchants took an active interest in developing the commodity at the source, that is, in sugarcane cultivation and sugar production. The reasons are probably the same ones that pushed merchants in sixteenth-century Venice or Genoa to be involved in the production of silk or woolen textiles: It helped them to cope with demand for these products or to obtain their product at a more competitive price.[11]

The Coffee Trade

The history of coffee has already been told many times over.[12] Coffee apparently originated in Ethiopia. Coffee trees were planted in Yemen, and the use of coffee as a beverage spread in the sixteenth century to the Hijaz and Egypt through members of Sufi orders who used it in order to stay awake at night for their *dhikr* (Sufi ritual performances). In spite of the resistance of some '*ulama*' to the use of this beverage they thought was intoxicating, it very soon spread from Egypt to most other parts of the Ottoman Empire, to Syria and then to Anatolia. The first two coffee-

houses in Istanbul were opened in 1554 by two Syrians, one from Aleppo
and the other from Damascus. Cairo at the turn of the century already
had numerous coffeehouses. One European traveler, Henry Castela, vis-
iting Cairo in 1600–1601, noted the presence of many very crowded
taverns where, at all hours of the day, people drank hot black water—
coffee was a drink he had obviously never seen before.[13] Johann Wild,
who visited Egypt a few years later, noticed, while in Dumyat, what he
called the *kahvekhans*, a Turkish word for coffeehouses, where people
were drinking boiled black water.[14] Wild's observation means that the
popularity of coffee had already spread from the capital to a provincial
town.

For Isma'il Abu Taqiyya, involvement in the coffee trade came fairly
late, the first written record of his dealings in this commodity dating from
1012/1603,[15] years after its introduction to Cairo.[16] By then, people had
been drinking coffee for some decades, and it had spread from the restricted Sufi circles to the general population. The switch to coffee did not
require major changes in trading patterns, because it could be bought in
the main Red Sea port, Jedda, where the spices were sold. However, at a
later date Isma'il Abu Taqiyya, with his partners 'Abdul-Qadir al-Damiri
and Mustafa al-Safadi, formed a *shirka* that took al-Safadi to Mukha, a
major coffee market. This port was apparently attractive to merchants
because, according to the Dutch East India Company records, the customs duties levied there were considerably lower than those in Jedda.[17]
To a certain extent, Abu Taqiyya was using the same agents and the same
legal tools, such as the partnership contract. But he did take a risk insofar
as he was investing capital in a fairly new type of commodity, with the
hope of finding a large enough market to make it lucrative. It would, of
course, be interesting to compare the development of the coffee trade
with that of the spice trade in terms of quantities and prices. The few
examples available, such as a contract dated 1014/1605 for a sale on
credit that included pepper at 20 *dinars* per *qintar* for the pepper and 10
dinars per *qintar* for the coffee, do not clarify the picture sufficiently,[18]
and we have no data to estimate which commodity was more profitable
during those years.

The rise of coffee consumption in the course of Abu Taqiyya's lifetime
was probably restricted to Egypt and to other Ottoman lands, with exports directed towards Anatolia, either through merchants in Cairo or
through Abu Taqiyya's agents in Bilad al-Rum.[19] Although some coffee is

mentioned in Abu Taqiyya's exports to Venice, it took some time before the habit of drinking coffee began spreading, and the drink did not gain popularity in Europe until the latter part of the seventeenth century.

At a time when coffee consumption was still a matter of debate among legal scholars, some of them severely condemning it as an intoxicant, a number of merchants of Abu Taqiyya's generation encouraged its consumption by the construction of coffeehouses. These were to play a vital role in Cairo's social life and culture. Right in the center of the city, Isma'il Abu Taqiyya built a coffeehouse when he and al-Damiri constructed their two *wikala*s. Ahmad al-Ruwi'i, likewise, built one in the quarter of al-Azbakiyya, an area undergoing rapid expansion at the time. No doubt, other merchants too realized that this was one way of increasing sales for a product that brought good profits. Through an agent he had in Dumyat, Abu Taqiyya was probably trying to find local markets in the provincial towns of Egypt, although the agent was probably also keeping his eyes open for foreign merchants, presumably from Syria and Anatolia, who were in search of coffee.[20] The coffeehouse, gaining popularity, was soon to be found not only in every town and city, but in some of these, in every quarter.

Sugar Production

The most important adjustment to Abu Taqiyya's economic activities and trading patterns was related to his involvement in sugarcane agriculture and the sugar industry. Through the activities of this merchant and his colleagues, we are able to see the links between the cultivation of cane, the extraction of sugar from it, and its export to markets abroad. The study of these particular individuals and their activities also sheds light on some aspects of more general matters, such as the relationship of the state or of the guilds to production.

The sugar trade was one of the most important economic activities of earlier periods, before the Ottoman conquest. Sugarcane was planted both in Upper and Lower Egypt, and numerous sugar refineries functioned in Fustat and later in Cairo and Bulaq. The sugar produced, which included a variety of types, was world famous and very much in demand in Europe. In the fifteenth century, the industry is said to have had lower production rates, and even certain imports of sugar in Egypt have been recorded.[21] The number of sugar refineries in Misr was said to have been drastically reduced in the fifteenth century, a fact historians have linked to the decline of the sugar industry in Egypt.[22] However, by the seventeenth century, sugar had once more become one of the major economic activities of Cairo. Whatever decline it had suffered in the late Mamluk period was remedied as this industry came to the fore once more. André Raymond has shown that the importance of sugar production in the economy of the country was sustained throughout the seventeenth century.[23]

To Abu Taqiyya and his contemporaries it must have been evident that about a century and a half earlier, sugar production had been a major economic activity. Even if the numerous refineries that someone like Sultan al-Ghuri, the Mamluk sultan who ruled between 1501 and 1516, had owned, in Bab Zuwayla and in Bulaq, were either not functioning or not functioning to full capacity, they may nonetheless have been visible to the inhabitants of Cairo. The most important merchants of these decades—Abu Taqiyya, al-Ruwi'i, Jamal al-Din al-Dhahabi—were involved in reopening the refineries and reviving this industry.

For Abu Taqiyya the change was not a simple matter of increasing his sugar exports: It meant a structural transformation of his network. So far, the network had been between major trading centers in various parts of the world—important towns and cities such as Istanbul, Damascus, Mecca, and Jedda—and had included merchants and people offering various services to them. Like any other merchant, Abu Taqiyya knew that the further he extended his network, the higher his profits would be. Early in the seventeenth century, he established a new set of networks with rural areas, notably in the Delta. He was now dealing with new groups of people, such as village *shaykh*s and *multazim*s, as well as facing new problems of transport and storage. This move from commerce to agriculture and production meant a major adjustment. Dealing in sugar, in fact, involved Abu Taqiyya in the various stages of production, from cultivation to export. And placing capital in a noncommercial enterprise, both artisanal and agricultural, involved him more deeply in the economy of Egypt in its various aspects.

Expectations of profits must have been quite high for Abu Taqiyya to undertake this project. In both the Ottoman Empire and Europe, demand for sugar was on the rise, and he could also see possibilities for its exportation across the Red Sea to Mecca, Jedda, and Mukha. Egypt was furnishing the Ottoman Empire with large quantities of sugar, but towards the end of the sixteenth century and the beginning of the seventeenth, that demand increased, probably as a result of the rise of population in Anatolia in the sixteenth century. Certainly Egypt was not the only sugar producer of the empire. Sugar refineries existed in Cyprus and were active at the time of the Ottoman conquest, but their output was destined for the imperial kitchen in Istanbul, as recent studies suggest.[24] The quantities these refineries produced were probably insufficient to answer demand, leaving the door open for sugar produced in Egypt to find numerous export outlets.

Moreover, in Europe, as Braudel points out, sugar until the sixteenth century had been a luxury item. For a long time, it was only available at apothecaries where it was sold as a medicine to relieve the sick. As one of the most expensive foodstuffs, sold by the ounce, it was considered a valuable enough gift to be given by one prince to another.[25] Then the use of sugar began to spread until it came to be found on everyone's table. This development occurred at a time when population was rising; the population of Europe, for example, is said to have doubled in the course of the sixteenth century. In other words, there seems to have been an increase in demand from several directions. Reports must have been reaching Abu Taqiyya—from the agent he had in Istanbul, from European merchants coming to trade in Egypt, and from the Jewish customs officials, *multazim*s, who were in close touch with Europeans, especially with Venetian merchants (they even had agents traveling to and from Venice). Sugar had long been in demand abroad. But apparently in this period, the rise in demand was dramatic.

Merchants in Cairo became involved in the various phases of the sugar trade. Isma'il Abu Taqiyya undertook financial arrangements with the landholders planting sugarcane. One such arrangement was the *salam shari'i* (advance payment for future delivery), an agreement for an advance payment to the person planting the sugarcane, which included clauses specifying that at a certain date, the merchandise, often already transformed into sugar, was to be delivered. Sugarcane, planted in January or February and harvested in October or November, requires an extensive capital investment in its initial stages, and the advance payment Abu Taqiyya made to the planter was therefore very welcome assistance. This kind of payment gave Abu Taqiyya priority in obtaining access to the produce. He was also getting it at a lower rate than the market price. The few available examples of prices show Abu Taqiyya paying between five and ten *qirsh* per *qintar* of sugar when he made these advance payments. He would presumably sell it for considerably more than that. In other words, this *salam* was a form of buying the produce on speculation, in the sense that he was paying for merchandise that would be delivered in the future. In practical terms, he was probably making the payments at the time that sugarcane was being planted, and the sugar was delivered shortly after harvesttime. In Muharram 1013/1604, the first month of the Muslim year, for instance, he was paying 450 *dinars* for 115 *qintars* of sugar to be delivered in Shawwal, the tenth month, of the same year.[26] Likewise in the second month, Safar, 1013/1604 he was paying 1264 *dinars* for the *sukkar kham* (dark sugar) that would be delivered seven months later at the beginning of Ramadan of that year.[27] For the producer, the payment helped finance the plantation until harvesttime; for Abu Taqiyya, it guaranteed that a certain amount of sugar would be delivered to him on a set day, and presumably he would make a good profit. These agreements were registered in the court books, but sometimes Abu Taqiyya wanted additional guarantees, in the form of a *rahn* or mortgage of a property (a house or the like) that he could take possession of if the agreement was not fulfilled.[28]

In addition to the *salam shari'i*, the court registers also record large loans *(qards)* Abu Taqiyya made to people involved in cultivating sugarcane. The loans were sometimes quite high: 148,000 *nisfs*, for instance, to the *multazim* or tax farmer in the province of al-Munufiyya who was planting sugarcane,[29] or 3,500 *qirsh* (105,000 *nisfs*) to Shaykh Muhammad al-Shanawani.[30] These loans could have been made as an inducement to the borrowers to fulfill Abu Taqiyya's demand for this commodity. The borrowers may have used these funds either to expand their agricultural production or to enhance their own positions—by buying *iltizams*, for example. They may well have done both, perhaps investing certain sums in the land and the rest elsewhere.

Merchants in Agriculture and Production

The involvement of merchants of Abu Taqiyya's generation in the agriculture of sugarcane is significant in many ways. Merchants were able to supply themselves with sugarcane in commercial quantities long before the emergence of large, privately owned estates, which did not make their appearance until the nineteenth century. Historians have linked commercial agriculture to forms of land tenure, arguing that landholdings in the

Ottoman period barely allowed peasants subsistence plus the taxes they had to pay the state and that commercialization occurred on a large scale only when the system of land tenure was changed in the nineteenth century.[31] This argument is based on the linkage of commercialization with private ownership. These views, however, are hardly upheld by the evidence. Commercial agriculture during this period was by no means limited to sugarcane. Egypt was exporting large quantities of rice to other parts of the Ottoman Empire. (The somewhat exaggerated figures that Vansleb provides in 1672 and 1673 are of 500 ships loaded with rice leaving Damietta every year for Turkey.) The same is true of flax, grown extensively and exported in many types of linen cloth. Johann Wild estimated that between fifteen and eighteen vessels carried linen to Constantinople every year.[32] Kenneth Cuno has argued with regard to the late eighteenth century that some landholdings were relatively large, even though the form of tenure remained the same.[33] He however implied that the existence of large landholdings was a feature peculiar to the period he was studying, whereas the evidence here points to its existence much earlier. Although no detailed study of land tenure in the sixteenth and seventeenth centuries as yet exists, the sources I have consulted clearly indicate that merchants often dealt with peasants who had fairly large pieces of agricultural land—far beyond what they needed for their families' subsistence. How widespread this tendency was is another question for future research to answer.

Yet this question can be argued from a different perspective. From the evidence that a number of crops were, in fact, highly commercialized during this period, it follows that the global agricultural output was well beyond the subsistence level, regardless of the type of land tenure that prevailed. This argument assumes that the landholders would be influenced by supply and demand, that is, by market forces; at times of relative prosperity, they could change land use from subsistence crops to commercial ones, if this tactic would give them a better revenue. There is a good argument that agricultural expansion during this period allowed production to go beyond the subsistence level. Stanford Shaw says that the expansion of cultivable land in Egypt in the late sixteenth and early seventeenth centuries was a result of the extension of irrigation.[34] Moreover, the extensive expansion of sugar production occurring during this period had to be accompanied by an expansion in the cultivation of cane. The injections of capital into agriculture by merchants like Isma'il Abu Taqiyya and 'Ali al-Ruwiʻi were certainly an important factor in the transformation of larger areas into sugarcane-producing land. Such transformations, however, took place as a result of increased demand from abroad, and the kind of land tenure that prevailed was not necessarily a barrier to market forces.

The mechanisms through which these transformations occurred varied. In many cases merchants dealt with *multazims*. The *multazims* were responsible for the collection of agricultural taxes from peasants but did not determine what the peasants should plant. However, because a *multazim* usually had to advance capital to allow the peasants to purchase seeds, to plant, to repair his instruments, to repair channels, he would probably be able to "convince" some of them to modify what they were planting. Moreover, a *multazim*, in addition to his right to collect taxes, was granted, as part of his tax concession, a small portion of land with which he could do as he liked. He could decide what he wanted to plant.[35] There was therefore some room for manipulation of the crops that were planted. Sometimes merchants dealt directly with the peasant landholders. Abu Taqiyya, for example, had dealings with a certain Shaykh Muhammad al-Shanawani, who had 60 *feddans* (unit of land measurement equivalent to 4200 square meters) of sugarcane in al-Munufiyya.[36] There were probably other mechanisms as well, but we know little about them.

The involvement of merchants in agriculture meant that their commerce was being integrated with production and that they were investing in the agriculture of a produce that they knew was in high demand in world trade. This is a phenomenon that some historians claim took place only in Egypt under Muhammad ʻAli, as a result of contact with the West and initiated by the state.[37] The system was obviously being applied earlier in certain sectors, and in the nineteenth century it was expanded to include others. The initiative for these undertakings was not, as it later became, the state's. Muhammad ʻAli controlled agricultural production and he could therefore decide which crops were to be planted.

This system allowed Abu Taqiyya and other merchants to have a measure of control over the quantities and the deliveries of goods they needed in their trade. Abu Taqiyya, for example, could presumably get fairly big quantities if he wished, given the amount of capital he was investing. Although some of the *salam* agreements were for more limited amounts of sugar, 110 *qintars*, 115 *qintars*, 250 *qintars*, or 336 *qintars*,[38] others were for much larger amounts, 820 *qintars*, 952 *qintars* or 1050

*qintar*s at a time.[39] Rather than having to base his calculations on un-
knowns, he could count on having fairly large amounts, at prices he knew
beforehand. This system not only permitted him to calculate his investments and profits with a certain degree of accuracy but also, at another
level, to link supply and demand, or supply in foreign markets to demand at
the source of production. He could decide to invest as much capital in loans
or advance payments to producers as his expectations for sales were high.

Whether they used loans or the *salam shari'i*, merchants like Abu
Taqiyya, al-Ruwi'i, and Jamal al-Din al-Dhahabi were to a certain extent
able to control the sugar market of Cairo. Others also played a part,
particularly the *sukkari*s, or merchants who specialized in sugar. The work
of André Raymond on the *sukkari*s has demonstrated that as of the beginning of the seventeenth century, they too suddenly emerged among the
wealthiest groups of Cairo.[40] They were probably also involved in the
same operations as the other merchants. With the money that merchants
put into agriculture, and the obligation the lenders had to provide them
with merchandise, they controlled sufficient quantities—at certain times,
in any case—to be able to manipulate the price. Because of favorable
conditions, Abu Taqiyya was actually selling sugar from his refinery,
wholesale, to other local sugar merchants, indicating that he had production in excess of what he could handle himself. Nevertheless, merchants
who exported sugar had to keep their prices at a competitive level so as to
be able to expand their markets outside of Egypt.

Most important, this situation indicates some extension of the sugar
industry from Cairo to the provinces, allowing merchants to cope with
increasing demand for this product. We would presume that there was
already a certain amount of know-how about sugar production in these
rural areas. Elyahu Ashtor has pointed out that in earlier periods some
sugar production had always been undertaken in or near the estates where
sugarcane was grown.[41] This was still true some centuries later, during
Abu Taqiyya's lifetime. Otherwise, simply to send equipment where no
one was familiar with the process of production would not have been of
much use. What the merchants of Cairo might have been doing was to
expand rural participation in the process.

Abu Taqiyya, like al-Ruwi'i, participated indirectly in the sugar production process taking place in rural areas. It appears that frequently the
people who were planting sugarcane also did part of the processing, such
as extracting the juice, on the site. This was a fairly simple process, done

by placing the sugarcane between two superimposed wheels turning in opposite directions. The juice extraction, which provided molasses (*'asal aswad*) was the first stage of the process. Sometimes it was to Cairo that the molasses was taken to be boiled down to sugar. Abu Taqiyya, however, encouraged having this last process done in the rural areas and accordingly sent his equipment, very large copper bowls in which molasses was boiled down, to where the cane was planted—al-Gharbiyya, perhaps, or al-Munufiyya. In 1033/1623, for instance, Abu Taqiyya was actually renting out such copper bowls, with his name inscribed on them.[42] Likewise, when al-Ruwi'i died, the inventory of his property included sugar processing equipment—again, large copper bowls—in the province of Munufiyya in the Delta area.[43] The sugar produced in rural areas was what would be called dark sugar (*sukkar kham*), which was both consumed locally and exported. But the most luxurious and expensive kind of sugar, white refined sugar (*sukkar mukarrar*), seems to have been produced only in Cairo, and this was presumably what was consumed in the imperial palace in Istanbul.

Abu Taqiyya's benefits from this pattern are obvious. First of all, it facilitated transport: The amount of cane required to produce sugar was bulky, but refined sugar was compact; thus, transport costs must have been much lower. It probably cut down on production prices too because labor was presumably cheaper in Munufiyya or Gharbiyya than in Cairo. (Even though labor costs were probably not very high in either the city or the rural areas, sugar production was labor intensive.) But for a merchant dealing in large quantities and whose interests were linked to international trade, what was of particular interest was to have the requisite amount of sugar ready when he needed it—when a shipment of goods was being sent across the Mediterranean or across the Red Sea. In terms of availability, then, the arrangements Abu Taqiyya was making with the sugarcane producers gave him priority treatment.

How much sugarcane was processed on the land and how much was sent to the refineries of Cairo remains a matter for conjecture. In any case, in 1012/1603, Isma 'il Abu Taqiyya acquired a sugar refinery (*matbakh*) called Matbakh al-Qawwas situated in Khatt al-Amshatiyin, in the center of Cairo, near his house.[44] Henceforth, it was in the center of the city that the sugar industry was situated, an indication of its growing importance. The description of this refinery in the *waqf* deed in which Abu Taqiyya endowed it, shows that a number of processes could be undertaken there.

The refinery had a space to put the sugarcane upon its arrival, and both juice extraction and cooking operations were done there. The sugar produced Matbakh al-Qawwas was of more than one kind: molasses, dark sugar, and refined sugar of varying qualities, depending on the way the refining was done. This refinery might therefore have handled all the stages, starting with the sugarcane, or it might have taken the dark sugar *(sukkar kham)* that was coming from the rural areas and transformed it into more expensive, whiter sugar. A *sukkari* was in charge of running these operations at Abu Taqiyya's refinery, and there must have been some arrangement between them to allow this *sukkari* to sell part of the product while Abu Taqiyya sold the other part.[45]

It is revealing to study the involvement of merchants in production because of the light this sheds on a domain we know little about: the way production was organized and its relationship to guilds. Many historians consider that production did not undergo any significant development because of the rigid controls that were imposed on it by the state or by the guilds themselves. It is quite likely that the guild structure was strengthened after the Ottoman conquest and that the guilds undertook some functions formerly in the domain of the *muhtasib* (market inspector), such as control on the quality of products,[46] but whether or not this was merely a way to consolidate the state's hold on these bodies is another matter. Historians of the old school, like Gabriel Baer, consider guilds of the Ottoman period to have been to a large extent state-controlled. Scholars like Pascale Ghazaleh, working on the basis of archival sources, challenge this view, considering state control to have been present but not all-encompassing.[47]

The controls set up by the guilds themselves is also a matter that has remained largely obscure. Guilds are said to have curtailed any innovative practices, restricting membership to their guild, and keeping those who were not members from exercising their profession. The guilds are also said to have controlled access to raw materials, *shaykhs* of the guild being in charge of distributing it among members. The court records of seventeenth-century Cairo confirm that guild members were expected to follow various rules and regulations set up to protect the interests of its members or to protect consumers. This is illustrated in a court case concerning the textile merchants of Wikala al-Mar'a in Bab al-Nasr; they were expected to abide by the rules regarding both the quality of the cloth and its width. Those who did not follow regulations were punished.[48] Another case deals with guild membership: A *tawqaji* (bonnet maker) is forbidden by the *shaykh* of that guild to practice this profession. If demand for a particular good was limited, guild membership was most likely to be restricted and attempts made to stop those who were not guild members from exercising a certain profession. If on the other hand, demand was high, or was rising, such a rule is unlikely to have prevailed. One way or another, the rules stopping someone from producing a particular item—if such rules existed in a specific guild—were not necessarily implemented when it came to persons in other professions or persons of prominence like merchants. People like Abu Taqiyya and al-Ruwi'i were not likely to be members of the sugar producers' guild, any more than the soap merchants of Jerusalem who owned soap factories were members of the soap producers' guild.[49]

Another important aspect of this matter is related to access to raw material. For certain guilds, this was a vital matter. Access to raw material was regulated to ensure that all guild members got a share. And yet it seems unlikely that such rules would have been applied in all guilds; if raw material was not in short supply, a guild might well have ignored these regulations. Isma'il Abu Taqiyya was dealing directly with the producers, and we do not find evidence of his passing through the guilds. The archives consulted for this period, as a matter of fact, did not have data showing that the guild prohibited the soap factory owners of Jerusalem or the sugar refinery owners in Cairo from obtaining their raw material— that is, the olive oil or the sugarcane—from the people who planted olives or cane. There is, consequently, a good argument for a guild organization that was not static but instead responded to varying conditions, such as the availability of supply or the growing international demand for a particular product.

The production of Abu Taqiyya's refinery, in addition to the sugar he got directly from rural areas, made relatively large quantities available for Abu Taqiyya to export. We have no way of knowing how much of this sugar was intended for export and how much for local consumption. What is clear is that his exports were directed to a number of different markets in various regions: to Jedda;[50] to Mukha;[51] to Damascus;[52] to al-Bilad al-Rumiyya;[53] to Venice.[54] About a half century after Abu Taqiyya's death, Vansleb observed the kind of commodity that was exported from Alexandria to Europe and in his list included a variety of types of sugar: sugar in large loaves, sugar in little loaves, sugar candy, in addition to what he calls sugar "soltani" and "sorbet"—terms for which we do not know the precise meaning.[55] Besides these exports, more sugar was sold locally and to merchants who eventually transported it abroad.[56] In order to export this commodity, Abu Taqiyya was making good use of the networks that he had been setting up at an earlier stage in his life.

The investments made by people like Abu Taqiyya, al-Ruwiʿi, Jamal al-Din al-Dhahabi, and other merchants in sugarcane agriculture and sugar processing probably had several consequences. In economic terms, the capital invested must have encouraged some expansion in sugar production in Lower Egypt, and revived this industry from the decline, or perhaps the crisis, of the fifteenth century, about which much has been written.[57] It probably also served to make Egypt's prices somewhat more competitive. For Abu Taqiyya to sell to his Venetian clients, the price he offered must have been more attractive than that of the sugar that was being produced closer by—in Sicily, for instance, or in Cyprus.[58]

The kind of adjustment that this shift represented was by no means unique to merchants in Cairo; it occurred about the same time in other parts of the Ottoman Empire. Suraiya Faroqhi has shown, for the sixteenth century, that merchants in Anatolia were investing in rural areas in order to get the products they were trading in or investing in the production of the textiles they needed for their trading. Village women in mid–sixteenth-century Central Anatolia, for instance, worked up the mohair wool for merchants in Ankara; camlet manufacturers in the villages of the Ankara region were dependent for their livelihood on merchants in Ankara who sold the camlets in Venice. Likewise, the Bursa silk merchants, studied by Haim Gerber, who exported silk textiles to many regions were the ones who provided the silk weavers with silk raw material.[59]

The involvement of merchants in the process of production continued until the eighteenth century, in textile production notably, and perhaps in other domains. ʿAli al-Jiritli has noted that until the start of the nineteenth century, merchants imported cotton from Syria, had it yarned locally by women, and then sent it to weavers that they supervised.[60] At the present state of our knowledge, we are unable to measure how widespread this practice was in Egypt, how many types of production were involved, and how many merchants or artisans participated. Nevertheless, we are forced to rethink the whole question of industrialization under Muhammad ʿAli and the extent to which we should consider it a revolution or an evolution —that is, part of a process that had started much earlier, without which his new policies could hardly have been implemented. In looking at industrialization this way, we see that it was more than the introduction of a new type of machinery: It was a type of organization and network without which the machinery alone would not have been efficient.[61]

At a somewhat later period—at the end of the eighteenth century and at the beginning of the nineteenth century, under Muhammad 'Ali—certain changes in the system began to appear. The Mamluks of eighteenth-century Cairo, in order to expand their commercial profits, were investing in land so as to get the amount of grain that they needed for their exporting ventures to France. The comparison between this situation and Abu Taqiyya's diverges in one major point: At the end of the eighteenth century, merchants' interests coincided with those of the expanding capitalist world economy, resulting in a situation where countries like Egypt were exporting agricultural products and raw materials to the capitalist world. Likewise, under Muhammad 'Ali, the changes he introduced in the economy by adjusting agricultural supply to demand in the European market, resulted in a closer integration with the European world economy at the expense of commercial relations within the Ottoman world economy. This process ultimately led after the mid-nineteenth century to the creation of a peripheral economy in Egypt, one that was dominated by the interests of a growing European capitalism. Two hundred years earlier, in contrast, the ventures of Isma 'il Abu Taqiyya were serving to expand both the production of sugar and the export of the commodity to distant markets. He was exporting finished products that were produced locally rather than agricultural products or raw material. Therefore, contrary to what some historians have maintained, decline did not set in once trade and industry fell out of the control of the administration, nor did a more lively trade with Europe necessarily weaken local structures. When the role of the state in the economic activities was reduced, other groups emerged to take its place.

Although the trade of Egypt during this period thrived essentially within the Ottoman world economy, we can still find evidence for a significant development of trade with Europe. One aspect can be observed in the trading links with Venice. The commercial relationship with Venice and Venetian merchants was a very old one. In European markets Venetian merchants had, even before the Ottoman conquest, played the role of distributors of Eastern goods in general and spices in particular. Very soon after the conquest, the Ottoman state confirmed that the Venetian merchants would maintain all the privileges they had had under the Mamluk sultanate, so that throughout the sixteenth century, they maintained an active commerce with the region, bringing in with them a variety of European goods, both for the local market and for exportation to further destinations, particularly via Jedda and Mecca. Consequently, Venetian merchants were very adversely affected by the emergence of the Dutch as major spice distributors in Europe, and their position was seriously shaken. If Venetians were losing ground as spice distributors in Europe, they may have been tempted to try their luck with larger quantities of sugar, to answer a growing demand for this product in Europe. We find occasional references to Venetian merchants operating in Cairo who also acted as intermediaries for persons in Cairo wishing to ship goods to Venice or to import goods from there.

At the beginning of the seventeenth century there was stiff competition between European trading powers for control of the Mediterranean trade, the Venetians slowly losing their control over what had largely been their domain, as their Dutch and French competitors pushed their way into the markets of Egypt and Syria. The competition took place at more than one level. On the state level, contacts with the administration in Istanbul aimed at obtaining privileges from the sultan for the merchants of the trading nations, cuts in customs duties, security for their merchants, consulates to protect them, and so on. Another kind of competition took place among the merchants themselves, bringing into play their ability to maneuver the market, a situation from which indigenous merchants may have derived certain advantages because of their familiarity with local conditions.

Yet when Abu Taqiyya took his trade to Venice, his intermediaries were not the Venetian merchants but the Jewish agents and assistants of the Jewish officials who ran the customs. They took a consignment of Abu Taqiyya's merchandise, traveled with it to Venice, sold it there, bought from the Venetian market the goods he had asked for, and finally returned and presented their accounts. He was therefore extending his network to Venice. The history of merchants from Ottoman lands in general, and from Egypt in particular, who worked in European trading centers is still an obscure subject. The kind of direct contact they may have had, the ways by which they extended their networks there, and the circumstances behind the expansion of their activities need to be studied further. It is particularly interesting and revealing that the merchants of Abu Taqiyya's generation were extending trading networks to Venice at a time when the commercial activity of Middle Eastern merchants is thought to have been curtailed by their European competitors. This expansion of their networks points to a vitality in their trading that has not been sufficiently brought to light. Their economic activity in the sugar trade allowed them to compensate for part of their losses in the spice trade. By the last decade or so of his life, Abu Taqiyya had clearly made the shift, in terms of the amounts of money he invested and the number of dealings that he had in relation to sugar.

The consequences of this restructuring were not only economic but also social. Once a system was set up, and a network of relationships was established in Cairo and in the rural areas, the control that it gave over the trade in sugar, both domestic and international, must have put at risk a large number of more modest ventures. Merchants who had only a small-scale business in sugar, or did not have the capital to invest in the way that al-Ruwi'i and Abu Taqiyya were doing, must have found themselves at a great disadvantage. Merchants who were able to control a commodity, especially an important one like sugar (even if their control was not total), were few in number, and this dominance further boosted their position within the merchant community. The situation thus consolidated the position of a small, powerful group at the top of the merchant hierarchy who fared better than other merchants. As a matter of fact, because a number of the merchants who followed this course of action were associated with the *shahbandariyya* (first 'Ali al-Ruwi'i, then Isma 'il Abu Taqiyya, and then Jamal al-Din al-Dhahabi), their successful commercial ventures probably contributed to enhance the position of *shahbandar* during this period.

Smaller-scale merchants with limited networks were less able to obtain information on supply and demand in markets in other regions and had less capital to invest in a new venture. They were therefore less likely to be able to shift their trading patterns. In other words, merchants of Abu Taqiyya's caliber, at the top of the hierarchy—together with the many less prominent merchants that they often included as business partners for a particular venture or on an occasional basis—were better placed to overcome a crisis than merchants of more modest means. In the final analysis, then, the situation resulted in a polarization within the merchant community: Those who adjusted to change enriched themselves enormously, and those who did not found themselves in a less comfortable position than they had been earlier. However, the merchant community was not equally affected by what was going on. Many more merchants would have been affected only in an indirect way—those, for instance, who exported Egyptian rice or linen, or those whose activities were concentrated in trade between Egypt and Syria.

The links that merchants established with the sugarcane producers, and the capital that they poured into sugarcane agriculture, also worked to the disadvantage of the smaller-scale sugar producers in Cairo. The owners of refineries, for instance, even when they were doing good business, might not have had the capital at Abu Taqiyya's disposal to purchase the raw material before it actually appeared on the market. It is logical to presume that they would therefore have been paying more for the raw material they needed to run their refineries than someone like Abu Taqiyya. Again, the result would have been a certain degree of polarization between those sugar producers who had priority in access to the raw material and those who did not.

What Abu Taqiyya, al-Ruwi'i, and al-Dhahabi, among others, had done when they involved themselves in agriculture and production was actually not new. A century and a half or two centuries earlier, similar initiatives were commonplace among Mamluk sultans and among powerful emirs like Qusun and Ibn Zunbur, who formed part of the ruling elite and played a prominent role in the political scene during the first half of the fourteenth century.[62] Sultan Barsbay, who ruled between 1422 and 1438, had taken a particular interest in sugar, monopolizing its agriculture and production. It was fairly common for sultans to own sugar refineries; Sultan al-Ghuri possessed a number of them. Often emirs who belonged to the ruling class too owned sugar refineries and were involved in the sugar trade, investing in a business that was known to bring about high profits. By Abu Taqiyya's time, these ruling groups had disappeared from the scene as a result of the destruction of the Mamluk Sultanate by the conquering Ottoman army. Their political successors, the Ottoman rulers —whether the pasha sent to govern Egypt or the administrators who accompanied him—showed no particular interest in making investments in the production of sugar. What is new about the early seventeenth century is the fact that merchants played a vital role in the process. This important activity was now being undertaken by an indigenous, economically active group rather than by those holding political authority.

The Economy and the State

The sugar business can be used to illustrate some of the ways that state intervention was felt in a major economic activity and some of the ways in which this activity was pushed by economic forces. Sugar was greatly in demand—locally, in other parts of the Ottoman Empire, and in Europe. An active private trade existed between Egypt and Anatolia; in addition, the government in Istanbul required a certain set amount of sugar every year for the imperial kitchen. This obligation had to be fulfilled before any sugar was sold in the market. Stanford Shaw provides the figures for these official shipments destined for the imperial kitchen in Istanbul: 800 *qintars* of sugar per year were being sent to Istanbul between 1572 and 1586; in 1586 the amount was almost doubled, to 1,400 *qintars* per year.[63] It was through the guild *shaykh* that arrangements were made for providing the sugar requisitioned by the state, and he had to make sure that guild members complied. These amounts were actually bought at market price, from what we can surmise from Abu Taqiyya's dealings with officials charged with these sugar purchases. In 1029/1619 he sold some 120 *qintars* of sugar to the *amin al-sukkar* (the agent in charge of collecting the tax in kind for sugar), for the *irsaliyya* (yearly remittance) shipment to Istanbul, at 20 to 30 *qirsh* per *qintar*.[64] That, roughly, was the market price. Once the treasury had obtained the amounts it required for its shipment to Istanbul, it did not impose other restrictions or limits on private purchases or production regarding either the supply of sugar for consumption in Egypt or that destined for export.

The position of the state might have been motivated by the fact that sugar production far exceeded the needs of the state. The mere 800 *qintars* a year that were being shipped (increased to 1,400 in 1596) probably represented a negligible portion of the total sugar production. A single purchase Abu Taqiyya made from a rural area sometimes amounted to close to a thousand *qintars*—with the difference, of course, that he was obtaining a rougher kind of sugar *(sukkar kham)*, while that sent to the imperial kitchen was the most refined. Other merchants may have been dealing in similar or larger quantities. The situation was therefore quite different from that which a number of historians have observed with regard to production of certain commodities in Istanbul or in Anatolia.[65] The Ottoman state was particularly concerned with obtaining products such as the textiles and hemp needed for its arsenal or the cloth needed for the uniforms that the Janissaries wore.[66] The relationship of the Ottoman state to trade and industry in Egypt was looser because of the great distance between this province and the center, and because of the interest of the central authorities in what happened in Istanbul rather than in the various provincial capitals.

As with the spice trade that the Mamluk sultans had monopolized, the end of the sultanate had allowed merchants to emerge and maneuver their businesses more freely. The large investments that the Mamluk ruling class had made towards sugar production were, a hundred years later, being made by the merchants. The evidence for the success of these investments is in the exports of sugar to Mediterranean and Red Sea ports. In other words, commercial expansion of the period was not conforming to the model of incorporation into the capitalist economy, whereby raw materials were exported and finished products imported. The sugar industry, strengthened by these heavy investments, played a role in keeping the balance that way.

Conclusion

The experiences of Abu Taqiyya and other merchants of his generation are quite revealing on a number of levels. Because much of Egypt's international trade consisted of a transit trade in commodities going to other destinations—whether Indian spices or coffee destined for Ottoman or European Mediterranean ports or European metals destined for further transshipment eastward—its relationship to the Egyptian economy as a whole is a matter of debate. One argument upholds international trade as a significant force behind economic change; another argument is that this kind of trade could benefit only the handful of merchants who could get a direct profit from it and could affect only one specific sector of trading, with little or no effect on the mainstream of economic activity. Because there are so many blanks in our knowledge of how the economy functioned during this period, with regard to both production and agriculture, it is difficult to draw a clear picture of conditions. Yet the findings here indicate that the role that merchants played in transforming economic activities was significant and, at certain levels, interconnected with agriculture and production. That is to say, demand for a certain commodity could bring about an increase in production or agriculture. Moreover, partly because of this economic activity and similar or parallel activities others may have undertaken in Egypt or elsewhere in the Ottoman Empire, the Mediterranean region remained an active and important center of international trade.

The adjustments that Isma'il Abu Taqiyya brought to his activities were changes coming from within the system, not from without. They were not the direct result of European impact, nor were they imposed by orders issued by the Ottoman state or the sultan. In financing agriculture and production, Abu Taqiyya as a merchant was doing what other groups had been doing at earlier periods. The methods he used were familiar ones; he was not inventing new forms but using the available ones to his advantage. In spite of the difficulties that were inherent in any period with so many changes in a relatively short time, Abu Taqiyya must have been materially compensated for the adjustments that he had made. All this tells us something about the framework within which he was functioning. The system must have had the vitality to confront challenges and to adjust itself to new situations. The efforts of the elite merchants of Cairo had contributed to put sugar produced in Egypt back in line with world demand for another century or so.

But what happened after Abu Taqiyya's lifetime? The question cannot be fully answered because the basic research has yet to be undertaken, —the rest of the seventeenth century needs to be explored more fully. Nonetheless, it is useful to point out some connections between the period of Abu Taqiyya's lifetime and the eighteenth century. The work of André Raymond has brought many aspects of the eighteenth century to light, and the evidence for continuity is apparent with regard to a number of points. In commercial agriculture and the export of locally produced goods, for instance, we can see a connection between the seventeenth and eighteenth centuries. We know that until the mid-eighteenth century, Egypt exported considerable quantities of linen to France, whence it was distributed to other countries.[67] The textile industry remained through part of the eighteenth century one of the industries that employed the most artisans, and its artisans were among the wealthiest in Cairo.[68] Export of linen was on the increase till the 1730s, when it constituted a third of all Egyptian exports to France.[69] Subsequently the imports of European cloth had an adverse effect on this industry.

The evidence also points to the continuity of the sugar industry. Raymond's research on sugar merchants indicates that according to their inheritance records, they remained, prosperous throughout the seventeenth century–in fact, down into the early part of the eighteenth. In other words, the importance of this commodity and the wealth it brought to those who dealt in it continued for some time after the disappearance of the generation of merchants contemporary with Abu Taqiyya. Raymond's figures show the sugar business at the end of the seventeenth century to have been among the most important economic activities of Cairo.[70]

Thus, although much research remains to be down on the few decades immediately after Abu Taqiyya's death, the evidence shows that some of the main features characterizing the period during which he lived were present for another century and a half—until again major structural changes were introduced.

5

Social Structures

Core and Periphery Changes

The financial position that Abu Taqiyya reached as a result of his involvement in the Red Sea trade, and later the sugar industry, had social ramifications. By roughly the second decade of the seventeenth century, his social position, which had gradually been rising, was becoming firmly established through the links he had formed with the people who were part of the power structure. As a result of such links, he and other merchants found themselves involved in changes of the political balance that they probably had not foreseen.

The transformations in the economic status of the elite merchants at the end of the sixteenth century coincided with the changes taking place in the power structure of the Ottoman bureaucracy, both in the center and in the provinces. Accordingly, the Abu Taqiyyas witnessed not only the evolution of the merchant group in Cairo but also much broader changes in the relationship between Cairo and Istanbul that affected other social groups as well. Spanning three generations—Isma'il Abu Taqiyya (d. 1624), his father, Ahmad Abu Taqiyya (d. 1596), and his son Zakariyya (d. ca. 1669)—were some of the major upheavals in the social and power structure. His father's lifetime coincided with the reign of Sultan Sulayman the Magnificent (d. 1566); probably more than any other sultan, Sulayman was able to control the power structure of the empire, and his military successes considerably expanded its boundaries. By the time of Zakariyya's death a hundred years later, the sultan no longer had the same power or authority; the bureaucracy had gained the upper hand, while the sultan himself had retreated to the background. A parallel restructuring occurred in the relationship of the center to the provinces. In Egypt, Ahmad and Isma'il Abu Taqiyya were contempories of some of the most prominent pashas who governed Egypt, such as Sinan Pasha (1567–68 and 1571–72), who eventually led a military expedition to Yemen and ended up as Grand Vizir in Istanbul, second only to the sultan of the Ottoman Empire; and 'Ali Pasha (1601–4), who like Sinan Pasha, was appointed Grand Vizir after being governor of Egypt. By the middle of the seventeenth century, however, the pasha's authority had become subordinated to that of the rising local military groups who contended with him, when a new power structure, consisting of high-ranking members of the Ottoman *ujaqs* (military corps) and the Mamluks, emerged. Here, as elsewhere in the Ottoman state, the general outcome of the conflict between the Ottoman authorities and local military groups was that the links between the capital and the provinces were somewhat looser than they had been. The whole period was one of social and political upheavals, in Egypt as well as in the other parts of the Ottoman Empire.[1]

Little is known about the social structure in Egypt in the decades that immediately followed its integration into the Ottoman Empire, that is, from 1517, the date of the Ottoman conquest, to the 1570s or 1580s. The Mamluk military elites who in the late seventeenth and in the eighteenth century reemerge as an important political and economic group, had not yet made their appearance in the political scene: most of the members of the Ottoman administration served too briefly to form a base for themselves in Cairo. Of merchants, until the generation of Abu Taqiyya, we know hardly anything, partly because few of them reached prominence. Unlike merchants from earlier and later periods, they left us no public buildings, for instance, to which their names were attached. Toward the end of the century, local elites, including merchants, began to emerge. This phenomenon, which occurred in many parts of the Ottoman empire, can be attributed to the changing balance in the power structure in Istanbul.

The classic work of Stanford Shaw on the administration of Ottoman Egypt indicates that the various military groups enhanced their power by gradually taking control of the major sources of wealth, the urban and rural *iltizams* or tax farms. This process started about the beginning of the seventeenth century and was completed in the eighteenth century.[1] However, there still remain many unanswered questions about the way this process came about and about the actors who participated in the process, directly or indirectly. Further study is needed for understanding the inner workings of various social groups that helped to shape these emerging structures, both in Egypt and in the other parts of the empire. Often the tendency is to observe how the top layers are affected, yet when such important changes take place, they leave their mark on many more social groups.

Merchant Roles

There is general agreement among historians about the direction that these changes in power structure were taking. However, up to the present time, historians have not paid much attention to the position of merchants in this process; none of the major works on this period—Shaw's, P. M. Holt's, or Michael Winter's, for example—mentions any role the merchants could have played in the power struggle during these decades. Perhaps they felt that too little was known about merchants and about the period in general to permit any hypothesis, or perhaps they also considered the part that merchants played insignificant. But now, with the material being uncovered in the court archives, it may be possible to have a realistic assessment of the role of merchants in public life and in power struggles, an assessment which is vital for our understanding of how society functioned at a time when social and economic transformations were taking place.

The economic reemergence of merchants during the period was accompanied by a social reemergence. During such a time of general social upheaval, the chances of social mobility were heightened, both for groups and for individuals within these groups. Therefore, an analysis of their relationships to the power structure can ascertain on the one hand, the shape that their changing social position took, and on the other, their role in the restructuring that was going on. That is to say, in this complex process merchants can be viewed both as a group affected by these changes and as individual participants in the process, who, backed up by their own recently improved economic conditions, stood to gain from the emerging situation.

In doing so, we can test a number of different models historians have formulated with regard to merchants' place in the social structure and their links to the power structure of premodern Middle Eastern urban societies. One model envisions the merchants as a constant source of revenue for the state, or for the rulers, because they handled cash or other forms of wealth, which either could be confiscated at will when the state was in need of funds or could be taxed at exorbitant rates, leaving the merchant with little of his personal wealth. In this model, as it is developed in some studies, the merchant is moved by political forces rather than by economic forces. His activity is controlled by rulers, by the state, or by state functionaries. His role is that of a passive partner, and his trade is guided by others than himself. Often subjected to extortions in one form or another, he had to take a defensive position, constantly protecting himself from rulers and greedy customs officials poised to get what they could from his profits.[2]

This image is, however, not entirely borne out by the empirical data from this period.[3] Confiscations did occur—and specific examples exist— but we need to find out if they were the norm or exceptional occurrences and, consequently, how merchants' behavior was adapted to these conditions. The data available for a period around 1600 show that merchants were not, in fact, constantly trying to hide their wealth for fear it would be taken away from them. Many of the wealthiest among them were quite comfortable exhibiting their success, making public their level of expenditure, and, significantly enough, investing in various kinds of ventures, an unlikely matter if merchants felt insecure or threatened. We therefore need to rethink these models in the light of the archival material that was not available when scholars formulated them.

Another model envisions the merchant as being too important to rulers and ruling classes to be marginalized. He provided them with imported luxuries that they desired, he brought slaves, he imported weapons, and therefore he served their purposes well.

Neither model proposes a role for merchants that is other than passive, used by ruling groups to serve their purposes but not influencing the direction of their actions in any way. His passivity and his inability to defend his interests are explained by the absence of powerful associations representing merchants' interests, similar to those in European cities.

By studying Abu Taqiyya and the other prominent merchants of his generation, we can test the applicability of these models by analyzing these merchants' relationship to the existing power structures and their role in the transformations taking place at the time. Were merchants of the time in any way involved in these events? If so, did they in any way either help to bring them about or influence the direction in which they were going? More specifically, as we follow the Abu Taqiyya family, we ask if they were passive onlookers during the social conflicts that helped to bring about these changes, or if their collusion with pashas, *multazims*, or Mamluks directed change one way or another.

Another question that has long been the subject of debate among historians is why merchants in the Ottoman world did not, like their counterparts in Europe, evolve into a separate corporate entity that could pressure the authorities with their demands. Part of the problem in questions of this kind is that they look for models and forms that are replicas of institutions that evolved only in Europe—and as the result of its particular historical development, the circumstances of which could hardly be duplicated. Such a question does not lead to a better understanding of the conditions prevalent during Abu Taqiyya's lifetime. By analyzing information from the archival sources, however, we can ascertain some of the parameters within which merchants had some bargaining power and the means they used to achieve their ends within the social structure of which they were a part.

Merchants and the Power Structure

Even though merchants were not active in the struggle for political power that was taking place between the Ottoman authorities and the local military groups—they were not after the tax farms (*iltizams*) the military groups wished to control, nor did they participate in the violence that exploded between the conflicting parties—they were not the passive onlookers that they are often pictured to be. One could, in fact, argue that the support of merchants for one group or another was a major factor that could tip the balance in its favor and, consequently, their weight in the political and social scene, because of their economic position, had to be taken into consideration.

Merchants had numerous and varied links to groups in power, as had always been the case. Karimi merchants, for instance, were in close touch with the ruling class during the thirteenth and fourteenth centuries. Sultans negotiated the security of merchants with the rulers of those lands where they traded. In return, they looked to the merchants when they needed funding for their military expeditions.[4] The position of Karimi merchants in the fifteenth century underwent an important change in this respect when Sultan Barsbay monopolized the pepper trade and many of them became commercial agents for the Mamluk sultans, whose orders and policies further regulated the Karimis' activities and to a large degree curtailed their actions.

What is of interest here with regard to the merchants of Abu Taqiyya's generation, is to define the shape that their links with authority took, or to describe the kind of relationship existing between a group excluded from political power and people in power, such as Ottoman pashas and members of the bureaucracy, members of the military corps, and customs officials. The elite merchants—the Abu Taqiyyas, the Ruwi'is, the Damiris, the Yaghmurs, or the Shuja'is, the 'Asis—had accumulated large fortunes from their business ventures, which made of them an economic force. In their dealings with the groups in power, whether these were mercantile or other kinds of dealings, merchants entered various kinds of relationships with each other: as partners in a particular venture, as loaners of money, as rivals or competitors for the same benefits in another venture. We sometimes find them cooperating with each other—in a matter of mutual benefit for example—and at other times in opposite camps. Although the merchants were relatively independent from the state, they nevertheless had to deal with groups in power and maneuver their way as best they could.

During Abu Taqiyya's lifetime, merchants had a complex position in relation to the political authorities or to elites who formed part of the power structure. On the one hand, even though merchants were an economic force, the relationship to those in power, whether the Ottoman pasha or the rising military elites, was an unequal one, and merchants could be pressured to do things that were not in their direct economic interest. On the other hand, we can perceive a reciprocity of interests between merchants and those in power that merchants one hundred years earlier did not have. Merchants had the bargaining power that their wealth gave them, a weapon they could use to negotiate their way through a deal, but they were under pressure from different sectors of the ruling elite to share a portion of their profits, through loans or advance payments. For a long time to come, they were going to have to deal with this matter as best they could.

To protect their interests against ruling elites, merchants tried, whenever possible, to emphasize the reciprocity of their links to those in power. One way to attain this objective was to emphasize, through different forms of expression, the mutual side of their relationship. Some historians have argued that when merchants accumulated great wealth, they were likely to try to hide it in order not to attract attention to themselves and the consequent possibility of confiscation by the rulers. It would appear, however, that this is far from the truth, at least in the case of the elite merchants of the period. To enable them to enter relationships in which the merchant was not the passive and submissive partner, people like Isma'il Abu Taqiyya, quite the contrary to certain interpretations, molded their life-style to resemble that of the ruling class. Not only was this more pleasurable on a personal level, but it also served a more important purpose: It put the merchant on the same social footing as his potential rivals, allowing him to form a relationship with members of the military ruling class on an equal footing.

No wonder then, that during the last two decades of his life, Isma'il Abu Taqiyya surrounded himself with many of the trappings of the "aristocracy" of Cairo. He was by that time *shahbandar al-tujjar,* a position that tremendously enhanced his social power. His household was a large one, with *tabi's,* (followers or clients who did not get a salary but could benefit from Abu Taqiyya's protection in return for their services), slaves, and servants; he employed administrative personnel, notably a secretary, *(mubashir)* to help run his accounts. In addition to this, his large family —with wives, concubines, and many children—must also have helped to enhance his social image. He lived in a large house that had numerous conveniences and accommodated visits from high-ranking personages. They could be received in the large reception hall, which was decorated in colored marble and lit in the evening by silver chandeliers; there they would be served meals on the Iznik plates—ceramic plates made in Iznik in Anatolia, which were fashionable at that time—that are mentioned in Abu Taqiyya's inheritance deed.[5] They were waited upon by many domestics. At that point in their relationship, Abu Taqiyya would have wanted to appear an equal, even if merchants did not have political or military power. This way of forming social relationships with those in power was one that occasionally brought results.

In the matter of appearance and the amount of money spent to enhance it, we perceive a cultural attitude diametrically opposed to a Protestant or Calvinist approach, which emphasized frugality even when wealth was available. The Islamic culture that Abu Taqiyya was part of expected a certain degree of public and private spending from one who had material means—partly for the benefit of those around him and partly for his own image, which was expected to be in keeping with his social position. This attitude indicates the relevance of culture in questions of an economic nature; even in matters where material interests were at play, cultural factors could play a vital role. Much in the same way that the "Protestant ethic" as a cultural trait may have been one of the factors behind the development of capitalism in Europe, other cultural traits were integrated in the economic approach of Middle Eastern merchants.

The major power groups to which Abu Taqiyya and other merchants were linked were, first, the members of the Ottoman ruling hierarchy—notably the pasha and the Qadi al-Qudat, who headed the political and judiciary systems—and then the high-ranking officers who headed the militias and the *multazim*s (customs officials) with whom merchants dealt on a regular basis. The Ottoman pashas of the second half of the sixteenth century may well have been direct competitors in Abu Taqiyya's trade. Given the fact that, for most of them, their appointment to Egypt was for only one or two years, it is somewhat surprising to see them involve themselves in the economic life of the country. Perhaps the fact that trade was so lucrative enticed them to invest in this activity, directly or indirectly. The precise contours of their trading activities are less well known than those of the merchants, however, because they were not using the court system in the same way. Occasionally, an explicit reference in historical texts alludes to this activity; for example, the historian Ahmad Shalabi indicates that Bayram Pasha (1035–38/1626–28) had a leaning towards trade *(lahu mayl ila al-tijara)*.[6] On a more concrete level, we know that some pashas, like Iskandar Pasha and Sinan Pasha, owned ships that sailed the Red Sea[7] and invested large amounts of money in building *wikala*s along major ports of international trade, such as Bulaq, Rashid, Alexandria, and Suez.[8] Their economic interests in Egypt were handled by their agents long after they had left their posts.

Also active in international trade were the Ottoman pashas of Yemen and, to a lesser extent, Abyssinia, the pashas of the different regions sometimes cooperating with each other in their trading activities and very often cooperating with the merchants of Cairo. According to one court case, Ahmad Pasha of Abyssinia owed *khawaja* Karim al-Din al-Burdayni and three other merchants in Cairo a sum of money; his loan was guaranteed by Ibrahim Pasha in Cairo, and it was through him that the money was returned to the merchants in 1032/1622.[9] The pashas were therefore direct competitors to merchants like Abu Taqiyya, the Ruwi'is, or al-Dhahabi, and, in fact, powerful competitors because they handled very large sums of money and had access to an infrastructure that was perhaps not readily available to merchants. Two examples illustrate the level of their wealth. When the storerooms in Cairo belonging to Mahmud, Pasha of Abyssinia, were opened when he died, the estimated value of the spices in them was close to half a million *nisfs*.[10] Similarly, the *wakil* (agent) of Hasan Pasha of Yemen in Cairo sold spices to the French consul there for the sum of 10,000 *dinars*, that is, close to half a million *nisfs*.[11] In addition to being competitors, the pashas occasionally made use of their political prerogatives in order to fulfill a successful commercial venture. The fact that the pashas would not be brought to court because of their position in the political structure, for instance, in itself put merchants in a weaker position.

Pashas sometimes conducted their trade through their own agents and at other times addressed themselves to merchants who had the expertise as well as networks in the major trading centers in the region. The trading relationship between merchants and pashas could take a number of forms, with the merchant acting as agent or as partner. In either case, the merchant could guarantee a margin of profit. Nevertheless, this was not the equal relationship of the ordinary *shirka* or partnership that merchants normally contracted. Accordingly, a merchant was likely to be making less money on a venture that involved high-ranking political figures.

A merchant probably did not have much choice but to enter such ventures if he was approached by the pasha. During Abu Taqiyya's lifetime, the Ottoman pashas still held sufficient authority as a governor, although this situation was starting to change. A merchant whose business interests were involved with those of the pasha would try to make the most of a situation he could not entirely control and attempt to obtain some form of benefit. A close link with the pasha could enhance the prestige—and the credibility—of a merchant. Once it was known that he was doing business with the pasha, this link with authority, if properly maneuvered, could shield merchants from confiscations.

Once Abu Taqiyya had penetrated the circle of Ottoman authorities, he became involved in a series of mutual favors and services. Very often, these were not directly related to trade or to any immediate material benefit. One Qadi al-Qudat asked him to perform a banking service: to transfer a sum of money, through Abu Taqiyya's agents, to a relative in Istanbul. Another Qadi al-Qudat, Muhammad Afandi, who later occupied the prestigious post of Qadi 'Askar of Rumeli, made Abu Taqiyya his agent *(wakil)* in running a plantation *(ghayt)*, Ghayt al-Ja'bari, close to Cairo, even after he left Cairo to return to Istanbul.[12] The services that a

Qadi al-Qudat could offer Ismaʿil Abu Taqiyya were numerous, given the merchant's close links to the court, especially that of Bab ʿAli. More significant, it was through relationships like this one that Abu Taqiyya's voice might be heard in Istanbul, because the Qadi al-Qudat's appointment in Cairo was usually short-term, not lasting more than a year or two. It is quite possible that Abu Taqiyya turned to relationships of this kind in times of crisis, such as when Mustafa Pasha confiscated a large sum of money from merchants.

The reciprocity of this kind of relationship is illustrated by Abu Taqiyya's links with one particular pasha. During his last years Ismaʿil Abu Taqiyya had had a close relationship with Fadli Pasha (also called Fadlalla Pasha of Yemen, who became famous for his dealings with the Dutch) and, to a lesser extent, Ahmad Pasha of Abyssinia.[13] Abu Taqiyya may never have met Fadli Pasha, who was governor of Yemen, and yet the volume of their business together was quite high. Fadli Pasha was probably interested in receiving merchandise from Egypt. According to Dutch East India Company records, one boat a year reached Mukha, an important transit center, from Suez, and the goods it brought were eagerly awaited.[14] These persons in authority who dealt in the same kind of merchandise as Abu Taqiyya could thus benefit from his networks and his expertise. Fadli Pasha, in particular, was known for the wide scope of his commercial dealings. The merchants of the Dutch East India Company whose ship docked in Mukha and saw him, noted in the company's correspondence how involved he had been in trade and the large amount of merchandise that passed through his hands. In the words of one of these Dutch merchants, pashas came to Yemen poor men and left it as rich men.[15] At the time of Abu Taqiyya's death in 1624, Fadli was in debt to him and the family had to make arrangements to get their inheritance from him. The details of their business relationship are not spelled out, but because Mukha was an important trading post, Abu Taqiyya may have been providing Fadli Pasha with Egyptian products in demand in Eastern markets, or he may have helped him in marketing the spices and coffee in the commercial centers where he had agents and employees working for him.[16]

Another group with whom merchants had close alliances were the customs *multazims*, many of whom were Jewish during this period. We do not know how this important position, which opened the door to much gain, came to be dominated by Jews; this is a matter that still needs to be researched. Here again, reciprocity was an important part of the relationship. The exactions of these customs officials are well documented. Johann Wild, who was in Egypt between 1606 and 1610, gives a vivid picture of how merchants were sometimes treated in customs when they arrived with their goods. In this case, the customs official asked the Persian merchant whom Wild was accompanying what his bales contained. Not satisfied with the answer that they contained pepper, he accused the merchant of hiding precious stones and pearls in them. In spite of the merchant's remonstrances, he split open the bales, and the pepper flowed out, to the merchant's dismay and anger. No precious stones or pearls appeared.[17] And yet such annoyances were not without their consequences. The merchant took the case to court, complaining that his merchandise had been ruined. The customs official not only had to gather up all the pepper he had spilled but also had to pay a fine. The incident that Wild narrates is thus of great interest because it shows the limits of the customs official's power and the role of the courts in such cases.

Theories formulated about exactions of customs officials often tend to provide a black-and-white picture: the customs official as the oppressor; the merchant as the oppressed, with no recourse. There is certainly some truth in this picture, especially with merchants of medium or modest scope, who were not strong enough to negotiate their way. Merchants with sufficient social weight, and with sufficient economic weight, however, entered into a dynamic relationship with customs officials, which could work to the benefit of one side or of the other.

In return for guarantees against exactions, Abu Taqiyya shared some of his trade with these customs *multazims*, sometimes selling them upon arrival a fair portion of the goods imported that arrived across the Red Sea at Suez, presumably at less than the price he would have sold them wholesale in the market in Cairo. These customs officials also bought portions of the goods merchants were exporting to Europe, so that here again, they were sharing some of the profits a merchant would have hoped to make. The records indicate that Abu Taqiyya loaned them large amounts of money, such as the sum of 2,720 *dinar*s in 1013/1604, to the two *multazims* of the spice customs, which included not only his advance payment for the customs dues and miscellaneous fees for his imports over a set period but also the spices they bought from him.[18] The fact that such dealings were recorded in court gave them a legal dimension that could serve as protection to the merchant. But the customs officials had other means by which they could pressure merchants for extra benefits outside the legal framework. We find the two customs *multazim*s of the Suez customs house, where the Red Sea goods arrived, Bayazid Bey Mir Liwa and *al-mu'allim* Musa b. Khalafa, somehow able to convince Isma'il Abu Taqiyya, himself an importer of spices, to buy from them some 106 *qintar*s of pepper, at roughly the market price, 15 *dinar*s the *qintar*.[19]

The pattern of lending the *multazim*s a sum of money that they could use to trade with is also evident in Abu Taqiyya's dealings with the Alexandria customs, where he reexported the merchandise that had come across the Red Sea in addition to exporting local products like sugar. For instance, he lent 1,700 *qirsh*, to *al-mu'allim* Shalum b. Murdukhay with the understanding that the duties for whatever goods Abu Taqiyya shipped to Venice or Bilad al-Rum (one of the Arabic names for Anatolia), or received from there would be deducted from this loan.[20] These customs officials were also intermediaries in importing European goods that they sold to merchants in Cairo—metals, copper, velvet textiles.[21] The losers, when such transactions took place, were the European merchants in Cairo, who saw in the customs official a dangerous rival with whom it was hard to compete.

One of the most important aspects of the merchants' relationships with the customs officials had to do with the expansion of their networks, which worked for both parties, in different directions. Again, reciprocity was vital. The archives indicate, especially for the late sixteenth century, a number of instances in which Jewish customs officials used merchants as their agents not only to ship their goods to Mecca, where they or their Jewish agents would not be able to penetrate, and sell them there, but also to buy spices and other goods in Mecca and ship them back to Cairo.[22] Through the merchants of Cairo the Jewish customs officials were directly extending their network to the Holy Cities of the Hijaz, where only Muslims could penetrate. There was a similar pattern in the other direction, across the Mediterranean to Venice. Abu Taqiyya and some of his colleagues were able to benefit from the links that these officials had with European trading ports. In fact, it was through the Jewish agents of these customs officials that Abu Taqiyya was able to penetrate the European market. Jews held a prominent position in the trade between the Ottoman Empire and Italy during the sixteenth and seventeenth centuries, especially with Venice.[23] Abu Taqiyya apparently had neither partner nor agent residing in Venice; he placed his orders directly either with Harun or with two brothers called Naharun and Shu'a. These persons, probably linked to a Jewish network to which the customs *multazim*s belonged, traveled to Venice, sold Abu Taqiyya's merchandise there, bought merchandise for him in the Venetian market, and shipped it to Alexandria.[24] The benefits of this opening to his network must have been considerable, especially in view of the fact that other sectors of international trade were in a crisis because Dutch merchants had penetrated the Asian spice markets and were attempting to control the spice trade with northern Europe.

The *multazim*s' support could also benefit merchants in regard to the capitulations or *imtiyazat* that Ottoman sultans granted to European trading nations, giving their merchants customs facilities and favorable customs duties in Ottoman ports. The capitulations granted to merchants from various European nations—the French and British, for instance—in the last decades of the sixteenth century and the early decades of the seventeenth allowed them a lower rate in customs duties than indigenous merchants, thus giving them an unfair advantage.[25] The extent to which these customs duties, favorable to European merchants, were implemented depended to a certain degree on the local customs officials. The *multazim* thus had to balance a number of considerations: He might try to get away with the nonimplementation of orders which came from Istanbul, a task that was obviously easier when the central state was weak, and charge European merchants duties higher than those agreed upon in the capitulations; or he might try to make up for losses incurred from lower rates paid by French merchants by imposing extra fees on merchants who did not benefit from trade agreements; or, if he considered the side benefits he obtained from the local merchants, he might take a course that was less detrimental to their interests. Merchants thus had to strike a balance in their relationships with the authorities. At times, the relationships may have attained a certain degree of equilibrium, and whatever material losses that the merchants had sustained were sometimes well compensated with gains, whether purely economic, social, or both.

Another group in power that merchants were linked to were the members of the military. At the beginning of the seventeenth century, they were in the process of consolidating their power base. Although Abu Taqiyya and merchants in general were not directly involved in the struggle between the Ottoman authority and the troops that started to manifest itself with some violence in the 1580s, circumstances drew them into this power struggle in an indirect way, involving them in a process that they may or may not have wished to be part of. Their involvement may well have served to tip the balance in favor of one of the warring parties.

A number of circumstances brought Abu Taqiyya in close contact with Mamluks and members of the military corps. Because they were in possession of some rural *iltizam*s, they were in a position to procure raw materials or commodities like sugarcane or rice for merchants. In the early 1600s some of them had started making their way into the urban *iltizam*s, including the customs of Suez, a very lucrative one because the spices and coffee coming across the Red Sea route were taxed there. In 1014/1605, for instance, Bayazid Bey (*bey* being a title given to officers who held important administrative positions) held this concession, sharing it with Musa b. Khalafa, the Jewish *multazim*.[26] It was in Abu Taqiyya's interest to maintain smooth relations with these people. On the other hand, there was some involvement of the military in the supervision of customs; according to Shaw, the pasha sent members of the Mutafarriqa corps to supervise the operations there and presumably to keep an eye on the *multazim*s.[27] Merchants may not necessarily have had direct dealings with the military, but it certainly did not hurt to keep on their good side.

One aspect of the struggle between the military elite and the Ottoman governor was a struggle over the control of the financial resources, notably the tax farms or *iltizam*s. A *multazim* or tax farmer had to pay a yearly sum of money to the treasury in order to get the right to farm the taxes of a certain *muqataʿa*. During the early years of the seventeenth century there were some significant transformations in this system. The military were in the process of expanding their hold over the tax farms. In fact, they penetrated all the urban *iltizam*s—taxes on production, services, and transport—with the exception of the customs houses, which remained predominantly with the Jews. Thus, for the military this decade also brought important changes.[28]

Some of the Mamluks and members of the *ujaq*s (military corps) who saw an opportunity for considerable financial gain in these *iltizam*s may either have not had the cash to make the initial payments to the treasury, which were sometimes quite high, or deemed it appropriate to use borrowed money rather than their own cash. It was from men like Ismaʿil Abu Taqiyya that such funds were available.

Merchants were not restricting their loans to the customs *multazim*s with whom they were doing business. During the first and second decades of the seventeenth century the military and the Mamluks relied to a certain degree on merchants for large loans of money. Like other merchants, Abu Taqiyya found himself forming alliances with the military—the members of the *ujaqs* and Mamluks—and he could hope to get a number of benefits from his links to these people. In the first place, the sugar business had put him in close touch with various members of military corps who were *multazims* of rural landholdings; he dealt with them in order to get the sugarcane and on various occasions made them large loans, perhaps as an inducement for getting the commodity he wanted at the time he needed it. In addition to these immediate factors, there was Abu Taqiyya's discomfort from the competition, not always fair, which he faced from the pashas who traded in international goods; it may have been this factor that pushed him to willingly provide the military group with assistance in their struggle against Ottoman authorities.

Abu Taqiyya's dealings with emirs were repeated and frequent. With Emir Nusuh b. 'Abdalla *Mutafarriqa,* for instance, who was *kashif,* a holder of an administrative position, in the provinces of al-Gharbiyya and al-Munufiyya, there were repeated deals in the course of the first decade of the seventeenth century, the emir procuring some raw materials, the merchant paying in advance and providing loans.[29] The sums involved were quite high. In 1029/1619, Abu Taqiyya loaned 148,000 *nisf*s to Emir Yusuf b. Husayn Jawish, *multazim* of a rural holding in the province of al-Munufiyya.[30] This is an indication of the amounts of money that were passing from the hands of prominent merchants to those of the emirs and beys.

At a time when the members of the *ujaqs* and the Mamluks were about to start the process of taking over a large part of the urban *iltizam*s, formerly held by civilians, this kind of financial help, in the form of loans, gave them an added impetus to go ahead in their project. The support from elite merchants could well have been one of the factors behind their control of more and more urban *iltizam*s, a major financial resource that at a later period they came to dominate more completely.

Within a few decades they had come to control many of these resources, and this must have been obvious fairly early. The emergence of these military groups, sometimes with some initial help from wealthy merchants, changed the power balance between the Ottoman pasha and the military groups that had predominated for most of the sixteenth century. Thereafter, the pasha's authority started to decline. The balance between center and province, or core and periphery, was tipping a little more towards the outer regions.

No wonder, then, that this shift of power aroused the anger of the pashas against merchants, with whom the Ottoman representatives in Egypt had had a relationship involving shared activity. This can explain why Mustafa Pasha, who ruled Egypt for about one year (1028–1029/1619–1620), a few years before Isma'il Abu Taqiyya's death, became enraged at what he could see happening before his own eyes—merchants giving financial support to military groups who challenged Ottoman authority, something he considered a form of treachery. To balance one group against another, Mustafa Pasha promised the troops that he would raise their pay. He also decided to confiscate large sums of money from the merchants of Cairo.[31] The historian al-Bakri reports that this pasha confiscated the sum of 33,000 *qirsh* from merchants, to their distress. He does not mention names, but it goes without saying that he would start with the wealthiest ones—people like Abu Taqiyya, Ruwi'i, and al-Dhahabi. The merchants reacted immediately by drawing up notarized deeds and sending them, along with their petitions, to the sultan in Istanbul. The results were encouraging because Mustafa Pasha was immediately recalled to Istanbul. This development must have pleased the troops, too, because he had not been paying their salaries regularly. The appeal of the merchants had succeeded—certainly with the support of the military, and perhaps also with a degree of support from the contacts some of them may have had with people in Istanbul, as was the case with Abu Taqiyya.[32] Whatever the case, this incident shows that by the second or third decade of the seventeenth century, merchants could play one force against another.

Shortly after these events, and within Zakariyya Abu Taqiyya's lifetime, the emergence of the Mamluk beys had been achieved. In 1631, six years after Abu Taqiyya's death, Musa Pasha assassinated one of the beys, Qitas Bey. The consequences of this act mirror the new balance of power that was achieved during the four decades. The beys immediately reacted, wanting to make sure that Musa Pasha was punished. Some of those who wished to kill the pasha finally managed to depose him. In the following two decades, political power had passed on to them, in the person of Radwan Bey, at the expense of the Ottoman authorities.[33] We can thus conclude that this story about the rise of local military groups, which has been retold many times, had many dimensions and was not simply a matter of the Ottoman authorities on one side and the military on the other.

In the meantime, there were other consequences of the links that Abu Taqiyya had forged. It is probably due to the connection with the Mutafarriqa corps, the corps to which he became attached, that Zakariyya obtained the title of *emir*.[34] Whether or not he did anything to deserve this title is a matter of speculation. In all likelihood he paid his way upward. But it is also significant that in the years following Isma'il's death, marriage alliances between the Abu Taqiyyas and the members of this corps drew the two closer, and these alliances extended the connections first made by Abu Taqiyya. In two of her marriages, his daughter Fatma (also called Stita) was joined to members of the Mutafarriqa.[35] The fortunes of the Abu Taqiyyas were, in some ways, parallel to those of the military elite. If Zakariyya had been a less successful merchant than his father, he had nevertheless managed to take the family one step closer in its connection to the ruling military elite. Mobility from one social group to another was therefore not impossible, but it was much more likely to happen in times of great social transformation, as this one was.

A new stage had been reached in the relationship between the Ottoman authorities in Egypt and local power groups. This was an important change, to which many factors contributed. There were also wider regional factors, the most important of which had to do with the relationship between the center and the periphery, the weakening of central power in Istanbul at the expense of stronger provincial entities. The local factors that were behind these transformations must certainly have differed between one region of the empire and another, and the full complexity of the situation is one that still has to be studied. As far as Cairo is concerned, we can argue that merchants had a role in bringing about these changes. It would be interesting to ascertain whether merchants played a similar role in other regions of the Empire and, if so, who the other actors may have been.

The Merchant in Society

A number of conclusions about the role of merchants in the late sixteenth- and early seventeenth-century society can be reached. First of all, the complex conditions of this period helped to change the condition of merchants. Their position was characterized by their structural independence from the ruling bureaucracy, both as an economic force and as a social force, in the sense that they were not tools of either the political forces or the bureaucracy. They constitute a group that had become a socioeconomic force to be reckoned with by those in power.

And yet merchants were often pressured into relationships that may not have been of their own choice. They negotiated with the different groups in power to protect their own commercial or economic interests. But ultimately, the position of merchants, which rose during those decades, speaks for itself. Although in Europe the guilds were behind many of the gains that merchants made in their struggle for power, the archival sources used here do not suggest any role that the guilds of Cairo may have played in the rise of merchants. As far as we can tell from available evidence, and until further research sheds more light on this matter, the power of merchants was personally based, and to a large extent, many of their objectives were attained in an informal way rather than through guilds.

•   •   •

It may well be that the great prestige attached to the post of *shahbandar al-tujjar* dates from this period. There had always been an organization that grouped merchants hierarchically and was headed by a prominent member. We know this from the Mamluk period. But the importance of the post emerges only in the Ottoman period, when its influence went beyond the circle of merchants and traders. Even though we know hardly anything of the decades that followed the Ottoman invasion of 1517, it seems likely that the stature of this position grew as the social economic position of merchants underwent important changes in the course of the half century covered in this book.

The changes that the merchant group experienced and the alliances they made with the military elite affected the structure of government in Egypt. Merchants had, in their own way, helped to shape the events that took place and the restructuring that followed because they were able to influence the actions of those in power and could therefore help to control the direction of the transformations taking place. The history of this period, in other words, was shaped not just by the Ottoman authorities and their representatives or by the local military groups who opposed them, but by merchants as well. Important as their role is to our understanding of how society was functioning at the time, and how different social groups were linked to each other by ties of mutual interest, it is one that has hardly been recognized. A reappraisal of the role of merchants in premodern Middle Eastern society is therefore likely to bring to light important perspectives.

The study of the changing condition of merchants can be put in context with other social changes in other parts of the Empire. Rif'at Abou El-Haj, for instance, has suggested that during this same period there were parallel changes in other groups—notably in the landowning class—appearing when public lands were transferred to public property.[36] There may have been other manifestations of the phenomenon in Cairo insofar as it implies social mobility at a time when the whole power structure was undergoing transformation. It also implies the emancipation of an economic activity formerly controlled by the bureaucracy. In other words, what was happening to merchants in Cairo may well have been one dimension of the broader picture of social change in the Ottoman state during roughly that same time. Much more research is needed, however, before we can get a clear picture of the changes experienced by various social groups in the different parts of the Ottoman Empire during this period.

These findings also push us to reconsider the view that the society of the period was divided into two distinct groups: the bureaucracy (rulers), on the one hand, and society (the ruled), on the other. The implication— that the links between the two groups were one-way only, with society providing the surplus in cash or in kind from which the ruling bureaucracy lived—neglects some vital aspects of the links between the two, notably the ties of interest, the rivalries, the competition, and the reciprocal influences and benefits between the members of the ruling bureaucracy and the merchants.

6

Shaping the Urban Geography

Cairo of 1600

Cairo was a city with which Abu Taqiyya could identify at several levels. As the largest city in the Empire after Istanbul, it was full of people of many nationalities and social groups: Some came from nearby regions like Syria; others from faraway lands in Africa; some were permanent residents, others only passing through. As a merchant, Abu Taqiyya would have had dealings with many of these people. Like other inhabitants of Cairo, he must have enjoyed its rich architectural heritage; he was particularly fortunate because he lived and worked in a part of the city that had one of the highest concentrations of major public monuments. Most important to him as a merchant, of course, was that he was living in one of the major commercial centers of his time. Cairo was the hub of his commercial activity because of its position as both a meeting point for a number of major trade routes and a center for the exchange of goods. From the Red Sea, from Black Africa, from Syria, from Venice and from Anatolia, merchants came with merchandise to sell and exchange or to transport to further destinations. The street linking its northern gates, Bab al-Futuh and Bab al-Nasr, to Bab Zuwayla in the south, was the busiest area of the city, heavy with traffic—beasts laden with goods to be transported into the city to one of the commercial establishments or leaving to start on a long journey.

Along that main thoroughfare and in close proximity to it stood the larger commercial establishments where the large-scale merchants carried on their business, the *khan*s and *wikala*s. Many of the major establishments were buildings that had once belonged to the Mamluk sultans— Sultan Qaytbay, Sultan al-Ghuri, Sultan Barsbay—and ruling emirs, like emir Qusun. In these buildings, some of them monumental structures, merchants and tradesmen now rented out space.[1] They stood out from other commercial establishments because of their embellishments, in colored marble and carved stone, and the inscriptions of royal founders on their entrances. The sight of these and other buildings was part of Abu Taqiyya's daily ride from his home to the two shops he shared with al-Damiri in the Silk Market, Suq al-Harir, or to another shop in Khatt al-Ghuriyya.

Cairo was also a major religious center, even though its position as the most important center of Islamic learning was seriously affected by its incorporation into the Ottoman Empire. Istanbul had taken over that role, and its growing number of colleges attracted the best professors and students. Although we know little about the attitudes of merchants in general and Abu Taqiyya in particular toward religious life in Cairo, within the commercial center that they moved in and in the areas in proximity to it stood some of the most impressive religious establishments of the city. Among these were the Azhar, both a mosque and a center of scholarship, with which many of the leading scholars of the time had connections, as well as some of the most popular Sufi establishments. Not far from Abu Taqiyya's house, in Darb al-Tahun in the northern part of the city, a number of Sufi *shaykh*s had founded *zawia*s (Sufi establishments), where their disciples gathered around them. The *zawia*s of 'Abdul-Wahab al-Sha'rani and of al-Ghamri were at walking distance, and their numerous disciples must have been visible in the neighborhood. The provisions that Abu Taqiyya eventually made in his *waqf* indicate his links to another Sufi order, the Sadat al-Wafa'iyya, which was, along with the Bakri order, among the more prestigious orders of Sufis, because this order received a share of the revenues of his commercial establishments.[2]

For all these reasons, Abu Taqiyya could identify with Cairo, for throughout his career, it had been a central focus of his activity and his interests. However, during the last decade of his life, when he was at the peak of his career as a merchant, the relationship of Abu Taqiyya to the city gained another dimension: He contributed to shaping Cairo's urban geography and left a landmark that was to bear his name for generations to come.

Merchants in Urban Development

Abu Taqiyya's contribution can be placed in a broader context. The analysis of the relationship of the merchants of his generation to the city and to urban development is one way of exploring another dimension of the changing relationship between state and society. In observing them undertaking some of the functions that had been a prerogative of rulers, we see what was part of the evolution of the socioeconomic condition of merchants during Abu Taqiyya's lifetime. This evolution of their position affected not only their economic condition, but a number of other aspects of their lives, of which urban development was one. In emerging to a high degree of visibility in the context of the urban setting of Cairo, Abu Taqiyya was part of a trend.

For the merchants, one consequence of urban development was that the expenditures for a commercial infrastructure to accommodate the increased volume of trade meant a heavy financial burden placed on their shoulders. We can only guess at the way that a merchant balanced the different, sometimes conflicting, considerations in making a decision to support urban development and investing in building a *khan* or *wikala* rather than using the money to expand his trade.

The high profile that merchants attained in the city is in marked contrast to the silence about them in the contemporary histories and chronicles of Egypt in Arabic. We find no mention of Abu Taqiyya, al-Damiri, Ruwi'i, or any of the numerous other merchants that appear frequently in archival sources, their role in the major events of the period not being important enough to justify mentioning them. Yet his generation left its mark on the city through the construction of public buildings: the little mosque of *khawaja* Karim al-Din al-Burdayni in the quarter of al-Da'udiyya as well as the mosque, elementary school, and public fountain that *khawaja* Ibrahim al-Mansuri built in Old Cairo. Streets and quarters still bear their names, notably Khan Abu Taqiyya Street, and the al-Ruwi'i quarter, today one of the busiest areas for hardware and aluminum goods.

Besides Isma'il Abu Taqiyya and al-Ruwi'i, several other merchants of this generation were involved in the development of the city or of its infrastructure, including Isma'il's brother Yasin, and *khawaja* Jamal al-Din al-Dhahabi, whose residence and *wikala* are among the buildings listed as national monuments.[3] It is significant that these were merchants of great prominence: Abu Taqiyya, al-ʿAsi, and al-Dhababi were all *shahbandars*; and Ahmad al-Ruwiʿi was the uncle of ʿAli al-Ruwiʿi, Abu Taqiyya's predecessor in the *shahbandariyya*. All of them were part of the elite sector of the merchant community, and therefore their acts cannot be taken as representative of the merchant community as a whole. Nevertheless, because of the amount of wealth that they were able to manipulate, what they did with it represented a trend of some significance in the broader context of the time. It is in the context of this emergence of merchants that Ismaʿil Abu Taqiyya's contribution to the urban geography of the city should be seen.

Merchants were not the only group to emerge in the urban scene of the time. Badr al-Qarafi, scholar and *qadi,* who died in 1008/1599, financed a little mosque off the main thoroughfare in Khurunfish street;[4] and Qadi Ahmad al-Nubi, still remembered by his development of the quarter of Darb al-Nubi in Azbakiyya in the northwest of Cairo,[5] was also involved in the construction of public buildings and the development of new quarters. The emergence of merchants was therefore part of a larger trend that mirrored some of the social transformations that were taking place during this period, with members of the indigenous population becoming more prominent.

The reasons for their emergence on the urban scene at that particular time are varied and complex. On the one hand, the city was undergoing urban growth. The numerous works of André Raymond on this subject have clearly shown the expansion the city underwent between 1517 and 1798. On the other hand, the groups who had traditionally been associated in Cairo with urban projects and with public construction were, for different reasons, dissociated temporarily from this role. Various hypotheses can be put forward to explain why a city like Cairo was growing at a period when everything else—economy, administration, law and order— are thought to have been in decline. Some historians see population growth as a general regional phenomenon that can be observed in a number of other cities of the Ottoman Empire, and of the Mediterranean in general.[6] Evidence for the growth of Cairo, Aleppo, and Tunis towards the end of the sixteenth century, for instance, is indicated by the transfer of the tanneries in these three cities, by sultanic order, from populated areas to areas in the periphery of the city. The reason for such transfers was that the urban fabric had extended to these establishments, and it was important, because of the odors and for hygienic reasons, to keep them at a distance from densely populated areas.[7] A further explanation is that the towns of the Middle East were places of refuge for rural populations when life in rural areas became too difficult.[8] Still another explanation is that in times of famine, which in Egypt were recurrent on account of its dependence on the yearly flooding of the Nile, food was easier to obtain in cities because the government had an interest in keeping the provisions flowing.[9]

During Abu Taqiyya's lifetime, significant urban transformations were occurring. Because some of these changes were instituted by merchants, and many of the important ones were in commercial areas, we can make a connection between the growth of the city and the development of its commerce, much in the same way that we can in the case of European trading cities. A thriving international trade, with the shift to the coffee trade and the expansion of the sugar industry, was one of the important driving forces behind the expansion of Cairo during this period, as in many other cities where periods of commercial prosperity brought urban growth. A similar phenomenon had occurred in Venice in the fifteenth century, when its thriving trade resulted in a building boom, in which colossal sums of money were spent; and in Antwerp, in the second half of the sixteenth century, a period of commercial prosperity, during which not only the city's population doubled but also its number of houses, and new squares and new streets were built.[10] Thus we can see a link between the expansion of these cities and their growing commercial activities.

The impressions that we get from many of the European travelers who visited Cairo during this period confirm that its commerce was active and prosperous. Michael Heberer Von Bretten, a prisoner caught by the Ottomans in Malta and brought to Cairo in 1585–86, found the city so enormous and so crowded that he did not doubt that it was larger than either Paris, Rome, or Constantinople.[11] His impression must certainly have been based on what he saw in the city center, which was the most crowded part of Cairo. A few years later, Johann Wild, the German who was in Cairo between 1606 and 1610, found its commerce extremely active and was impressed by the stalls full of stones, spices, precious sweet-smelling woods, beautiful turbans, and fine cottons that came from the East. He saw the corals and woolen cloth that the Venetians brought, and he found that the merchants from Constantinople had little merchandise to bring with them but came to buy products in Cairo and take them away.[12]

One of the immediate reasons for the emergence of merchants on the urban scene at that particular time was that a vacuum had been created when first the Mamluk sutans and ruling emirs and then the Ottoman pashas—both groups that had in the past been actively involved in urban projects—were no longer important actors on the scene. The imperial past of the city was a daily reality that the inhabitants of Cairo saw all around them, especially in the city center. Abu Taqiyya, who spent most of his time within the core of the city center, could see in his daily ride from his house at Darb al-Shabrawi, off the main commercial thorough-fare of Khatt al-Amshatiyyin, to the market of Suq al-Warraqin or Khan al-Hamzawi, the numerous examples of royal buildings. Immediately upon leaving Darb al-Shabrawi, the dead-end alley where his house was, he faced the delicately carved stone facade of the old Fatimid Mosque of al-Aqmar, a royal construction. As he rode on, in a few minutes he reached Bayn al-Qasrayn, the heart of the city, where on his right was the imposing dome of the mausoleum of Sultan Barquq; nearby was the college and mausoleum of al-Nasir Muhammad b. Qalawun, which was surmounted by a lace-like minaret. Only a little farther and Abu Taqiyya was riding by the facade of Sultan Qalawun's complex, with his mausoleum, college, and *maristan* or hospital. When he looked up, he could see the inscription, carved in stone from one end of the building to the other, with the glorious titles the Sultan had bequeathed upon himself: *sultan al-iraqayn wal misrayn,* Sultan of the two Iraqs, the Arab one and the Persian one, and the two Egypts, Upper Egypt and Lower Egypt; *malik al-barrayn wal bahrayn,* king of Africa and Asia and of the two seas, the Mediterra-nean and the Red Sea; *sahib al-qiblatayn,* guardian of the two *qibla*s (holy places) of Mecca and Jerusalem, where Muslims faced when praying; *khadim al-haramayn al-sharifayn,* protector of Mecca and Medina.[13] That was one of the most impressive landmarks in Bayn al-Qasrayn, and many people on their way to work would look up at it.

For a while after the disappearance of the Mamluk rulers from the scene, their role in urban development was taken up by the Ottoman governors, who concentrated their efforts mainly on the port towns of Bulaq on the Nile and Rashid and Alexandria on the Mediterranean.[14] Within a few decades after the Ottomans took Egypt, the construction that took place there—warehouses and storerooms, shops, baths, elemen-tary schools, religious buildings—multiplied the facilities of Bulaq. Mosques like the one that Sinan Pasha constructed in that river port introduced a different style, imported from Anatolia by the new patrons. This was, however, only a phase—limited in time, and limited in scope to the main ports. After the mid-eighties, the Ottoman governors were less inclined to interest themselves in urban projects. They became deeply involved in a long power struggle with the military, which absorbed much of their energy and recurrently erupted into violent incidents—in one case, costing the life of one governor, Ibrahim Pasha, surnamed al-*maqtul* (the assassinated).

At this point, merchants of Abu Taqiyya's generation could afford to invest some of their money in the construction of public buildings because they were neither directly involved in the struggle for power between the military groups and the representatives of Ottoman authority nor openly siding with one party or the other. Then, they handled wealth they had accumulated from their commerce. They had other reasons to want to own or develop urban property. Owning a commercial establishment, a mill, or an apartment building brought in regular revenues, particularly advisable in times of monetary instability. During Abu Taqiyya's lifetime there had been an important currency transformation. At the start of his professional career, the main coins in use were the golden *dinar,* called the *sharifi* (worth 40 *nisfs*) with the local silver *nisf.* By the time Abu Taqiyya died, the *dinar sharifi* had become a rarely used coin and was replaced by the silver *qirsh* (worth 30 *nisfs*). The shift from gold to silver and the resulting monetary crisis probably caused a certain degree of instability. It was probably thought not advisable to keep large sums of loose cash for long, for fear of loss of value. Urban investments in such times of crisis were therefore likely to increase.

In addition to this, urban property, especially if endowed in *waqf,* had long been considered both a way of diversifying assets and a protection against confiscation. A government with a short money supply was the least likely to put its hands on a *waqf* property and more likely to look for cash. One such incident is recorded in the early seventeenth century. The merchants of Abu Taqiyya's generation personally experienced such a confiscation when Mustafa Pasha decided to confiscate some 30,000 *qirsh* from merchants. One factor may have played to Abu Taqiyya's advantage in this unpleasant situation. At that time, he had just finished the construction of his second *wikala,* which must have cost a fortune to build. At that particular moment, on 20 Muharram 1029, when Mustafa Pasha started the confiscations, Abu Taqiyya turned the *wikala* into a *waqf*, immune to confiscations of this kind. We are left guessing as to whether news had reached him of impending trouble or whether the confiscations had just started and he immediately decided to take action and endow the building, which had been finished almost a year before. Whatever the case, his act was well timed, for he had spent a large sum to build the two *wikala*s and probably had less loose cash than at normal times. He had also protected his property from confiscation.

The fact that merchants invested in urban property rather than keeping their cash for trade is a subject that has raised some controversy. Some historians consider this type of spending to be "conspicuous consumption" of money that merchants could have applied more usefully to their trade than to religious or charitable buildings, which were of no direct benefit to them and cost a great deal. The same criticism has been applied to the construction undertaken in Cairo by the Mamluk sultans. This, however, is one phenomenon that cannot be explained simply in economic terms, or in terms of the immediate financial returns to be expected. Instead, it has to be explained in cultural terms if we are to understand the motivations for such patterns of behavior. We have to understand this phenomenon in the context of an urban society in which any kind of public construction was in the hands of individuals rather than states or governments—a feature that certainly must have fostered a sense of responsibility among those who had wealth to develop urban infrastructure. But there were also certain benefits to be had.

There is no doubt that Abu Taqiyya enjoyed making a good appearance and seemed to like his role as a well-known public figure—that was, in one sense, part of the role of being a *shahbandar*. His major construction projects were undertaken when he was *shahbandar*, and he may well have had the enhancement of his position in mind when he did so. Merchants, however, had other reasons to want to attain visibility in the city. Having one's name attached to a public building, institution, or street could serve a number of purposes. The Mamluk sultans had used their monumental structures to further their own glory; their large, imposing buildings, with forceful inscriptions set exactly where the eye of the passerby would see them, were symbols of power. The architecture of the Ottoman pashas likewise displayed symbols of Ottoman power and hegemony, although many provincial features were incorporated.[15] Merchants too could further some of their objectives by using the same formula. Building a mosque, a public school, or fountain was a sign of success, a manifestation of wealth, and led to a significant objective: improving a merchant's credibility and his credit and, indirectly, widening his sphere of activity.

However, the reasons behind the concern for public construction that the merchants of Abu Taqiyya's generation showed was part of a broader social trend of which they were part. For a social group that was in the process of upward mobility during this period, visibility was an important means of obtaining recognition and social prestige. Much in the same way as the rites associated with the *shahbandariyya* had allowed Abu Taqiyya to form a public image, his public buildings left to stamp on the urban geography of the city. Years after he died, generations of Cairenes recalled him in terms of the urban landmarks associated with his name, in the same way as his colleague al-Ruwi'i remained in the public memory because his name became associated with the quarter he developed. Therefore, buildings not only brought economic benefits but also helped in developing a public image for their builders.

Because merchants were important actors on the urban scene, they could have a hand in the direction that urban transformations were taking. Two trends are evident in the urban development of Cairo during the decades of Abu Taqiyya's lifetime: The first was an expansion in the commercial part of the city, and the second was an expansion in the western outskirts, in al-Azbakiyya. In both developments we can discern a significant role played by merchants. Though for different reasons in each case, and using different methods, Abu Taqiyya took part in both.

Constructing New *Wikalas*

Not surprisingly, merchants' primary interest was in commercial establishments and in those parts of the city where commercial activity was concentrated. This explains why so many commercial structures were erected and why the commercial zone of Cairo was extended. Merchants would have been the first ones to feel that the existing structures were insufficient for their needs—if, for instance, during the height of the trading season, timed by the pilgrims' caravan to and from Mecca or the seasonal arrivals and departures of Red Sea ships, they were not finding the space for the storage of their merchandise available. Archival sources indicate that at least seven *wikalas* were built by merchants during the couple of decades before and after the turn of the century, a phenomenon of considerable significance. Two of them, in Bulaq, were constructed by 'Abdul-Qawi al-'Asi, and the other five were erected in the center of Cairo: the two *wikala*s built jointly by Isma 'il Abu Taqiyya and 'Abdul-Qadir al-Damiri; the *wikala* that Yasin Abu Taqiyya built in al-Rukn al-Mukhallaq; Wikalat al-Shuja'i in Khan al-Khalili; and Jamal al-Din al-Dhahabi's *wikala* near Suq al-Sagha. The construction of new *wikala*s, with their multitude of functions, and the scale of their buildings, can be taken as an important indication of the commercial situation during the period from the end of the sixteenth century to the early seventeenth. Only a very active trade and prospering commerce would have justified this kind of construction.

Prominent merchants found it advantageous to have their own individual places of business. If nothing else, it reenforced their position vis-à-vis other merchants. In addition, a *wikala* brought in revenues from the rent of both the shops on its outside and the living units on the upper floors. Abu Taqiyya and al-Damiri, for instance, received the handsome sum of 16,500 *nisf*s as one year's rent for the smaller of the two *wikala*s they built.[16] The global result of such construction activity was that the commercial infrastructure of Cairo was appreciably expanded in a fairly short time, providing facilities for more merchandise to be handled and stored.

Another dimension to the development of the commercial infrastructure can be discerned. For Abu Taqiyya, the construction of these major commercial establishments was the culmination of years of investment in various forms of infrastructure to support trading activities—for example, buying a portion of a *wikala* in a town in the Delta to support his activities in that region; or buying half a ship in the Red Sea, where so much of his trade was concentrated.[17] As business expanded, he was developing an infrastructure to support it.

A very significant change in the domain of urban development can be attributed to Isma'il Abu Taqiyya and 'Abdul-Qadir al-Damiri. The two *wikala*s in the street, Khatt Sirr al-Maristan, that they jointly financed were more than just two new commercial establishments: These buildings, in fact, started the transformation of a street from residential to commercial use. Before the two merchants started their construction, Khatt Sirr al-Maristan was a quiet residential street, with houses on either side. After they had finished, the street was gradually transformed into a commercial thoroughfare.

Behind the Qalawun Hospital *(maristan)*, the street called Khatt Sirr al-Maristan was very close to the commercial heart of the city, notably, Bayn al-Qasrayn, the city center; Suq al-Nahhasin, the coppersmiths' market; and Suq al-Sagha, the market for precious metals and jewels. Bayn al-Qasrayn, probably the most crowded part of Cairo, was the location for a number of urban institutions, such as the hospital and the courts of Salihiyya Najmiyya, Qisma 'Askariyya, and Qisma 'Arabiyya. Very close by was the court of Bab 'Ali. Accordingly, people came there from all over the city. On days when Abu Taqiyya wished to avoid the crowded center of Bayn al-Qasrayn as he rode home, all he had to do was turn left at Suq al-Sagha and in a few minutes he could be in Khatt Sirr al-Maristan, taking him to Khatt al-Khurushtuf, where Yasin Abu Taqiyya and Laila had their houses; then one more turn right took him back to the main street, very close to his own house. This street therefore had a double advantage: It was close to the heart of the city and easy to get to from the main street, both very important requirements for the large *wikala*s that had to be reached by loaded beasts carrying the merchandise that would eventually be stored there. For Abu Taqiyya, it was also very close to his house at Khatt al-Amshatiyyin.

Because the project was quite a large one, it took years of planning and preparation. In 1017/1608, Abu Taqiyya and al-Damiri signed a written agreement to build the *wikala*s in partnership, fixing the share of each—three quarters for Isma'il and one quarter for 'Abdul-Qadir.[18] We can only conjecture as to why the two partners who, in all their previous business deals had shared by half whatever capital or profit was involved, now altered this pattern. It may have been that al-Damiri was more reluctant to put aside the large amount of money such a project would require. Very possibly, too, the independent deals that Abu Taqiyya had made, especially with the sugar trade, had brought in huge profits, in which al-Damiri had had no involvement.

One of the big problems Abu Taqiyya and Damiri had to take care of was acquisition of land. In a densely populated city like Cairo, it was extremely difficult to obtain a building site in such a choice area. The difficulty for these two merchants was compounded by the fact that the buildings in Khatt Sirr al-Maristan were all fairly small houses, inhabited by people of modest standing, like the textile dyer, Shams al-Din Muhammad b. Salama;[19] or Shaykh Abul Tib b. Mansur, who sold ointments.[20] In order to get a piece of land large enough to build their establishment, a large number of people had to be approached and convinced to leave their homes to find other places to live, so that their houses could be torn down. This was no easy task. Some of these people actually owned house and land, and others had built their houses on *waqf* land, so that in addition to the complications of dealing with people, there were complexities concerning the legal status of the land, which was partly private property, partly not. From certain persons, such as the *waqf* supervisor of Qalawun's *maristan*, Abu Taqiyya rented plots of land; sometimes these were of very modest dimensions, such as one plot measuring 13 *dira'* × 13.5 *dira'* and another 9.5 × 16 *dira'*[21] (the *dira'* measures about 65 cm). For the larger of the two *wikalas*, which was finished by 1619, Abu Taqiyya and Damiri had acquired some eleven plots of land from the original owners and users. It had taken them some years to negotiate with, convince, and sometimes pressure the owners or the renters of these little plots, one after the other, until they could acquire the two enormous plots where their two *wikalas* still stand opposite each other. This change in land configuration was in itself a major transformation.

During the many years when the project was being realized, first the smaller *wikala*, *al-wikala al-sughra,* on the west side of the street, then the large *wikala, al-wikala al-kubra,* on its east side, Abu Taqiyya watched the work progressing, on his way to or from the market. First there were the extensive clearing operations, then the foundations were built, and finally he could see the buildings begin to appear. At long last, years later, as soon as he entered Khatt Sirr al-Maristan, he could see the two monumental entrances of the *wikalas* across from each other towering above. From then on, Khatt Sirr al-Maristan was no longer a street to be taken to escape the noise or crowds of Bayn al-Qasrayn, but one to which people came specially. For merchants, the buildings together brought to the real estate market over one hundred and twenty storerooms *(hasils)* for rent. Merchants like al-Ruwi'i, who immediately rented space there, found facilities for themselves and for their clients right there in the building: a *masjid* or little mosque, a coffeehouse, and a public fountain at the corner of the larger *wikala*. 'Abdul-Qadir al-Damiri moved into the small house built at the corner of the *wikala* and made an opening so that he could get into his *hasil* without having to leave the house. And of course, Abu Taqiyya himself used the *hasils* to store and sell his spices, coffee, and sugar. For ordinary people, the upper floors of the *wikalas* offered living units for rent, sixteen in the smaller *wikala* and twenty-nine in the larger one. As a result, many more people were going to inhabit this street than before.

The brilliant insight that Abu Taqiyya and al-Damiri had in choosing this spot for their urban investment is proven by the later developments in Khatt Sirr al-Maristan. Slowly but surely, the trend he and Damiri had started was followed by others, and one *wikala* after another replaced the private houses on this street, until the street consisted of one *wikala* after the other,[22] much like the main commercial thoroughfare lying parallel to it. The street had been transformed from a residential to a commercial area, the commercial zone of the city being thereby considerably expanded. Because the *wikala*s of Abu Taqiyya and Damiri were the first structures of their kind, and because they were the largest as well, it was these buildings that stood out. As a matter of fact, the street became identified with the Abu Taqiyya building. About two decades later, when a merchant by the name of *khawaja* Ahmad al-Khatib built a *wikala* adjacent to one of the Abu Taqiyya/al-Damiri buildings, the two *wikala*s were being referred to as *'imarat* (building complex) al-Khawaja Isma'il Abu Taqiyya. In other words, for some reason, the name of Abu Taqiyya became attached to this area, and that of al-Damiri fell into obscurity. About the reasons that could have brought this about, we can only hypothesize. Perhaps it was that Isma'il Abu Taqiyya had been a *shahbandar* and was a prominent figure in society. Perhaps, also, it was a difference in character, and Abu Taqiyya had sought to attain fame and to acquire visibility, while al-Damiri had not.

Large-scale urban transformations were never very frequent, given the difficulties and the expense. Often it was rulers who were responsible for such changes, as had happened a few years earlier when the Ottoman sultan had issued orders to have the tanneries south of Bab Zuwayla transferred to Bab al-Luq. The configuration of land was accordingly changed, the large plot of land where the tanneries had been located being divided into small plots and built up. In some cases, it was a powerful political figure who instituted changes of this sort; for example, about two decades after Abu Taqiyya's death, Radwan Bey transformed the site south of Bab Zuwayla, constructing a huge complex that included his palace, a market, a *wikala*, and several other buildings. The Abu Taqiyya/al-Damiri project, though important, was not the only such project initiated by merchants. In Bulaq, the river port of Cairo, the same phenomenon had occurred: the two *wikala*s of a *shahbandar*, 'Abdul-Ra'uf al-'Asi, started the transformation of the street parallel to the main commercial thoroughfare, incorporating residential areas into the commercial zone. These examples of urban transformation taking place within a short time are of great pertinence to our understanding of how and why Cairo expanded during this period.

Abu Taqiyya and the other merchants of his generation had concentrated their major efforts and their finances on those projects that were immediately linked to their commercial activity. Moreover, there were a number of reasons why Abu Taqiyya in particular and merchants in general were more closely linked to the central part of the city than other inhabitants of Cairo. His two residences—that in Darb al-Shabrawi, an alley opposite the al-Aqmar Mosque, and the other in Darb Tahun off Suq Amir al-Juyush—were located there, very close to the main commercial thoroughfare of the city. This was the pattern that most of his merchant colleagues adopted—living in homes close to the commercial part of the city, close to their business premises: in al Saba' Qa'at for *khawaja* Nur al-Din al-Shuja'i; behind Madrasat al-Ghuri, for *khawaja* Ja'far 'Amir.[23] This pattern applied not only to the very wealthy merchants, living in large and comfortable houses, but also to the merchants with limited capital and restricted networks, whose houses, off the market area or close to it, sometimes contained only three or four rooms. A similar trend was noted by André Raymond for a later period.[24]

Moreover, all the other Abu Taqiyyas—Laila, Sayidat al-Kull, and Yasin—lived in the vicinity of Khatt al-Khurushtuf, near Isma'il's home. The reasons are obvious. Living near the center or off the main thoroughfare was convenient not only for the merchants, who were close to the places where they worked, but also for their families. Nearby were the numerous *suqs* (markets) and goods of all kinds. If 'Atiyat al-Rahman wished to buy jewelry for herself or her daughters, Suq al-Sagha, the market for precious stones and jewels, was a few minutes away. If they wanted silks and velvets, which Laila Abu Taqiyya loved dearly,[25] several markets for luxury textiles were in the vicinity—Suq al-Sharb, Tarbi'at al-Harir, and Suq al-Warraqin, for example. Along the main thoroughfare were the most important markets: the spice market in the city center near Khan al-Khalili, where Christophe Harant, the Bohemian nobleman who traveled to Cairo in 1598, saw Persian merchants displaying their brocades, rich textiles, and other merchandise;[26] the copper market, Suq al-Nahhasin, next to it; the market for silk, Suq al-Harir not far away; and slightly off the main road, the slave market. These were only a few of the numerous markets along the thoroughfare. The wide variety of merchandise available there attracted local customers, people from outside the city, and foreigners.

Merchants also found there the numerous services for transporting, storing, and weighing goods. Even though the Abu Taqiyyas had a private *hammam* (bath) in the house, that did not necessarily prevent either the men or the women of the house from using a public *hammam*—Hammam al-Sultan Inal was the closest to the house. Likewise, with the Qala-wun Hospital close by, a doctor could be summoned if a child was ill. In other words, living in the center of Cairo, unlike living in the closed residential areas (*haras*), meant that a whole range of public amenities was available within close reach.

We might therefore imagine that Abu Taqiyya's connections to Cairo were limited to the city center, where he lived and worked. But his relationship to the city did not rest solely on commerce; it had other dimensions, not directly linked to the core of his professional occupation. Although Abu Taqiyya's links with the city center always remained vital, various circumstances pushed him to forge links to other quarters.

Development of al-Azbakiyya

Merchants played a significant role in the development of al-Azbakiyya as an elite quarter, in northwest Cairo, during this period. Their decision to buy or build secondary homes along the banks of Birka al-Azbakiyya was prompted by the fact that they had reached a level of wealth, allowing them to spend fairly large sums of money for pleasure, entertainment, and image building. By moving to these waterside houses beside a lake *(birka)* for holiday pleasures, they were in fact following a fashion that the political rulers had initiated much earlier.

They may also have been prompted by a desire to get away from the disturbances occasionally taking place in the streets of Cairo at that time. In 1586 a troop revolt was precipitated by 'Uways Pasha's decision to solve the shortage in treasury funds that year by salary cuts for troops. The conflict between the military and the Ottoman authorities brought about recurrent street violence, disruptive for people in the vicinity. At least once, the disturbances occurred in areas close to where the Abu Taqiyyas were living. The soldiers stormed into Bayt al-Qadi, the residence of the Qadi al-Qudat, which in fact was no other than the Bab 'Ali where Isma'il Abu Taqiyya was a constant visitor, for the Qadi al-Qudat sent

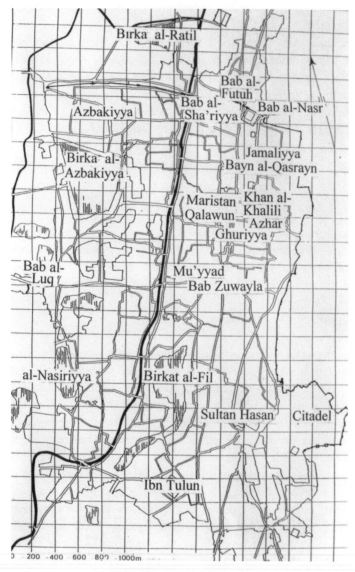

4. Cairo. Courtesy of the author.

from Istanbul resided in a large palace, part of which housed the court of Bab 'Ali. Once they attacked passersby in Rukn al-Mukhallaq Street, where Yasin Abu Taqiyya built his *wikala*, which was only a few steps away from Isma'il Abu Taqiyya's residence.[27] Thus merchants like Isma'il Abu Taqiyya who could afford to have secondary homes at a certain distance from the hub of the center might move there with their families in times of trouble.

Isma'il Abu Taqiyya chose to have his house on the banks of Birka al-Azbakiyya. Birka al-Azbakiyya was the largest of the many lakes in and around Cairo, which included Birka al-Fil in the south of the city and Birka al-Ratli in the north. Filled with water at the time of the Nile flood, these *birka*s, especially Birka al-Azbakiyya, provided diversions for the inhabitants of Cairo. On these outings they could enjoy not only the gardens and fields but boating along the banks, with food and often music as well.

Of the various *birka*s in the city, Birka al-Azbakiyya was the one closest to Abu Taqiyya's house; he could reach it by riding through Suq Marjush, and across Bab al-Sha'riyya. At the same time, it was far enough from the areas where there was trouble. Once he was there, peace and quiet prevailed. A house on the banks of the Azkabiyya was pleasant for a family vacation, anyway—with the green fields, the water, and the fresh air. It was quite different from his house in Darb al-Shabrawi; the windows of the house opened on the *birka,* and there was a view and a breeze, which the house in the city lacked. Behind the house stood the field of Ghayt al-Hamzawi. Once settled in their waterside house, the family could enjoy the same pleasures that members of the ruling elite had enjoyed. Boating was a favorite pastime, and the houses built along the *birka* had their own boating facilities; people in the house could, on the spur of the moment, descend the stairs, get on the boat, and sail around the large lake.

For a long time, Birka al-Fil, to the south of the city, had been the most aristocratic location, with one palace after another along its banks, so that the lake was entirely surrounded by these residences. The merchants of Abu Taqiyya's generation followed this model with Birka al-Azbakiyya. Compared to Birka al-Fil, space was more readily available because in the early 1600s only a few buildings stood there, mainly on its eastern bank, where the mosque of Azbak stood. It must have given the merchants some satisfaction to be able to enjoy the same pleasures that the military elite was enjoying in the more aristocratic Birka al-Fil. Abu Taqiyya, Muhammad Ibn Yaghmur, 'Uthman Ibn Yaghmur, and Sulayman al-Shuja'i built houses close to each other on the northeastern corner of the *birka,* where they could come either when times in the city center were troubled, or when on a feast day or a holiday, they went for an outing.[28]

Abu Taqiyya had other links with the Azbakiyya quarter, which was the fastest growing part of Cairo during these years. More than anywhere else in the city, the urban expansion could be readily observed: A number of the fields and gardens to the north of the *birka* were being divided into building plots and rented out to people who eventually built on them. The garden in the *waqf* foundation endowed by 'Ali al-Farra, the gardens belonging to Shaykh al-Turi, an empty plot forming part of the *waqf* property endowed by Mustafa Katkhuda, and the Sudun Garden were all divided up between 1006/1597 and 1011/1602, and the built-up area of the city increased.[29] These new areas were inhabited mainly by the middle class—artisans, shopkeepers, textile workers, and such. As these areas close to the Azbakiyya lake started to become inhabited, infrastructures were needed to fulfill some basic needs, such as sanitation, water supply, schooling, and places of prayer.

At this point in time, it was neither the sultans of Istanbul, nor their representatives in Egypt, nor even the emirs and Mamluks who provided this infrastructure, but merchants, notably Ahmad al-Ruwi'i and Isma'il Abu Taqiyya, and scholars like al-Qadi Ahmad al-Nubi.[30] The most extensive works were those of Ahmad al-Ruwi'i, who built a mosque, elementary school, public fountain, and public bath, in addition to a number of artisanal workshops in the quarter that still bears his name. His buildings were important enough to become the core of a new quarter in this northwestern part of the city. Of lesser scope was the mosque that Abu Taqiyya built, or, more correctly *re*built: It was an old building fallen into ruins, belonging to the *waqf* of one his wife's relatives, a certain *khawaja* Salih al-Ahaymar.[31] And in the same vicinity, Qadi Ahmad al-Nubi built a little mosque, Jami' al-Nubi.

The changing relations between the state and society had allowed new groups to make their contributions to the geography of the city. The disappearance of the Mamluk sultans was followed by a period of urban development sponsored by the Ottoman pashas. Subsequently, the indigenous inhabitants of Cairo made important contributions to the development of an urban infrastructure in the city. The buildings that merchants and scholars constructed—for the most part, small structures in a modest garb—did not claim to rival either the architectural jewels the Mamluk sultans had left or the structures associated with the Ottoman state. Although their buildings, did not possess the grandeur of royal Mamluk construction, their social significance—as the urban contribution of a rising group of prosperous merchants and as material evidence of an important social phenomenon—is undeniable. For Abu Taqiyya himself, and for other merchants who were part of the same trend, the changing relations between state and society had meant a greater financial burden for merchants in developing a commercial infrastructure. But they had also been given a chance to develop greater visibility and, consequently, greater prestige and social power, which enabled them to consolidate the wealth that they had accumulated through their commercial activity.

It is easy to picture Abu Taqiyya, at the peak of his career as *shahbandar*, having built up for himself a reputation among the inhabitants of the city, not only professionally, as a great merchant, but generally speaking, as a person of note—generous to the poor, as the provisions he made for the patients of the Qalawun Hospital show, and with a high degree of social power. And as he passed through the main street of Cairo every day, to and from work, from his house in Darb al-Shabrawi to the other house in Darb al-Tahun, or when he and his family members took the Marjush road to ride to the house on the banks of the Birka al-Azbakiyya, the people who saw him identified him by his bearing, by his clothing, and by his retinue of servants and followers who accompanied him. Very likely, his passage along the street was, on a small scale, an event reminiscent of the larger and more important ceremonials that accompanied the passage of important officials like the pasha or the Qadi al-Qudat. The people in the street must have made the connection between him and the great buildings he had erected near the city center. These had rapidly become landmarks that people in the city identified with Abu Taqiyya. The house where the *shahbandar* lived, moreover, must also have become a landmark of sorts, reflecting his status because it was more luxurious and larger than the houses around it.

7

Family Life in the Abu Taqiyya Household

Isma'il Abu Taqiyya found his way home in the late afternoon after a long day filled with negotiations, meetings, and arrangements with clients. Taking the main thoroughfare with its heavy human traffic and the many beasts of burden led by shouting muleteers, he could barely lift his eyes as he was passing in front of Qalawun's mausoleum, the large dome that indicated he was approaching home. A few more minutes, then he turned left near Aqmar mosque to the quiet street of Darb al-Shabrawi. As he entered the courtyard of his house, it was not silent, but it had a different kind of sound from the street, softer because there were children's voices. The color was brighter than the beige stone facades he had ridden along, for inside, trees and plants now met his eyes, and instead of the film of dust in the street there was a well-watered courtyard. There were numerous domestics and slaves, looking after beasts in the stable, working the well to provide everyone in the house with water every day, watering the garden, or burning the fuel to heat water for the bath. The green of the garden provided a fresh breath of air. He dismounted his horse, the men in charge of the stable led the beast away, and Abu Taqiyya walked into the house.

Moving from the outside—the market and his numerous meetings with clients or partners, the courthouse and its noisy plaintiffs—into the inside of his home meant entering the world of family, children, intimacy, and privacy. His years as *shahbandar* had turned him into a public figure of sorts, and this was reflected in his appearance, his clothing, and his home. He not only enlarged his house but also adorned it with luxurious objects. The list of household objects in the inheritance deeds drawn up after his death includes silver chandeliers, numerous copper objects, and Iznik bowls and plates.

More significant than these material comforts were the modifications to his family structure that resulted from his own rise to prominence. In observing how family life in the house of one wealthy merchant was organized at one moment in history—and at one particular stage, notably when Abu Taqiyya had reached maturity of years and had attained the social prestige that came with his success in the market—we can study the roles played by the family members as well as their relationships to him, to each other, and to the outside world. Despite the widely held view to the contrary, the family was not isolated from the outside world: The social and economic conditions that affected Abu Taqiyya's career left a mark, not only on the material conditions of his family, but also on family structure and interpersonal relationships.

The study of family life, moreover, shows how within the patriarchal structure that was dominant in this society, individual family members who were endowed with special abilities could make their voices heard and direct a course of action involving other family members. The structure, while solid and respected by those concerned, did not necessarily crush individuality or stifle initiative. More specifically, we see some of the women of the house—notably, among Abu Taqiyya's wives and daughters —emerge in multiple roles and in positions of strength in relation to other members of the household, largely because of their own personalities. Their wishes were taken into serious consideration by family members who were more highly ranked in the family hierarchy. In spite of the practice of polygamy, they compare, on the whole, quite favorably to women in France and England of the late sixteenth and early seventeenth centuries. Although more European women may have had access to education, they had less access to property, even when it was their own, and much less ease in terminating their marriages if they so wished. Moreover, for a variety of reasons, witch-hunts in France, England, and Germany intensified during that period. Most of the victims were, of course, women who, for one reason or another, were marginalized and persecuted in their societies.[1]

In the last decade of his life, when Abu Taqiyya was at the peak of his career, his family and household were also being restructured. It was larger and more numerous, but, more significantly, it was also more hierarchical in form, presumably as a result of wealth and numbers. In a sense, in any patriarchal family structure, the dominant form in the Middle East and many other cultures, the father had a more elevated position than his wife and had authority over his children as well. That would have been the case with the Abu Taqiyyas as with other families all along. But what is interesting to observe in this particular case is how the patriarchal structure took a particular form when associated with greater wealth and status; how this structure helped Isma'il Abu Taqiyya shape his relationships with his own brother and sisters, his wives and concubines, and his children; and how they reacted to his rising status. To a certain extent, Abu Taqiyya helped to define the shape that this structure took, in a way that would not only consolidate his position within the family but also enhance his public image, as head of an important family.

An analysis of the functions and the limits of family structure can be helpful in understanding the complex relationships within it. Most studies on family have concentrated their interest on the formal structures, and their conclusions, based on the study of these structures, have emphasized the fact that in the upper echelons of society, family life was much more prescribed than in lower ones, and that the rules regulating behavior were very rigid, especially with regard to women. And yet a perusal of the numerous court cases in which the family was implicated show that this is only one part of the picture, not the whole picture. The nature of the sources used here reveals a level of reality beyond what is the strictly formal aspect of family structure. They allow us an occasional, but very valuable, glimpse of the levels of personal and sometimes intimate relationships within the family. Such glimpses allow us to see the individual— his feelings and reactions to certain conditions or situations. More important, they show us how much (or how little) an individual could move within the hierarchical structure of which he was a part—that is, how supple or rigid it could be. In other words, within a hierarchically structured family, there was some leeway for individual family members, including Isma'il himself, to find channels through which to express their whims or desires, or take a personal initiative. We therefore catch glimpses of the family structure as it was lived by those who formed part of it.

The family structure thus appears as a malleable form, shaped and defined, in varying degrees, by the social and economic forces acting on it from outside. The general condition of elite merchants during this period and their rise to prominence in urban society left a mark on their family structures. Their new place in the social hierarchy of Cairo was paralleled by a new kind of hierarchy inside the family. Nevertheless, family life was also shaped by the members who formed part of it—in this case, by Abu Taqiyya himself, the most prominent family member, but also by other family members who at different times and under different circumstances found a chance to push matters in one direction or another.

Family, as studied from this perspective, emerges as a form that is dynamic and changing. Important as blood ties were, the way a family was structured could be influenced by a number of circumstances around it. It could be modified by various social and economic conditions that could change with time. Moreover, the people who formed part of the family could also be instrumental in shaping it.

Extended Family

Isma'il's relationship to his brother and sisters had had its ups and downs but, as time passed, it came more and more to center on him. There had been friction when they were young people. Isma'il and Yasin had once taken a dispute between them to court; and Budur, Sayidat al-Kull, and Laila had once even gone so far as to accuse Isma'il in court of having cheated them out of their father's inheritance—a particularly disagreeable event, which could have been solved within the family circle in order to avoid making their dispute public. It is impossible for us to know exactly what was behind these accusations, because Isma'il was able to produce the documents proving his innocence. But it would be highly unlikely for the sisters to accuse Isma'il in court without solid evidence. A certain amount of jealousy may have poisoned their relationship as young people, because the sisters could already see that Isma'il's fortunes were surpassing both their own and their father's.

Isma'il's accumulation of wealth in the years that followed these unpleasant incidents did not disrupt family ties between him and his siblings, but restructured them along more hierarchical grounds. By the time that Isma'il reached the peak of his career, the sisters and brother were probably obliged to acknowledge a status that the rest of society had already recognized. The relationship underwent change, and the new links between them were expressed in different ways. Isma'il wished to have a close relationship with Yasin but did not want to involve him in his financial matters. One of the expressions of this relationship between the two brothers was in the desire for physical proximity, though without sharing the same house or living together. They lived near each other by choice. Isma'il's house was located in Darb al-Shabrawi. When, in 1017/1608, Yasin decided to build a house, he chose a location in Khatt al-Khurushtuf that gave the house one facade on Darb al-Shabrawi. The houses were thus very close without being adjacent. That Laila was living in her residence in Khatt al-Khurushtuf may or may not have been because she wished to continue living in close proximity to her brothers. But one way or another, the three lived only a stone's throw from each other.

There were other manifestations of the changing relationship between the two brothers. Isma'il, as the elder brother, and the wealthier of the two, made provisions in his *waqf* for part of the revenues to go to Yasin and his children. Because the founder of a *waqf* was free to choose the beneficiaries, the inclusion of Yasin and his children in the *waqf* was an expression both of a family attachment that he chose to manifest and of his own role as head of the family and giver of gifts to those around him. In his major *waqf*s—that is, the two *wikala*s and the sugar refinery— Isma'il made provisions for the income to be divided between him and Yasin. The income of the refinery was equally divided between the two of them; that of the first *wikala* between his children and Yasin's children; and the second *wikala*, between his children, Yasin, and Ahmad b. 'Ariqat, Laila's son (and his son-in-law). As the giver of these benefits, Isma'il was also emphasizing his own position within the extended family structure, for he certainly must have known that the one who gave was the one who controlled.

Marriage and Concubinage Alliances

The kind of marriage alliance he had made as a young man was quite different from that of his later years. Two facts guided the change, his rise in status and his tighter integration into Cairene society. He had started by choosing spouses from within a small circle, notably, from among family members and members of the Syrian community, often *humsi*s. His later alliances followed a more open pattern. The archival sources provide us with rich data on these marriage patterns, which we can trace over a fairly long period. Between the 1580s and the 1590s, the Abu Taqiyyas' circle of friends and relatives was dominated largely by Syrian merchant families from Hums. Their business contacts seem to have followed a similar pattern during those early decades, but this pattern was more marked at home. Therefore, as the young Abu Taqiyyas had approached marriage age, the choice of marriage partners had naturally gone towards the families they were in close touch with. For a few years, both Isma'il and his sisters Laila, Budur, and Sayidat al-Kull were married within a small and restricted group, the close family—their cousins, children of their uncle ʿAbdul-Raziq—and other merchant families who, like them, were newly settled in Cairo. Of these, the closest to the Abu Taqiyyas were the Ibn ʿAriqats, later known simply as the ʿAriqats, a family of prominent merchants from Hums. The ʿAriqat family had many branches, but at least one branch had arrived in Cairo at roughly the same time as the Abu Taqiyyas.

It is clear that Ismaʿil adopted this pattern in his marriages to Badra b. ʿAbdul Rahman Ibn ʿAriqat and to Rumia b. ʿAbdul-Raziq Abu Taqiyya. His marriage to Badra, a young woman whose husband had recently died, took place some time between 1586 and 1592.[2] She suffered other losses during this period: the death of her father on the route to Hijaz (Darb al-Hijaz) around 1586, shortly after they had settled in Cairo; and in 1591, the death of her only brother, Muhammad.[3] The closeness of the two families from Hums was certainly an important factor in his decision to marry her. In addition, she obviously had comfortable means, the *muʾakhar* (deferred bridal-money payment) alone amounting to 800 *dinars*, not to mention her successive inheritances. It may have been during the same period that Ismaʿil married Rumia b. ʿAbdul-Raziq Abu Taqiyya, his first cousin. The families of the two brothers, Ahmad and ʿAbdul-Raziq, were close to each other, and this was an alliance that satisfied both his father and his uncle.

At this period in his life, the marriage patterns Ismaʿil followed were very similar to those of his sisters. All three sisters—Laila, Budur, and Sayidat al-Kull—married within the community of Humsi merchants. As a matter of fact, Laila remained within the Abu Taqiyya and Ibn ʿAriqat families in all of her three marriages: Her first husband, father of her son Ahmad, was *khawaja* Abu Bakr ʿAriqat; her second husband was her cousin Ahmad Abu Taqiyya (who died in 1025/1616); and her third, married fairly late in life, was *khawaja* ʿAbdul-Nabi b. Zayn al-Din ʿAriqat.[4] It is only at a later stage that divergences between brother and sisters became obvious. Ismaʿil's circle of acquaintances expanded with time, and the patterns he followed in his later marriages reflected his growing number of friends and associates and the wider contacts he made as the years went by. This tendency towards marriage from outside the closed circle of Humsi merchant families became even more pronounced with his own children, who married into the circle of scholars and even of emirs. The choice of partners was thus not only a channel for social mobility but also one of the channels through which this family of Syrian origin became more integrated into Cairene society. Later, when the Abu Taqiyyas became part of the upper layers of Cairene society, we find that they undertook fewer marriage alliances within the Syrian community in Cairo. The men of the family, generally speaking, tended to break this pattern earlier than the women.

In Isma'il's marriages to both Badra and Rumia, there had been a sense of family duty on his part, and a desire to fulfill a social obligation that his circle expected of him. This sense of family duty seems to have been less developed in Yasin, the only one among the brothers and sisters who did not follow this pattern. By the time that Isma'il decided to marry 'Atiyat al-Rahman b. *khawaja* Abu Bakr al-Ahaymar, a family of Egyptian merchants, he was probably well established financially and socially: One successful venture after another had gained him a reputation as one of the most astute merchants in Cairo. This time there was no particular sense of duty involved in his choice. He probably had known her family—that is, her father or her grandfather—either from the market or from their place of residence. The acquaintance could have been formed in Suq al-Warraqin. Isma'il had a shop there, as did 'Atiyat al-Rahman's maternal grandfather and perhaps her father as well. This same grandfather was also owner of the house where Isma'il was to live for many years, a house he had founded in *waqf*. He may also have known about her qualities that were to become so evident later, her intellectual abilities and her personality. 'Atiyat al-Rahman, who was to outlive Isma'il by many years, was also the only one of his wives to bear him a son who survived, thus gaining a special position in the family.

His fourth and last marriage was different from all three of the others, following a pattern closely associated with the military elite, that of marrying enfranchised slaves of Eastern European origin. It was shortly after 1017/1608 that Isma'il married his fourth and last wife, Hana', at a time when he had passed his fortieth year. She was a Georgian. Hana' had been the wife and freedwoman *(ma'tuqa)* of his colleague *khawaja* Abul Nasr al-Tarabulsi, with whom he frequently did business. After Abul Nasr's death in 1017/1608, Isma'il continued having partnerships with his young son Muhammad. But why, at this point in his life, did he wish to marry another wife, when he already had three other wives and numerous concubines in the house and was already the father of several children? The reason, we can gather, is that Hana' must have been beautiful, and he was probably very taken with her. The only daughter she had, Stita, seems to have been equally beautiful, for she had marriage offers while her elder sisters were still unmarried.

Aside from whatever personal attractions Hana' may have had, there must have also been social reasons for Isma'il to marry a fourth wife. Even though polygamy was commonly practiced, the majority of polygamous marriages included two or sometimes three wives. Among Abu Taqiyya's merchant colleagues there were diverse marriage patterns. *Khawaja* Muhammad Ibn Yaghmur, for example, seems to have been monogamous; the wife he married in the 1590's, Fatma b. Zakariyya, was the only spouse to receive an inheritance from him in 1024/1615. Interestingly enough, this had been one of the conditions mentioned in their marriage contract.[5] When 'Abdul-Qawi al-'Asi died, on the other hand, his immediate heirs were his one son 'Abdul Ra'uf and his grandmother, but no wives.[6] Others, like 'Abdul-Qadir al-Damiri, had three wives. Marriage to four wives was a rare occurrence among the inhabitants of Cairo, except for the very wealthy. The archives, moreover, show that Abu Taqiyya had made full use of his prerogative to own a number of concubines: another sign of wealth and status, invariably present in the large households of emirs. During a time of social mobility, which the society of Cairo was experiencing in those years, to acquire some of the appearances of the ruling elite had its social significance.

The choice and the number of marriage partners show that he had ordered his private life in accordance with his public life and his growing stature as an elite merchant. He could afford having a very extended household—with all it entailed in terms of space, services, and expenses —and there was a certain prestige in being at its head. It enhanced his social position to have a large house full of servants and slaves that people could point out to as they passed his street.

Hierarchies in the Household

Life inside the house was organized along hierarchical principles and divisions of space. This feature of inner organization is typical of wealthy households, which had plenty of room. The larger and the wealthier a household, the more the hierarchical organization was evident, both in the way that guests were received and in the way that the different members of the family occupied certain spaces.

Spatial organization of the private section of the house was such that on coming home from work, Isma'il would, depending on circumstance (for example, whether he was alone or with guests), spend his time in the more formal or the less formal section of the house. He might bring with him a colleague or acquaintance as he came back home, or they might join him later and spend the evening with him. For the less formal visits, small halls around the courtyard could accommodate his guests. As his mercantile ventures increased and he became a more prominent member of the merchant community, he had more visits from people in the higher social strata, including the emirs and Mamluks with whom he had entered into business relations, as well as his own colleagues whom he met with in his daily dealings in the market. When he received formal visits, he directed himself to the hall *(qaʿa)* on the ground floor, a large room with marble decoration and a high ceiling that made the air cooler and also provided an atmosphere of grandeur. This room was likely to be close to the entrance of the house so as to be at a distance from the family area. If he wished to stay out in the open air—on a summer evening, for instance —he could climb up the staircase to the loggia *(maqʿad)* overlooking the courtyard and watch what was going on below, who was coming in and going out of the house. For guests spending the night, a common occurrence in those days, there was a sleeping area *(khazna nawmiyya)* attached to the hall, where mattresses were spread out.

For the less formal visits there were smaller halls. Friends and colleagues like the Damiris and members of the Syrian community in Cairo came to visit Isma'il. It may have been that Syrians in general and Humsis in particular were frequent visitors to the Abu Taqiyya house—perhaps they were distant relatives, or had had some family connection with the Abu Taqiyyas back in Hums, or simply considered Isma'il their informal spokesman, given his position of leadership in society.

When his guests were gone, Isma'il might go to the living quarters upstairs, using one of the two or three staircases leading to the upper floors. Upstairs, in the family area, there was also a hierarchical organization of space. The inner space of the upper floors was divided into *maskan*s (lodgings), of unequal size and comfort, reflecting the social hierarchy in the house. A lodging could be a single modest room, or it could be a large apartment of two or three rooms, service spaces, and a toilet.

The household—with Abu Taqiyya's four wives and numerous concubines, employees, *tabi*'s, servants, and slaves—had a spatial organization that mirrored the different social status and social power of those living in it, rather than a spatial division by sex, with all men on one side and all women on the other. Moreover, this spatial organization provided Abu Taqiyya with access to its various parts more or less when he wished. Nevertheless, it also provided those persons who used these parts of the house with a measure of control over their own spaces and their own privacy.

Hierarchies in the house affected wives, concubines, and children. A wife's status could depend on her personal wealth or the fact that she had mothered children, boys in particular. 'Atiyat al-Rahman, for instance, was mother of Abu Taqiyya's only surviving son, Zakariyya, and four daughters, Jami'a, Umm al-Hana, Zayn al-Tujjar, and Tahira. She was, moreover, from a wealthy merchant family herself. There were differences in status between a barren wife, like Badra or Rumia, and a mother, and between a wife and a concubine.

Concubines were differentiated by two criteria. First, if they fathered his children, they were referred to as *mustawlida*. A *mustawlida* had a number of advantages. According to Islamic law, she was granted a certain degree of protection, because she could no longer be sold. Moreover, the children of a *mustawlida* were considered by law to be free-born, following their father's status, not slaves; consequently, they shared their father's inheritance like any of the children borne by a wife. A *mustawlida* did not herself inherit any part of her master's fortune. At his death, a *mustawlida* became free, rather than being considered as part of the inheritance, which was the case with other categories of slaves.[7] Provisions were very frequently made for them in *waqfs*, both in terms of revenues they would receive at their master's death and in terms of their continued residence in the family house, so that a minimum was assured for them. Although no such provision has been traced with regard to Abu Taqiyya's *waqf,* the absence of such does not necessarily mean that he did not provide for them. Informal arrangements may have existed. If there were no provisions for them, these women would certainly have been left in a precarious position after their master's death. Either their children, who had a share in their father's inheritance, would support them, or they married. In the case of one of Isma'il's *mustawlidas*, Sayma al-Bayda, she finally ended up with a small share, which reached her indirectly, when, shortly after his own death, one and then a second of her infant daughters died. Their share of their inheritance was divided between their siblings and her. In addition to legal protection, the social prestige of a *mustawlida* was enhanced by the very fact of mothering her master's children. It was, in other words, a privileged position in the household, and certainly one that distinguished the *mustawlida* from the other concubines.

A second criteria that gave concubines status was related to their origin (*bayda,* meaning white, used for East Europeans, such as Bosnians, Georgians, or Russians; *habashiyya* for Ethiopians, and *sawda,* black, for Africans). In the market for slaves, price differences existed between black, Ethiopian, and white slaves, a fact that was certainly reflected in their status and ranking within the household.

Thus a whole set of criteria determined the place of wives and concubines in hierarchies of power or privilege within the household. Behind these formal structures, we can sometimes perceive the more intimate realities of Isma'il's relationships. In his later years, life had brought him a number of painful circumstances—disappointments and personal losses. One of these was the death of Hana' bint 'Abdalla al-Bayda, the last of the four wives. It was perhaps with his concubine Sayma al-Bayda that he found some consolation for his loss, for in those last years, he spent more and more time with her. She bore him his last two children, one shortly before his death, Salha, and shortly after giving birth, she became pregnant again, delivering her second daughter, Fatma, only after Isma'il had died in 1624.

These hierarchies were reflected in the way that the house was used. 'Atiyat al-Rahman, for instance, would surely have lived in one of the larger and more comfortable lodgings. Not only was she from a notable family of merchants, and had her own private fortune, which helped to boost her prestige, but she also had five children, so she actually needed more space than the other wives. Having the best, or one of the best, lodgings in the house, in itself gave her a special position in the house in relation to the others living there. And yet, at another level, it was obvious to 'Atiyat al-Rahman as the years went by that her husband's emotions were centered elsewhere—that it was in the daytime that she saw him, when he was around the children. He was spending his nights with others. Except for Tahira, her last born, others were bearing his children.

We would guess that Badra's apartment would be smaller since she had no children. The same sort of hierarchy would presumably have been applied to concubines as was to *mustawlida*s. There were probably many possibilities and arrangements. In the house of Isma'il's colleague, *khawaja* Nur al-Din al-Shuja'i, for instance, three of his deceased son's *mustawlida*s shared a lodging in the family house in Khatt al-Saba' Qa'at, according to the *waqf* deed.[8] There might have been a similar arrangement in Isma'il's house. Or perhaps, because he was enlarging it, each one of these *mustawlidas* would have a lodging of her own.

Servants and slaves were lodged, in the other parts of the house, at some distance from the family. In all likelihood, some kind of hierarchy was respected by the various groups, although we know much less about the way servants and slaves lived or about the spaces that they occupied than we do about wives. Some houses contained a quarter or a large room for women slaves (that is, the unprivileged ones to whom their owner devoted no particular attention).

The concept of private and public spheres, a matter of great significance to the family, has been applied by scholars to the Islamic family in different ways. For some, *private* means the house and the family members it encloses; *public* means the world outside. Others associate *private* with women and *public* with men. The division between the two has often been understood to be strict and rigid, with little or no transgressing between the one and the other. In reality, these models of private and public spheres are usually not based on observation of a particular society or class but on generalizations that englobe all Islamic societies regardless of time, place, or class.

The analysis of the Abu Taqiyya family challenges this view both with regard to the division between men and women and with regard to the rigid divisions between the private and public spheres. For instance, at the level of the house itself, there was no evidence that women were confined or secluded in specific areas of the house. Neither Isma'il's house nor Yasin's (nor, as a matter of fact, the residences of other contemporary merchants that are described in deeds), contained a *harim*, or fixed space intended for the women of the house. The concepts of privacy, in terms of space, and the divisions between private and public spaces were more fluid than we have been led to think. This fluidity can be illustrated by the hierarchies of space, from the more private (the living unit) to the less private (the public parts of the house like the courtyard or bath) to the semi-public (the closed street where they lived) to the public (the main street). Similarly, several degrees of privacy can be discerned in relation to people who had access to the house, or even to the family section of the house. In other words, the move from the private sphere to the public one was not an abrupt one, and the barriers between the two were not rigid. In between the black and the white were several shades of grey.

Movement between the public and the private depended upon different criteria and conditions. Adjustments could be made, when necessary, to accommodate a particular situation without impinging on anyone's privacy.

The fact that wives spent much of their time within their own lodging does not necessarily mean that they lived in confinement and seclusion; in fact, they had a large measure of control within their living spaces. Someone of 'Atiyat al-Rahman or Badra 'Ariqat's standing had her own slaves to take care of her personal needs, independently of those of her husband's. In fact, Laila, Isma'il's sister, had obtained a formal undertaking from her husband to buy her a slave, and to replace her if she died. Wives of their rank also had *tabi*'s (that is, clients or followers), to do things for them, in return for some compensation or favor. Thus a wife of their social standing had her own structures that were parallel to, but distinct from, those of her husband's.

It was in their lodgings that these women received their visitors, mostly immediate family and relatives. 'Atiyat al-Rahman kept close contact with her mother and nephews. Badra had a large tribe of 'Ariqats, some of whom were now allied to the Abu Taqiyyas by marriage. Rumia's father remained close to her. These and other close or more distant family members had access to the lodgings on the upper floor. We know that extended family visits often took place, and close relatives often spent the night. Because houses did not have bedrooms, all that was needed to accommodate overnight guests were mattresses, which were spread in a corner of the room. Each of these lodgings therefore constituted a private space in which a wife received her own close circle of people who had access to it, including her family and relatives.

Wives who were property owners managed most of their business from their lodging, receiving when necessary the people who helped run their affairs. Badra and 'Atiyat al-Rahman, in particular, who were *waqf* supervisors for various family foundations, could partly manage their business through intermediaries. *Waqf* records had to be kept, with revenues and expenditures carefully recorded. If repairs were needed, some action had to be taken. If a tenant left, another had to be found. The person in charge of these routine matters had to keep the *waqf* supervisor informed of what was going on. If he had to enter a wife's private space, he may have done so under certain conditions—as, for instance, her wearing the veil inside her own house, which she normally would not have done.[9]

At times, however, they had to attend to matters personally. 'Atiyat al-Rahman was shrewd enough to know that no matter how wealthy her husband was, with all the wives and children he had, her share would not amount to much, and it made sense to her to attend to her property as well as she could.[10] She had already proven her personal abilities, as a result of which she had quite early been made *nazira* (supervisor) of her father's *waqf* property. Although she had two brothers, 'Ali and Hijazi, who were also beneficiaries of this *waqf,* she was the one chosen as the most capable of the three. Sometimes she seems to have been overcareful with money, which may explain why she and her mother, accompanied by Isma'il, went to the court of Bab 'Ali, where Farah, her mother, declared having borrowed 150 *riyals* from 'Atiyat al-Rahman, a very businesslike way of dealing with a family member, especially as this was a relatively modest sum.[11] 'Atiyat al-Rahman, like Isma'il, knew, or perhaps had learned from him, the importance of legal guarantees and putting things in writing in the court registers. On outings such as these, to the courts crowded with claimants and plaintiffs, 'Atiyat al-Rahman, with her expensive clothing and striking presence, was served with a rapidity and efficiency that not everyone could get. The spaces within which 'Atiyat al-Rahman functioned could therefore expand or retract, according to the circumstances of the moment.

The trace of some of the relationships with members of the Syrian community can be detected. Even though on a number of levels the family's Syrian origin tended to be forgotten, on the private or intimate level the picture was different. Within the circle of people who had access to these apartments, the proportion of Syrian visitors—relatives, in-laws, and close family friends—was relatively high. We can observe this phenomenon quite clearly at the time of Isma'il Abu Taqiyya's death, when his numerous female heirs, three surviving wives and three adult daughters, each looked for an agent to represent her interest in court and to settle her share of her inheritance with the merchants who owed him goods or money, either in Cairo or in other commercial centers where he had been doing business. Each of these delegated a person who would represent their interests, someone that they knew and trusted. For the most part, they chose persons of Syrian origin, whether or not they were family members. Badra 'Ariqat, for instance, mandated her relative, 'Uthman 'Alay al-Din 'Ariqat, and he seemed to carry out her wishes satisfactorily. Likewise, Fardus Abu Taqiyya was represented by her husband, *khawaja* 'Abdul-Mu'ti 'Ariqat. Rumia Abu Taqiyya's business affairs were taken care of first by her father, then by Ahmad 'Ariqat. Finally, perhaps dissatisfied with the way that her interests were taken care of by Ahmad 'Ariqat, she mandated a Syrian called Ahmad Ibn Siddiq *al-Humsi,* who does not seem to have been related to her. Likewise, Jami'a mandated a Syrian merchant called *khawaja* Muhammad b. Ahmad *al-Humsi* al-'Attar to represent her interests. Thus the close links with Syrians were maintained in the home at a time when Abu Taqiyya's public life was becoming more and more integrated into the society of Cairo.

Because none of the lodgings was entirely independent, certain links, defined individually, between the different lodgings had to be kept. All of them, for instance, shared the basic conveniences of the house—the courtyard where the children played, the well that provided them with their daily needs in water, the stables where the beasts who transported them on their outings were kept. The house had a private *hammam* (bath), a great luxury; most houses did not have such a facility, and people usually went to the public *hammam*s, of which Cairo had several dozen. The *hammam* was made up of two or three rooms with progressively higher temperatures, and a little pool in the hottest room. That too had to be shared, and depending on the kind of relationship that existed between Badra and 'Atiyat al-Rahman or Rumia at any particular moment, they might either make arrangements for one of them to use the *hammam* on a particular day and ask the others to keep away, or decide to share it and enjoy its relaxing vapors, getting massaged while chatting. This is a good example of the fluidity of private space in the house. A space that everyone shared, like the bath, became private for a certain time when one of the women was using it; or, in other words, it became part of her own private space temporarily, until she was through and someone else used it.

Even though wives spent much of their time inside the house, neither it nor the boundaries of their lodging constituted a rigid barrier between them and the world outside. Their living space, in fact, could extend or retract, depending on circumstances, between the lodging or *maskan* and the areas of the house they had to share with everyone else. Occasionally, either visits to relatives or business done in court or elsewhere took them outside the house. Likewise, for people coming in to visit, interaction between the visitors of the different persons was very likely to be taking place. The word *confinement,* so often applied to wives in Middle Eastern societies, with its connotation of a condition resembling detention, is somewhat misleading when we look at the situation from close range. Although life revolved around the home, a number of openings linked the women to the world outside. Among these was the fact that her finances were independent from those of her husband. Here again, it is enlightening to compare the situation of women with property in Egypt with that of their counterparts in Europe. In Stuart England, for instance, a wife lost her property rights upon marriage. Her husband alone could administer it, making her totally dependent on him. Marriage made her in the eyes of the law the equivalent of a minor.[12] Things were not much better in prerevolutionary France, where marriage usually gave the husband total power over his wife's assets.[13] In fact, the financial standing of a wife was a significant factor in the power relations within the household, and one that people like 'Atiyat al-Rahman were particularly capable of handling well.

The Abu Taqiyya Children

For Abu Taqiyya, to have many children was to fill the house and bring life to it. Like many others, he believed that "he who has children does not die" *(man khallaf ma mat)* because they would carry his name and keep his memory alive. And when one grew old, they would be there to support one *(ginah al-shakhs wuladuh:* "children were a person's shield"). A high infant mortality rate would certainly have prompted him to have as many children as possible. Like many parents in premodern societies, he had probably lost some children in the course of his long years of marriage. This kind of information is not recorded, but we can guess that for someone who was in the married state for thirty-two years (first mention of a wife dating from 1592), and who had four wives and many concubines, only a high child mortality can explain the fact that he was survived by only two married daughters, Fardus and Jami'a, and one unmarried adult daughter, Umm al-Hana. His seven other children were minors. The high mortality rate is illustrated by the deaths, not long after his own death, of the baby girl born to his concubine Sayma al-Bayda, and the baby's infant sister, one shortly after the other. The epidemic of 1028/1618 is said to have taken the lives of 635,000 persons (in the words of al-Bakri) most between fifteen and twenty-five years of age.[14] It is quite possible that there may have been losses in Isma'il's family as the result of this epidemic. One generation later, of all of Isma'il's offspring, only three, Fardus's son and Zakariyya's daughter, bore children who reached maturity; many died in infancy, childhood, or youth. If Zakariyya had ever had boys, they did not survive to maturity. And in the meantime, the son that Yasin had borne, 'Umar, had also died as a young man, shortly before his father.

As in most other families, the children in the Abu Taqiyya household would have been brought up to show the greatest respect to their parents, who would have instilled in them obedience. Edward Lane, in his *Manners and Customs,* says that one of the most heinous crimes a person could commit was disrespect to his or her parents, and that consequently it was very rare to hear of an undutiful child.[15] The relationship between Abu Taqiyya and his children might well have fit into the pattern that Lane describes. Moreover, for someone like Abu Taqiyya, who must have had an overpowering personality, there must have been little doubt among the other members of the household, and certainly among his own offspring, about the degree of respect or obedience owed to him, whether they were girls or boys, minors or adults, or whether they were married or unmarried.

Yet the children were far from being an undifferentiated lot. Even among children, a hierarchical structure of sorts existed, based not only on age and sex but also on personal qualities. Obedience and respect are sometimes equated with total submission and self-effacement, but that was not necessarily the case. In spite of the sometimes dry nature of archival documents, certain personalities emerge rather energetically, while others remain in the shadows. Isma'il's children are no exception; some being vocal and articulate, while others were either quiet or unassuming. In one or two instances, we find them to be particularly forceful in the way they express themselves.

The destinies of Abu Taqiyya's children were shaped by a number of factors, biological and social, beyond their control. Big age differences existed between his children; the last one of them, a girl, was born posthumously, at the time that two of his daughters, Fardus and Jami'a were married. Another important difference was between the male and female offspring. Except for the long-awaited Zakariyya, all of Isma'il's other children were females. No wonder, then, that so much hope was put on the boy, who was eventually going to take up the family business, and he was probably treated accordingly. Of the large fortune Isma'il eventually left, Zakariyya would get the largest single share, because he inherited double the girls' share. But evidently his father thought that even with that, he needed to make special provision for him. Isma'il Abu Taqiyya endowed a large number of urban properties, among which was a sesame press *(sirja)* in Maqs, a mill *(tahun)* in al-Jamaliyya, and a public bath *(hammam)* in Suq al-Ghanam.[16] All of the income was earmarked for the sole benefit of Zakariyya and to the exclusion of his sisters, thus guaranteeing him a handsome income that he would not have to share with the other family members.

The family would have also certainly differentiated between children of a wife and those of a concubine. At least five of his children were mothered by concubines: Fardus and Fadila by Hajir al-Bayda; Fatma and Salha by Sayma al-Bayda; Amna by Razia al-Bayda. The spatial hierarchy of the house emphasized these differences, for the children would lodge with their mother in more or less favored parts of the house. It is easy to imagine that 'Atiyat al-Rahman, who came from a merchant family, and her children would look upon the concubines and their children with some disdain. The pejorative terms *ibn al-jaria* (son of a concubine) and *bint al-jaria* (daughter of a concubine) have remained with us till today. Very likely, 'Atiyat al-Rahman would instill in her own children a sense of their own prestige as offspring of a wife. Nevertheless, children of concubines mingled with the other children in the playground of the house, the courtyard. They were, moreover, fully entitled to receive their shares of their inheritance, because they were themselves freeborn.

Other Household Members

The household of a wealthy merchant did not consist only of his wives, concubines, and children. Many other people either lived in it or had daily contact with it. Isma'il, for instance, employed a Coptic secretary *(mubashir),* called Ghubrial, to keep the daily accounts of his business, and perhaps of his home as well. Copts were known for their training in keeping accounts and were often employed in private households among emirs. Moreover, there were several *tabi'* connected with the house, some of whom probably also lived there, some of whom were Syrian, others were enfranchised slaves, who might be doing a multitude of little jobs in the house. The word *tabi',* sometimes translated as "client" or "follower," does not have a satisfactory equivalent in English. It indicated a connection to a notable person that implied a certain degree of servitude. However, rather than receiving wages, a *tabiʿ* was repaid with protection and with the prestige attached to the master.

The house also had a multitude of slaves bought in the slave market and servants who worked on a wage basis, who were responsible for the usual household chores of cleaning, cooking, and washing, as well as taking care of the stables and beasts, providing water from the well for house use—for the bath when needed—and running errands for the various family members. How many of them the household used is impossible to tell. The only indication of numbers that we have is when Ismaʿil fell very seriously ill in 1621 and, wanting to do a good deed before he died, had nine of his slaves enfranchised: three Abyssinians, one from Takrur, and five others simply referred to as *aswad* or black. This by no means meant that they left the house but was simply a change in their legal status.[17] There may, of course, have been many more.

Ismaʿil Abu Taqiyya's house therefore lodged many people. As his status and prestige grew, the house at Darb al-Shabrawi underwent major enlargement. Rather than move into another house, big enough to accommodate his growing needs for space, he acquired the property next door in 1011/1602 and, by opening the wall between the two buildings, integrated it into his own house. He thus gained an extra courtyard, two *qaʿa*s or halls, a *maqʿad* (open loggia or portico), a stable, a bath, a well, and two storerooms.[18] By the time that the interior was finished, Abu Taqiyya's residence had become almost as large and luxurious as a palace, with the conveniences usually found in the residences of the ruling class: a bath, a well, a stable, a mill; many large, decorated halls with marble fountains whose flowing water helped cool the room; and plenty of space to lodge his family and followers and to receive his guests. One document that was issued after Abu Taqiyya's death lists some of the household items and shows how these were divided among the heirs: three wives, three adult daughters, and the minors whose share was handed to their guardian. Ismaʿil Abu Taqiyya's little library went to the minors, as did his silver candleholder and two swords. They also inherited some Iznik plates and some pieces of copperware. Each of the women received some of the Iznik plates; and various copper items, such as plates *(sahns)*, large platters *(sufras)*, and candleholders were divided among the other heirs. This kind of amiable division saved them from having to sell these household items to divide the proceeds among them.[19]

Beyond the Formal Structures

Each family member was thus aware of his or her hierarchical standing, in his or her own group (siblings, wives, concubines, or offspring), and in the general household that Isma'il headed. Important as the biological differences among the Abu Taqiyya offspring were, and crucial as the hierarchical structure of the household was, the destinies of the various family members were not shaped by these factors only, but also by a complex set of changing socioeconomic conditions that affected the family, which we can best trace over a long period, and by the personal qualities of the individuals making up the family. Even though the family and household structure was very hierarchical, in certain areas it was fluid enough to allow for individual voices to be heard and personal initiatives to come to fruition in spite of the unequal structure; and even though structures and hierarchies were very important, relationships also existed beyond, or independently of, such structures.

The study of marriage patterns among the Abu Taqiyya children reveals the changing status of the family. Those who married earlier tended to derive less benefit from his status than those who married later (including the marriages that took place after he died). The first daughters who were married were Fardus and Jami'a, the former the daughter of a concubine and the latter the daughter of 'Atiqat al-Rahman. Both of them were married to members of the 'Ariqat family, a merchant family from Hums who had settled in Cairo, and an old family acquaintance of the Abu Taqiyyas. That both girls—one the daughter of a wife, and the other the daughter of a concubine—married men of similar standing tells us something about the status of the offspring of concubines. Moreover, both men were linked with Hums and both were merchants; that is, they were very much within a circle of people with close ties to Syria that were professionally connected to the merchant community.

A different pattern started to emerge towards the end of Abu Taqiyya's life, and continued thereafter. The case of his young daughter Fatma, who also had the name of Stita, is very interesting. Fatma/Stita was the daughter of his Georgian wife, Hana', who had previously been a concubine of one of his colleagues. Shortly before Abu Taqiyya's death, she got a marriage offer that was by far a better match than her sisters' spouses. The prospective groom, *mawlana qadi al-qudat* Ibrahim Afandi b. Dia' al-Din Ahmad, sent a marriage intermediary *(khatib)* to Abu Taqiyya with appropriate gifts, gold chains with rubies and emeralds, to ask for Fatma/Stita's hand in marriage.[20] The offer was accepted, but before the marriage could take place, Isma'il had died, and in the meantime Ibrahim Afandi was transferred to al-Diyar al-Rumiyya. The family had second thoughts about the match, for reasons we can only conjecture. They may have objected to the departure of Fatma/Stita, who was still a minor, to a distant land. More likely, however, they thought she could do even better, for very shortly after her father's death, in 1035/1625, Fatma/Stita was married to Muhammad, son of an emir in the Mutafarriqa corps, emir Ahmad b. *al-sayyid al-sharif* Ibrahim.[21] By means of this alliance, she penetrated a new circle, the ruling military class, the pattern in all three of her marriages.

The penetration into the upper strata through marriage alliances initiated by Fatma/Stita was followed by other female members of the family, both the daughters of Abu Taqiyya's wives and of his concubines. Umm al-Hana, daughter of 'Atiyat al-Rahman, married a secretary in the Imperial Treasury of Egypt *(al-khazina al-'amira)*, Qadi Shams al-Din Muhammad Ibn al-Muhalhal al-Jizi; and Amna, daughter of a concubine called Razia al-Bayda, married a *shaykh al-Islam* named Muhammad b. Taj al-Din al-Amini al-Hanafi. By the following generation, Zakariyya's daughter Karima married the holder of one of the most prominent positions in the religious hierarchy and in the society of Cairo, the head of the Sadat al-Wafa'iyya order, Abu Qasis 'Abdul-Wahab.[22]

Like Abu Taqiyya himself, his offspring too married at first within a restricted Syrian merchant circle, then eventually included spouses from outside this circle. Marriage alliances of his daughters and granddaughter included members of the highest social strata of Cairo. For the women of the family, change had come more slowly.

Isma'il Abu Taqiyya's reputation, which survived him by many decades, continued to have a bearing on the way his children conducted their private lives, some of them making good use of the benefits that could accrue to them through the weight Abu Taqiyya's name had, even within a marriage relationship. Of all Isma'il's children, the one who through the court documents appears to be the most forceful is neither the son, nor the eldest of the children, but one of his young daughters, Umm al-Hana, who when he died in 1624 was an adult but still unmarried. Endowed with the strong personality of her father, Umm al-Hana also had a heightened sense of her own worth and a sensitivity to the advantages she could get from the family name and the prestige attached to it. These qualities emerge in the form that her marriage contracts took —more specifically, from the kind of clauses or conditions included in the contract, which were intended to impose certain restrictions on her husband's behavior, both in her marriage to a Persian merchant in 1035/1625, and her marriage in 1041/1631 to a secretary in the Imperial Treasury.[23]

To a certain extent, the conditions of her marriage contracts were in keeping with accepted social and legal practice in Cairo during that time. Marriage contracts of the period show that it was quite common among traders' and artisans' families to include in the contract two or three clauses that regulated the question of polygamy, often limiting the husband's possibility of marriage to a single wife. Some contracts specified the kind of lodging the couple would have and sometimes also indicated the amount of allowance a bride should get. This flexibility in the marriage contract is another aspect in which the position of these urban women can be compared with their contemporaries in France and England. A study on women in England shows that until the end of the eighteenth century, divorce with the right to remarry could be obtained only by an Act of Parliament and was, in effect, granted only to husbands who proved their wives had been adulterous.[24]

The clauses in Umm al-Hana's marriage contracts were, however, much more restrictive for the husband than normal contracts, as her marriage contract with Qadi Shams al-Din Muhammad Ibn al-Muhalhal al-Jizi, secretary in the Imperial Treasury, in 1631, clearly shows. The prospective husband already had two wives—one living in Jiza and the other in Misr—and a *mustawlida*. Umm al-Hana agreed to marry a polygamous husband (because she herself had had two previous marrages), but he was not to take any more wives or any more concubines. Nor was he ever to lodge them either in the same house with her or in close proximity to her. Even within a polygamous marriage, there could therefore be certain restrictions placed by the wife. And even in a marriage to a high-ranking official in the government, the Abu Taqiyya bride could get extremely favorable conditions. She had, in addition to the habitual clauses that numerous marriage contracts contained, an unusual set of additional clauses that show her ability in manipulating the situation to her favor. Her contract, notably, included a clause that was Umm al-Hana's way of making legal what in fact was a moral injunction in Islam: for husbands to treat their wives equally, and not to favor one above the others. Because the law did not have any provisions for the punishment of a husband who violated this rule, she took matters into her own hands, by including a clause in the contract, which was binding and therefore grounds for divorce if violated. It stated that if he was in Cairo, he was not to spend more than two consecutive nights away from the house—that is, one night per wife—without a good excuse *('uthr shar'i)*, unless he obtained Umm al-Hana's approval as well as that of her mother and her brother.[25] Among the hundreds of cases of marriage contracts registered in the court books, it is very rare to find clauses that were so strict on the husband. We can explain it in this particular case, both by Umm al-Hana's forceful personality and by the social power that the Abu Taqiyyas continued to have.

The nature of the sources used here permits us to penetrate into the more personal aspects of family life and see how the fortune of the Abu Taqiyyas was sometimes shaped by special relationships that functioned independently of the family's hierarchical structure. A few hints emerge from the court records that allow us to see beyond the more formal structures into the more private aspects of Isma'il's life. In his later years, his yearning for a son to support him as he grew older and weaker and his awareness that Zakariyya was not able to give him this satisfaction led him to rely more and more on Ahmad Ibn 'Ariqat and to involve him closely in his affairs. Ahmad was his nephew, son of his sister Laila. He had also become Isma'il's son-in-law by his marriage to Jami'a. As Isma'il's energy decreased, he more and more often called upon Ahmad to do things for him and to share some of his responsibilities. Isma'il empowered him in court to act on his behalf, and he sometimes involved him in his business affairs. When he founded his *waqf* in 1619, he made Ahmad supervisor of this large foundation after his own death, to administer its revenues and expenditures and to see that they were handled according to his wishes. Ahmad was thus empowered to distribute the revenues among the other beneficiaries of the foundation (that is, Isma'il's offspring), a sign of the trust that Isma'il put in him. What Isma'il's failing health no longer allowed him to do in his later years, Ahmad 'Ariqat was to take over—both professional and family responsibilities. In return, Isma'il included him, with his own children, as a beneficiary of his *waqf* on the large *wikala*, a special privilege that he did not confer on his other son-in-law, Fardus's husband. Ahmad, in other words, had become for Isma'il the son that he did not have, and he relied on him in matters where his own son Zakari-yya, still too young, could not be of help.

Isma'il's relationship to his son-in-law went beyond strict family re-quirements and shows a special warmth that went beyond formal struc-tures. In his relationship to 'Abdul-Qadir al-Damiri, we can discern a similarly informal relationship between two friends, to which certain pat-terns of family behavior were applied between persons with no blood ties. This relationship was shaped entirely by their own initiative rather than by any family obligation, yet in many ways it was similar to a family rela-tionship—in its longevity, in the common material interest shared by the two friends, and in their desire for physical proximity. Damiri and Abu Taqiyya had started out as neighbors in the *suq* where they had their shops. They not only became inseparable business partners for some forty years but also came to own and endow property jointly. But common material interest was only one side of the relationship. At one time, Damiri was renting a house on the street where Isma'il lived, Darb al-Shabrawi, near Aqmar Mosque. No wonder, then, that at the time of Isma'il's death it was 'Abdul-Qadir al-Damiri who immediately came and offered his services to the bereaved family, an offer taken up by 'Atiyat al-Rahman and her daughter Jami'a and Umm al-Hana—for a while, at least. On one level, Damiri was thus included in the family circle and treated like a family member.

In spite of the importance of family hierarchies, individual expression could emerge from a wife or a daughter, occasionally with sufficient force to have an impact on the family. A singular group of court cases dating from 1035/1625 show an important aspect of family relationships coming to the fore. These are related to the inheritance of Isma'il Abu Taqiyya. At the time of his death in 1034/1624, only three of his ten children (an eleventh posthumous child was born later) were adults; the others were under the guardianship of Ahmad 'Ariqat, Isma'il's nephew and son-in-law. Ahmad 'Ariqat had been chosen as their legal guardian by Isma'il himself. During the month of Hujja 1031/1621, he fell seriously ill and thought the end had come. Lying in bed and unable to move, anguished at the thought of what might become of his very young children, he made his deathbed arrangements in the presence of a court official brought to his home for that purpose. He made his nephew and son-in-law Ahmad 'Ariqat the guardian of the minors, Zakariyya, Zayn al-Tujjar, Tahira,

Amna, Fadila, and Stita, in addition to the unborn child his concubine Sayma al-Bayda was bearing. Ahmad ʿAriqat was to buy and sell property for them, undertake transactions on their behalf, and buy their clothes for them, without extravagance. Upon their reaching their majority, he was to give them what was their share of the inheritance.[26]

When Ismaʿil did die three years later, the minors reacted forcefully against Ahmad ʿAriqat. Although it is difficult to pinpoint any particular misdemeanor on his part, there must have been some feeling that he was manipulating their finances to his advantage. If that was the case, then Ismaʿil's trust had not been well-placed, and he had misestimated Ahmad's loyalty. Whatever the reason, in mid-Jumada I 1035/1625, Zayn al-Tujjar was the first to send a *wakil* to the *qadi* to claim on her behalf that she was fifteen and wished to be declared a major so that she could take over the responsibility of her fortune. The *qadi* acceded to this request and soon it was followed by similarly successful undertakings by Zakariyya, Fadila, Fatma/Stita, and a little later, Amna, allowing them to become financially independent, despite the resistence that ʿAriqat tried to put up.[27] Time showed that their judgement of Ahmad had not been wrong, for a court case registered years later contains hints of his irregular management of the Abu Taqiyya–Damiri *waqf* that he supervised. ʿAtiyat al-Rahman, with her clear and astute mind, may have quickly understood what was going on and realized that the heirs were not getting their rightful shares. She may well have instigated the children to take matters in their own hands by presenting their case to court, even though three of these children (Fadila, Fatma/Stita, and Amna) were not hers. But, again, in a society which emphasized the role of the family as mediator of family quarrels, this was no small matter. And its consequences for the future of the family were also very important, if we concede that Ahmad ʿAriqat was manipulating funds to his advantage. The earlier these were released from his control, the better for those concerned.

Fragmentation and Restructuring

Ismaʿil Abu Taqiyya had held a large family together and had helped to structure it in a way that reflected his own position and accommodated the needs that this position created. His death shattered this structure—wives, concubines, and children could no longer be held together in quite the same way. This became apparent quite rapidly and was manifested in more ways than one. There was no one to replace him as head. His only son, Zakariyya, was a minor. His brother Yasin perhaps chose not to take on this role with Isma'il's family. The few more years that Yasin was to live were painful ones, with the loss of all his children, including one young man, 'Umar, who had reached maturity. By 1041/1631, Yasin too had passed away. And Ahmad 'Ariqat, on whom Isma'il had placed much trust, seems to have aroused the mistrust of the family. For a while after Isma'il's death, the family seems to have passed through a turbulent period before reaching a more settled phase with a new family structure.

One of the painful moments for the family in the years following Isma'il Abu Taqiyya's death was when, disoriented, they left the house on Darb al-Shabrawi, the place where they had spent many years—where as children they had played.[28] Soon thereafter, the Darb al-Shabrawi house was rented out to strangers. In a sense this brought to a close a chapter of their family history. Leaving the house where Isma'il had spent so much of his time in fact meant the separation of the people who had been held together by his presence. Each looked for another suitable place to reside. Badra moved into a house in the neighborhood. 'Atiyat al-Rahman, Zakariyya, Umm al-Hana, and Tahira stayed in another house belonging to the family, at Darb al-Tahun. We do not hear much more of Rumia. She may or may not have moved into separate lodgings. Similarly, Sayma al-Bayda, who had given Isma'il some warmth in his last years, was eventually married to an emir from the Mutafariqqa corps. And Amna, the child of one of Isma'il's concubines, was at one point living in a house her father had owned in Khatt al-Khurushtuf.

The second generation of the Abu Taqiyya family was restructured after Isma'il's death and given a new form, centered around neither Ahmad 'Ariqat, nor Yasin, nor Zakariyya, nor the girls' husbands, but around 'Atiyat al-Rahman. The aging widow gathered her married children and grandchildren around her. Their individual shares of Isma'il Abu Taqiyya's inheritance, given the large number of heirs, came to little, and it made sense for them to pool it by sharing a common household.

This restructuring was not simply the result of prescribed rules of behavior—it came to pass partly because of Umm al-Hana's initiatives in manipulating those close to her. Her two marriage contracts show her role in redefining the Abu Taqiyya family structure in the late 1620s and early 1630s. Umm al-Hana was instrumental in forming a family structure that was both matriarchal and matrilocal. This structure was set forth in contractual terms in her marriage contracts. Both husbands—first al-Qazwini, then Ibn al-Muhalhal—agreed to move into 'Atiyat al-Rahman's residence, where Zakariyya was living with his mother at the time. He himself was married and he had brought his wife to live with his family.[29] The elements of matriarchy are apparent from the clause to which al-Qazwini and Ibn al-Muhalhal had agreed, to live with Umm al-Hana's mother, her brother, and her sisters and their husbands without creating problems.[30]

And thus 'Atiyat al-Rahman came to be the head of the household and family, with a certain level of authority over her own offspring as well as their spouses. She had outlived Hana, Badra, and Rumia by many years. She had seen her children grow up and get married, and now she could take on a new role in the family, as head of the household, commanding respect from those around her, and having her wishes fulfilled by them. With her in the house were Zakariyya with his wife and children, as well as Umm al-Hana with her husband and eventually their little boy, Muhammad. And next door, in the house Isma'il had built for her, connected to the family house, were Jami'a and Ahmad 'Ariqat. She continued as supervisor of her family's foundation, handling its revenues and expenditures. In addition, 'Atiyat al-Rahman helped her children to care for their own property, so they could benefit from her long experience in managing finances.

But this situation, like the one before it, was also transitory, and within a few years, it too came to an end. The first shock occurred with the untimely death of her daughter, Umm al-Hana, around 1045/1635 (followed by that of Umm al-Hana's child, Muhammad). The family was again deeply affected. Umm al-Hana had possessed her father's ability to cement family relationhships, and the absence of her decisive personality left a sense of deep gloom. (When, sometime later, Zakariyya had an infant girl, he named her Umm al-Hana, after his sister.) But this was not the end of their personal losses. Shortly after, in 1053/1643, Jami'a too died. Her death was followed four years later, in 1057/1647, by that of her husband, Ahmad 'Ariqat, who had for so long been a central figure in the Abu Taqiyya family.[31] 'Atiyat al-Rahman, now in her sixties, felt her energies diminishing. Relying more and more on Zakariyya to do things for her, she gradually moved away from center stage, until her own death some five years later.

8

Conclusion

Ismaʿil Abu Taqiyya had experienced a significant change of fortune during his lifetime, which had brought him more personal prosperity and more social influence. This was, to a certain extent, the result of a number of successful commercial ventures. More importantly, his life was contemporaneous with a series of significant global changes that had a bearing on his own existence. In Cairo, as in many other commercial centers, the increased intensity of world and regional trade could be felt. Abu Taqiyya, as a well-established merchant with extended networks, was affected by this situation in the same way as merchants in India coping with increased demand for Indian textiles, for example, and merchants in Europe faced with the growing consumer demand of more prosperous populations. Even though the beginning of capitalist expansion of Europe has been traced to the sixteenth century, for nearly two centuries after that, commercial relations between European merchants and merchants like Abu Taqiyya seem to have been maintained on equal terms, rather than one partner dominating the other. European merchants at this stage were still primarily interested in the purchase of consumer products for customers who now wanted commodities from numerous and diverse sources. The search for markets for European products was only to occur in the eighteenth century and later.

Thus, we should reconsider many of the views regarding trade and of production in the region after Europeans had penetrated the spice market in Asia and developed the Atlantic sea route. These were momentous events, which affected world trade and eventually led to colonial domination. Although these events may seem to have pushed the region outside the center of activity and brought devastation to the economy and to the fortunes of Middle Eastern merchants, the study of merchant activities allows us to analyze the region in terms of the processes taking place there. These processes were affected not only by European penetration of Asian trade but by numerous other factors as well, some of which were adverse to economic activity, while others stimulated it. Therefore, instead of viewing the economy of the region in the seventeenth century as that of a passive South, where nothing important happened, in contrast to a dynamic North with a monopoly on change, we can trace some of the important trends affecting regions both north and south of the Mediterranean and study how they were affected or how they helped shape these trends.

The life records of Abu Taqiyya, moreover, allow us to reconsider the position of Egypt within the commercial history of the Ottoman region. Although the integration of Egypt into the Ottoman Empire changed its political status from the center of an empire to that of a province, we have to be careful about generalizations concerning its peripheral position, what one historian has described as the "backyard" of the Ottoman Empire.[1] The political conditions that followed Egypt's integration into the Ottoman state did not necessarily entail economic or commercial marginalization. There were, in fact, certain benefits to be gained from belonging to the Ottoman commercial space, or the Ottoman world economy, as some scholars have called it. Commercial ties were intensified between the different regions. From the sixteenth to the eighteenth centuries, regions like Syria and Anatolia were not only major trading partners with Egypt but also major consumers of its sugar and textiles. The growing populations of the cities in those regions were a significant factor in the increase in demand for certain goods. Indeed, this "marginal" area, far from the administrative center of the Empire, was creating significant commercial patterns, which helped to revitalize trade.

As highly centralized as the Ottoman administration was during this period, in regions like Egypt, located at a distance from the capital, the economy was much influenced by local and regional factors. That the sugar industry had a long history in Egypt, for instance, was a significant factor in its revival at the end of the sixteenth century. The traditional trade routes which crossed through Cairo—from North Africa, Black Africa, the Red Sea, Sinai, and the Mediterranean Sea—which had long been in use, were not abandoned. Some actually became more active as a result of Egypt's integration into the Ottoman world economy. Perhaps these developments in Egypt's economy had a bearing on the Mediterranean region as a whole and that changes in trade, agriculture, and industry were more than isolated incidents. The development of sugar and linen production on a large scale, notably, and of the transit trade in coffee must have had repercussions beyond Egypt's borders, which future studies may well uncover. For the time being, what the life records of Abu Taqiyya indicate are the wide diversity of economic patterns and the importance of local conditions existing within the Ottoman world economy. This diversity between one region and another, whether a result of historical development or of geographic factors, has been downplayed by scholars who have studied the non-European world as a single bloc as well as by scholars of Ottoman history who have tended to deemphasize regional differences. The records also indicate that a dynamic economy was bringing about significant tranformations in a region regarded as peripheral both to the Ottoman center and to the European world.

The study of the period between the end of the sixteenth century and the beginning of the seventeenth through an analysis of the activities of merchants can be justified on a number of levels. In the case of the merchants themselves, the position they attained during this period can be regarded a trend of considerable significance. Their affluence was more than an economic improvement in their position, affecting only the material well-being of one particular group. It marked the lives of merchants on many levels—social, legal, cultural, and private. When merchants like Abu Taqiyya, al-Damiri, the Ruwi'is, or the Shuj'is became wealthy, they became actively involved in the construction of public buildings that gave them visibility, they formed links of different kinds with the ruling elite, and they ordered their private lives—the kind of house they lived in, the households they set up, and/or their family structure—to their new realities.

These changing conditions of merchants allowed them to leave a mark on the wider scene in Cairo, because they increased their involvement, direct or indirect, in the political scene. The changes taking place did not revolutionize the social structures of the time. At the top of the hierarchy, the military—whether Ottoman militias or Mamluks—still dominated the power structure; merchants and scholars still had a lower position. Nevertheless, the weakening of the structures at the top gave indigenous merchants a chance to boost their positions in relation to the power structure. Less state intervention in commerce meant they could have a freer hand in running their affairs, according to whatever criteria that they judged to be the most advantageous to them.

The life records of Abu Taqiyya and his merchant colleagues allow us to see the links between international trade, agriculture, and production. These merchants were essentially interested in the profits they could make from long-distance trading, and yet we can see how this was linked to other aspects of the local economy. In Egypt, as in Yemen, patterns of agriculture had to be adapted in order to cope with new levels of demand —for coffee, for textiles, or for sugar. The fact that the merchants of Abu Taqiyya's generation involved themselves in agriculture and production is of great significance for our understanding of economic conditions. It suggests that during the period in question, the impetus for change was instigated by the rise in demand for certain products. Investments in agriculture and production served the purpose of those who eventually sold or exported these goods, at least insofar as certain products were concerned. Our understanding of these processes, however, will be incomplete as long as we do not study rural and agricultural conditions. We have to assume that changes were taking place in the kinds of crops being cultivated. It would also be of primary importance to study the history of major commodities like textiles—especially linen, a very important local industry and export item throughout the period from the sixteenth to the eighteenth century.

The adjustments that merchants made and the mechanisms that they used during this period of adaptation to changing conditions were those offered by a traditional society. Merchants like Abu Taqiyya were dealing with trading partners and trading systems of various origins and from diverse regions of the world while they themselves were functioning from within a traditional system, using the legal tools and commercial structures and institutions that were part and parcel of their environment and had, for the most part, existed for a long time. In spite of the restrictions that various traditional structures imposed, these were far less rigid than we tend to think. Rather than viewing these structures only as obstacles to any initiative, we can understand the situation better by considering them as frameworks within which different forms of action were sanctioned. Certainly, such a concept implies the imposition of rules of behavior, but not entirely at the cost of all initiative. The traditional structures within which merchants functioned, whether social or economic ones, were, in these times of flux, being adapted to diverse conditions or adjusted to meet particular needs.

Nevertheless, the conditions within which merchants functioned sometimes imposed their own restraints. The investments of merchants in trade and industry were undertaken within certain limits. Even when large sums were involved—in the form of loans or advance payments for commodities—the type of investment Abu Taqiyya made did not involve a long-term commitment. A merchant invested in the planting of sugarcane as long as he estimated a demand for it, or as long as he considered his export market would absorb the quantities he had. The amounts of money he invested were never too large to be irretrievable, mainly because they were short-term investments. If the following year, trends changed, he could transfer his investment elsewhere with no great loss. Thus, the capital flowing in from the city to the country and from merchants to producers had definite benefits for sugar production and maintained it at a high level for over a century. But, at the same time, the financial commitment of merchants to a larger-scale sugar production, which might have involved a relatively high investment over a long-term period, was not something that interested merchants like Abu Taqiyya and his contemporaries.

Likewise, the activities of merchants were challenged by certain constraints, this time of a sociopolitical nature. Even though by Abu Taqiyya's lifetime, commerce was not subjected to the controls of a state economy and merchants could, for the most part, conduct their business free of state intervention, they nevertheless had to spend some money for political purposes, sometimes sharing their trade with individuals in power or advancing them loans. Potentially this was a detrimental factor in their commercial activity, because it could mean that the capital a merchant could have invested in an economic activity was being spent elsewhere. Abu Taqiyya made loans to Mamluk emirs, advance payments to customs officials, and traded on behalf of pashas. As matters stood, however, the generation of Abu Taqiyya fared better than others. In the eighteenth century, for instance, Mamluk emirs, a growing force, involved themselves much more actively in international trade than their counterparts two centuries earlier. In 1600 the Ottoman pashas were no longer a major force, and the military elites had not yet fully consolidated their power but were in the process of emerging as a major force on the political scene, and that was essentially where they concentrated their efforts.

The conditions prevalent during those years call for a reconsideration of chronology with regard to economic and commercial history. The early seventeenth century ushered in trends of great significance in the commercial history of Egypt. They probably survived until the beginnings of incorporation, sometime towards the mid-eighteenth century. Sophisticated trading techniques were adopted, in many cases similar in form to those we know to have been used much later, although they were not as extensively used as in the nineteenth century. Some of the features that have been related to incorporation into the European capitalist world economy—the links between agriculture, production, and trade, notably —in fact were taking form during Isma'il Abu Taqiyya's lifetime. Abu Taqiyya and other merchants of his generation were involved in the various stages of sugar production—from agriculture, to refining, to export.

In the nineteenth century, these techniques were much more systematically applied, and engendered considerably higher revenues. And yet, unlike conditions in the nineteenth century, the activity of merchants in the seventeenth century led to expansion in the production and export of local finished products. After the middle of the nineteenth century, Egypt was, more and more, producing raw materials and importing finished products. Moreover, the profits of these ventures, during Abu Taqiyya's lifetime, went to local rather than to European merchants or their agents, as would be the case in the nineteenth century with the development of a dependent economy. This view supports Peter Gran's contention about the development of the indigenous economy, functioning within its own terms, prior to the period of European penetration.[2]

One of the important conclusions here is the continuity of earlier developments and those of the nineteenth century. Instead of the traditional approach of dating the beginning of modernization to 1800, I suggest that certain aspects of the changes taking place then were part of a process that started long before—during the lifetime of Abu Taqiyya. We can, in other words, argue for a process of *evolution* rather than *revolution*. Modernization, as it occurred in the nineteenth century, is linked to Western influences, and to a certain extent shaped by them. A number of features linked to this Westernization constituted ruptures with the past. I suggest that the process of modernization prior to 1800 was different from that which came later: Ruptures occurred, among which were the emergence of the nation-state in the particular form it took in the nineteenth century and the development of technology and its effect on society, and these ruptures helped shape the direction modernization took. We can thus study these ruptures as such, not as a beginning that had no basis in the past.

From that viewpoint, the developments taking place under Muhammad 'Ali can be seen in a different light. On the one hand, the industries that emerged then did not suddenly erupt but very likely had been built upon by artisans who had for a long time been trained in large-scale commercial production, much the same as their counterparts in Europe on the eve of the Industrial Revolution. Moreover, Muhammad 'Ali did not invent commercial agriculture but expanded it and extended state control over it. He was not the first to link export to agriculture, but his policies intensified the process of linking agriculture to industry and trade and put agriculture under government supervision, with the aim of integrating Egypt more into the world economy. Even though his efforts in this domain were crucial and the mechanisms he used were more systematic than those of his predecessors, we can nevertheless understand the changes of the nineteenth century in the light of what came before. On the other hand, evolution does not necessarily imply a smooth and clear line of development. We cannot minimize the importance of the changes occurring in the late eighteenth century and the nineteenth: Certain major phenomena taking place then marked the beginning of structural changes in the economy. Among these is the gradual decrease in export to Europe of finished products, a phenomenon accompanied by an increase in imported European cloth. André Raymond has observed this trend occurring towards the latter part of the eighteenth century. The local textile industry suffered the consequences, losing some of its European markets. A parallel phenomenon is evident with regard to sugar, for which there had been demand in Europe. The spread of sugar refineries, provided with sugarcane from America, in Marseilles and elsewhere, decreased this flow.

Accordingly, we can better understand why more land in Egypt was being converted to other cash crops more in demand and fetching higher prices, this time essentially raw materials rather than finished products. Peter Gran's study of the late eighteenth century postulates an expansion of agricultural land that was producing grain in answer to the great increase of demand for this product in France. Trends like this one marked the start of incorporation into the world economy. Muhammad 'Ali's policy continued the process of integration into the European world economy but attempted to curtail the process of peripheralization by his creation of new state-run industries. By the mid-nineteenth century, the process of peripheralization was greatly accelerated under his successors.

What all this clearly points out is that it is very dangerous to attempt to understand the modern period or the nineteenth century simply by looking at two or three decades before that, especially as most historians admit that the last years of the eighteenth century were a period of great crisis. To treat the last quarter of the eighteenth century as a period typical of a few centuries preceding it is ahistorical. Indeed, as I demonstrate, we cannot understand the modern period without going back to the sixteenth century, to understand the roots of many of the developments that came later. That century is the source for some of the phenomena that historians have heretofore dated to much later periods. This book should, in other words, lead to a reevaluation not only of the sixteenth and early seventeenth centuries but of the nineteenth century as well. I hope that future studies will show the geographical extent of the transformations taking place in Egypt about 1600 and the parallels that can be found elsewhere in the empire. It might also be relevant to explore the way these trends may have delayed or helped to define the shape of the process of incorporation into the European world system. Questions of this nature have as yet to be addressed.

The changing role of the state is a crucial one in the long-term economic and commercial history of the region, much the same way that it was in the economic history of Europe. In the sixteenth and seventeenth centuries, the weak state allowed groups such as merchants to reemerge and play a more prominent role, both economically and socially. This process was accelerated at the end of the eighteenth century, when Mamluk grandees involved themselves in the lucrative commercial activities of merchants. Muhammad ʿAli, with the strong centralized state he developed, was an interruption. Subsequently, the intervention of European powers, much more politically centralized than they had earlier been, changed the situation. Saʿid and Ismaʿil could not control massive European penetration, and peripheralization took on new dimensions. In earlier times, the absence of state controls had widened the scope of activity of merchants. By the nineteenth century, the state's weaker position worked to the disadvantage of local merchants, the new conditions favoring European merchants. The European capitalist system, now rapidly expanding, was backed by strong states and solid infrastructures that paved the way—with armies and with missionaries—for their own trade. Complaints of European merchants were taken up by their consuls and ambassadors directly with the sultan in Istanbul. There was no such support system for merchants in Egypt or other parts of the Ottoman Empire to protect them against the advancing European traders. Indigenous merchants did not have the same direct recourse to authority. Their structures and associations had not, historically, developed along those lines. Indigenous merchants were therefore not only competing with European merchants and with better technology in production, but also with states, and against these they could not defend themselves.

Appendix

Notes

Glossary

Bibliography

Index

Appendix
Genealogy

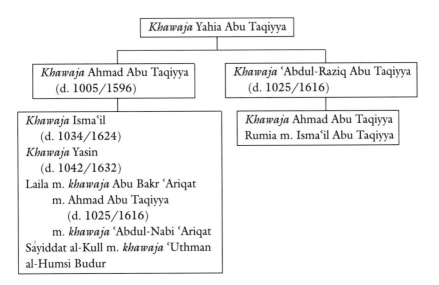

Khawaja Yahia Abu Taqiyya

Khawaja Ahmad Abu Taqiyya
(d. 1005/1596)

Khawaja 'Abdul-Raziq Abu Taqiyya
(d. 1025/1616)

Khawaja Isma'il
(d. 1034/1624)
Khawaja Yasin
(d. 1042/1632)
Laila m. *khawaja* Abu Bakr 'Ariqat
m. Ahmad Abu Taqiyya
(d. 1025/1616)
m. *khawaja* 'Abdul-Nabi 'Ariqat
Sayiddat al-Kull m. *khawaja* 'Uthman
al-Humsi Budur

Khawaja Ahmad Abu Taqiyya
Rumia m. Isma'il Abu Taqiyya

Khawaja Isma'il Abu Taqiyya

Married to:
Badra b. 'Abdul Rahman Ibn 'Ariqat (d. before 1044/1634)
Rumia b. 'Abdul-Raziq Abu Taqiyya
'Atiyat al-Rahman b. *khawaja* Abu Bakr Ahaymar (d. 1063/1652)
Hana' al-Bayda (d. before 1034/1624)

Children:
Fardus (married *khawaja* 'Atiya 'Ariqat; then Qadi Shihab al-Din Ahmad b. Hijazi)
Jami'a (married Ahmad 'Ariqat, d. 1053/1643)

Umm al-Hana (married *khawaja* Muhammad al-Qazwini; then Qadi Shams al-Din
  Muhammad Ibn al-Muhalhal al-Jizi, d. 1045/1635)
Zayn al-Tujjar (married Qadi Ibn al-Muhalhal after Umm al-Hana's death)
Zakariyya (d. by 1080/1669)
Fadila (married *khawaja* Mustafa 'Alay al-Din al-Shami)
Tahira (married *khawaja* Mansur Ibn al-Warraq)
Fatma/Stita (married Muhammad b. emir Ahmad b. *al-sayyid al-sharif* Ibrahim
  Mutafarriqa, then emir Muhammad b. Kiwan, then emir Bashir Agha Muta-
  farriqa)
Amna (married Shaykh Muhammad b. Taj al-Din al-Amini al-Hanafi)
Fatma (died in infancy 1034/1624)
Salha (born after Abu Taqiyya's death, died in infancy 1034/1624)

Zakariyya Isma'il Abu Taqiyya

Karima (married Shaykh Sijada al-Sadat al-Wafa'iyya Abu Qasis 'Abdul Wahab in
  1058/1648)
Umm al-Hana (married Shaykh Zayn al-Din 'Abdul-Latif b. al-Qadi Ahmad Hijazi in 1088/1677)

Notes

Reference to court cases are abbreviated as follows: an abbreviated form for the name of the court *(BA:* Bab 'Ali; *SN:* Salihiyya Najmiyya; *Q.Ask:* Qisma 'Askariyya; *Q.Arab:* Qisma 'Arabiyya), followed by the number of the volume, the case number, the date, and the page. The system of double dating is used when the original documents provide the date in *hijri,* i.e., according to the Islamic calendar in use at the time.

Introduction

1. Stanford Shaw, *The Financial and Administrative Organization and Development of Ottoman Egypt, 1517–1798.* (Princeton, N.J.: Princeton Univ. Press, 1962); Michael Winter, *Egyptian Society under Ottoman Rule, 1517–1798* (London: Routledge, 1992).

2. André Raymond, *Artisans et Commerçants au Caire au XVIIIe siècle* (Damascus: Institut français de Damas, 1973); Haim Gerber, "Social and Economic Position of Women in an Ottoman City, Bursa 1600-1700, " *IJMES* 12 (1980): 231–44; Amnon Cohen, "Le Rouge et le noir, Jerusalem style," *Revue du monde musulman et de la Mediterranée* 55–56 (1990): 140–49.

3. The remains of this court house are known today as Bayt al-Qadi.

4. Abraham Udovitch, *Partnership and Profit in Medieval Islam* (Princeton, N.J.: Princeton Univ. Press, 1970); Haim Gerber, "The Muslim Law of Partnership in Ottoman Court Records," *Studia Islamica* 53 (1981): 109–19.

5. Works like Wilhelm Heyd. *Histoire du commerce du Levant* (Leipzig: O. Harrassowitz, 1886) and Elyahu Ashtor, *Levant Trade in the Later Middle Ages* (Princeton, N.J.: Princeton Univ. Press, 1983), both based on European sources, tend to over-emphasize the importance of trade between the Middle East and Europe and to neglect trade with other regions.

6. Huri Islamoglu-Inan and Caglar Keyder, "Agenda for Ottoman History," *Review* 1, no. 1 (1977): 33–35.

7. The role of the court as a civil institution is analyzed in Nelly Hanna, "The Administration of Courts in Ottoman Cairo," in *The State and Its Servants: Administration in Egypt from Ottoman Times to the Present,* ed. Nelly Hanna (Cairo: American Univ. in Cairo Press, 1995), 44–59.

8. *BA* 126, 324 (1058/1648), 99.

1. Perspectives on the Period

1. Halil Inalcik, *The Ottoman Empire: The Classical Age, 1300–1600* (London: Weidenfeld and Nicolson, 1973), 4; Peter M. Holt, *Egypt and the Fertile Crescent 1516–1922* (Ithaca: Cornell Univ. Press, 1966) 61–70.

2. Bernard Lewis, *The Emergence of Modern Turkey* (London: Oxford Univ. Press, 1968); Stanford Shaw, *History of the Ottoman Empire and Modern Turkey* (Cambridge: Cambridge Univ. Press, 1987).

3. Fernand Braudel, *The Mediterranean and the Mediterranean World in the Age of Philip II*, 2 vols., trans. Sian Reynolds (New York: Harper Colophon Books, 1976).

4. Rifaʿat Abou-El-Haj, *The Formation of the Modern State: The Ottoman Empire, Sixteenth to Eighteenth Centuries* (Albany: State Univ. of New York Press, 1991), 6–11.

5. Resat Kasaba, *The Ottoman Empire and the World-Economy: The Nineteenth Century* (Albany: State Univ. of New York Press, 1988), 18–19; Huri Islamoglu-Inan, "Agenda for Ottoman History," in *The Ottoman Empire and the World-Economy,* ed. Huri Islamoglu-Inan (Cambridge: Cambridge Univ. Press, 1987), 47–52.

6. Immanuel Wallerstein, "The Ottoman Empire and the Capitalist World-Economy: Some Questions for Research," *Review* 2, no. 3 (winter 1979): 389–98.

7. André Raymond, "L'Impact de la pénétration européenne sur l'économie de l'Egypte au XVIIIe siècle," *Annales Islamologiques* 18 (1982): 226–27.

8. Raymond, "L'Impact de la pénétration," 231–33.

9. Peter Gran, *Islamic Roots of Capitalism* (Austin: Univ. of Texas Press, 1979), 6–11.

10. Kasaba, *The Ottoman Empire and the World-Economy,* 11–18; Ilkay Sunar, "State and Economy in the Ottoman Empire," and Islamoglu-Inan, "Introduction: 'Oriental despotism' in world-system perspective," both articles in *The Ottoman Empire and the World Economy,* ed. by Huri Islamoglu-Inan (Cambridge Univ. Press, 1987), 63–65, 7–11.

11. Hamilton R. Gibb and Harold Bowen, *Islamic Society and the West* (London: Oxford Univ. Press, 1957), 212–13.

12. Eric J. Hobsbawm, "The Crisis of the Seventeenth Century," *Past and Present* 5 (1954): 46–49.

13. Hugh R. Trevor-Roper, "The General Crisis of the Seventeenth Century," *Past and Present* 16 (1959): 44–51.

14. Abou-El-Haj, *Formation of the Modern State,* 6–7.

15. Braudel, *The Mediterranean and the Mediterranean World,* 1: 211–12, 444.

16. A court documentation for Mamluk Cairo has not been shown to exist.

17. Marc Bloch, *French Rural History: An Essay on Its Basic Characteristics,* trans. Janet Sondheimer (London: Routledge and Kegan Paul, 1966) 102–12.

18. Robert Brenner, "The Agrarian Roots of European Capitalism," in *The Brenner Debate: Agrarian Class Structure and Economic Development in Pre-Industrial Europe,* ed. T. H. Aston and C. H. E. Philpin (Cambridge: Cambridge Univ. Press, 1987) 213–15.

19. Peter Gran, *Islamic Roots of Capitalism.*

20. Thomas Ashton, *The Industrial Revolution, 1760–1839* (New York: Oxford Univ. Press, 1964), 18–41.

21. Peter Gran, *Islamic Roots of Capitalism,* 3–6.

2. Merchants and Merchant Families

1. Raymond, *Artisans et commerçants,* 579–81 and the footnotes therein.

2. Bruce Masters, *The Origins of Western Economic Dominance in the Middle East: Mercantilism and the Islamic Economy in Aleppo, 1600–1750* (New York: New York Univ. Press, 1988), 15.

3. Christophe Harant narrates that he took a ship from Gaza on 22 Sept. 1598, arriving at Damietta on 29 Sept. See *Le Voyage en Égypte de Christophe Harant* (Cairo: Institut français d'archéologie orientale, 1972), 24–27.

4. Merchants taking this route entered Cairo at Bab al-Nasr, the northern gate of the city. They were taxed there on the merchandise they were carrying with them. See Nelly Hanna, *Habiter au Caire: les maisons moyennes et leurs habitants aux XVIIe et XVIII siècle* (Cairo: Institut français d'archéologie orientale, 1991) 20.

5. Hanna, *Habiter au Caire,* 102.

6. Jean Sauvaget, "Les caravanserails syriens du hadjdj de Constantinople," *Ars Islamica* 4 (1937): 98-121; al-Muhibbi, *Khulasat al-athar fi a'yan al-qarn al-hadi 'ashar,* (Cairo: al-Matba'a al-Wahabiyya, 1284 H.), 2: 214–17.

7. *BA* 58, 820 (1000/1591), 334.

8. *SN* 459, 163 (986/1578), 56–57.

9. Najm al-Din al-Ghazzi, *al-Kawakib al-sa'ira bi-a'yan al-mi'a ashar,* ed. Jabra'il Sulayman Jabbur (Beirut: Muhammad Amin Damaj, 1949).

10. M. de Chabrol, "Essai sur les moeurs des habitants modernes de l'Egypt," *Description de l'Egypte, Etat Moderne,* 2: 391. Chabrol's estimates on literacy in Cairo are borne out by the large number of elementary schools *(kuttabs)* the members of the Expedition found, many of which have left remains. These little structures were generally built above public fountains *(sabils).*

11. One should note that both Isma'il and Yasin, later in their lives, built *sabil-kuttabs* attached to their *wikalas.*

12. *Dasht* 106 (1000/1591), 642.

13. *BA* 54, 98 (995/1586), 25.

14. *SN* 470, 968 (995/1586), 236.

15. *BA* 64, 609 and 618 (1004/1595), 143 and 145.

16. *Q. Arab* 12, 275 (1005/1596), 184.

17. *BA* 102, 1318 (1029/1619), 205.

18. C. G. Brouwer and A. Kaplanian, *Early Seventeenth-Century Yemen* (Leiden: Brill, 1988), 94–97. This work presents selections from the Dutch East India Company records.

19. Terence Walz, *Trade Between Egypt and Bilad al-Sudan,* (Cairo: Institut français d'archéologie orientale, 1978), and "Trading into the Sudan in the Sixteenth Century," *Annales Islamologiques* 15(1979): 211–33.

20. Raymond, *Artisans and commerçants,* 2: 580.

21. Thomas Phillip and Moshe Perlmann, eds. *'Abd al-Rahman al-Jabarti's History of Egypt: 'Aja'ib al-athar fi al-tarajim wa'l-akhbar* (Stuttgart: Franz Steiner Verlag, 1994), 378–79.

22. *Q.Ask* 33, 515 (1028/1618), 349.

23. *BA* 98, 3546 (1025/1615), 478.

24. Edward William Lane, *The Thousand and One Nights*, 1838, reprint (Cairo: Livre de France, 1980) 223, 228.

3. The Structures of Trade

1. See, for instance, Raymond, "L'Impact de la pénétration," 217–35.

2. Benjamin Braude, "International Competition and Domestic Cloth in the Ottoman Empire, 1500–1650: A Study in Underdevelopment," *Review* 2, no. 3 (1979): 437–51; Rhodes Murphey, "Conditions of Trade in the Eastern Mediterranean: An Appraisal of Eighteenth-Century Ottoman Documents from Aleppo," *JESHO* 33 (1990): 35–50.

3. Niels Steensgaard based his model on Van Leur. See *The Asian Trade Revolution of the Seventeenth Century* (Chicago: Univ. of Chicago Press, 1974), 22–41.

4. *The Origins of Western Economic Dominance*, 47–68.

5. Al-Dimishqi's often quoted classification of merchants into three types, traveling merchants, stationary merchants, and hoarders, is also a simplification of a much more complex situation, because there were many types of traveling merchants and many types of sedentary ones. See S. D. Goitein, *A Mediterranean Society*, vol. 1, *Economic Foundations* (Berkeley: Univ. of California Press, 1967), 157–61.

6. Christophe Harant, *Voyage en Egypte*, 199.

7. Bernardino Amico da Gallipoli, Aquilante Rocchetta, and Henry Castela, *Voyages en Egypte des années 1597–1601* (Cairo: Institut français d'archéologie orientale, 1974), 77.

8. Udovitch, *Partnership and Profit*, 5–6.

9. Ronald Jennings, "Loans and Credit in Early Seventeenth-Century Ottoman Judicial Records," *JESHO* 16 (1973); Gerber, "Muslim Law of Partnership," 109–19.

10. *BA* 103, 1648 (1031/1621), 486.

11. *BA* 97, 147 (1023/1614), 18.

12. *BA* 63, 431 (1003/1594), 86.

13. *BA* 75, 3080 (1010/1602), 849-50.

14. Raymond, *Artisans et commerçants*, 301–4.

15. *BA* 118, 358 (1046/1636), 89–90.

16. Walz, "Trading into the Sudan," 226–33.

17. *BA* 71, 1064 (1009/1600), 304–5.

18. *BA* 86, 718 (1015/1606), 111.

19. *BA* 87, 811 (1016/1607), 192.

20. *BA* 87, 809 (1016/1607), 191.

21. *BA* 87, 810 (1016/1607), 191.

22. *BA* 87, 811 (1016/1607), 192.

23. Abraham Udovitch, in *Partnership and Profit*, notes, for instance, that in Maliki law, a partner had the right to sell on credit, even if this right was not specifically conferred in the contract. That was the kind of obligation Abu Taqiyya was seeking to avoid.

24. *BA* 86, 715 (1015/1606), 110–11.

25. *BA* 71, 1064 (1009/1600), 304–5.

26. *BA* 86, 718 (1015/1606), 111.

27. *BA* 86, 717 and 718 (1015/1606), 111.

28. *BA* 82, 290 (1012/1603), 69.

29. *BA* 103, 412 (1031/1621), 134.

30. *BA* 90, 452 (1017/1608), 102; *BA* 98, 2162 (1025/1616), 275.

31. *BA* 82, 444 (1012/1603), 92.

32. Goitein, *A Mediterranean Society,* 241–44; Joseph Schacht, *Introduction to Islamic Law* (Oxford: Clarendon, 1964), 149.

33. K. N. Chaudhuri and Irfan Habib, "European Trade with India," in *The Cambridge Economic History of India,* ed. Tapan Raychaudhuri and Irfan Habib (Hyderabad: Orient Longman, 1982), 395–98.

34. Raymond, *Artisans et commerçants,* 298–301.

35. Michel Tuscherer, "Le Pélérinage de l'émir Sulayman Gawis al-Qazdughli, *sirdar* de la caravane de la Mekke en 1739," *Annales Islamologiques* 24 (1988): 163.

36. Raymond, *Artisans et commerçants,* 108ff. Johann Wild, who accompanied his Persian master on the pilgrimage, took the overland road from Suez to ʿAqaba, then sailed to Jedda; that is, he traveled partly by land and partly by sea. See Johann Wild, *Voyages en Egypte, de Johann Wild, 1606–1610* (Cairo: Institut français d'archéologie orientale, 1973), 28–29.

37. *BA* 98, 2162 (1025/1615), 275.

38. *BA* 86, 718 (1015/1606), 111.

39. *BA* 90, 1739 (1017/1608), 382.

40. *BA* 86, 717 and 718 (1015/1606), 111.

41. *BA* 94, 427 (1021/1612), 89.

42. *BA* 64, 609 (1004/1595), 143.

43. *BA* 97, 147 (1023/1613), 18.

44. *BA* 97, 147 (1023/1613), 18.

45. *Q.Ask* 38, 126 (1034/1624), 116.

46. Fernand Braudel, *Civilization and Capitalism, 15th–18th Century,* vol. 3, *The Perspectives of the World,* trans. Sian Reynolds (New York: Harper and Row, 1982–84), 480–81.

47. *BA* 96, 1870 (1023/1613), 289.

48. *Q.Ask* 36, 238 (1032/1622), 143.

49. Wild, *Voyages en Egypte,* 45.

50. *BA* 85, 2368 (1014/1605), 421.

51. *BA* 82, 646 (1012/1503), 120.

52. *BA* 98, 189 (1025/1616), 26.

53. *BA* 97, 283 (1024/1614), 37.

54. Goitein, *A Mediterranean Society,* 164–69.

4. Shifting Patterns in Trade

1. Abou-El-Haj, *Formation of the Modern State,* 5–6.

2. Immanuel Wallerstein, Hale Decdeli, and Resat Kasaba, "The Incorporation of the Ottoman Empire into the World-Economy," *The Ottoman Empire and the World-Economy,* ed. Huri Islamoglu-Inan (Cambridge: Cambridge Univ. Press, 1987), 88–97; Immanuel Wallerstein and Resat Kasaba, "Incorporation into the World-Economy: Change in the

Structure of the Ottoman Empire, 1750–1839" in *Economie et société dans l'empire ottoman,* ed. Jean-Louis Bacqué-Grammont and Paul Dumont (Paris: Centre nationale de la recherche scientifique, 1983), 335–53.

3. Halil Inalcik, "The Emergence of Big Farms, *ciftliks:* State, Landlords and Peasants," in *Studies in Ottoman Social and Economic History,* ed. Halil Inalcik (London: Valorium Reprints, 1985), 113 and "Capital Formation in the Ottoman Empire," 135.

4. M. N. Pearson, "Merchants and States," in *The Political Economy of Merchant Empires,* ed. James Tracy (Cambridge: Cambridge Univ. Press, 1991), 63.

5. Frederic C. Lane, "The Mediterranean Spice Trade: Further Evidence of Its Revival in the Sixteenth Century," *American Historical Review* 45, no. 3 (Apr. 1940): 580–90; Braudel, *The Mediterranean and the Mediterranean World,* 549–54.

6. Braudel, *Civilization,* 3: 211–16.

7. Jack Goldstone, "Trends or Cycles?" The Economic History of East-West Contact in the Early Modern Period," *JESHO* 36, no. 2 (May 1993): 104–19.

8. Fernand Braudel, *Civilization and Capitalism, 15–18th Century,* vol. 2, *The Wheels of Commerce* (New York: Harper and Row, 1982–84), 468.

9. Braudel, *Civilization,* 3: 220.

10. Braudel, *Civilization,* 2: 190–94.

11. Fernand Braudel, "The Mediterranean Economy in the Sixteenth Century," in *Essays on European Economic History, 1500–1800,* ed. Peter Earle (Oxford: Clarendon, 1974), 10–13.

12. Raymond, *Artisans et commerçants;* Ralph Hattox, *Coffee and Coffeehouses: The Origins of a Social Beverage in the Medieval Near East* (Seattle: Univ. of Washington Press, 1985), 3–28.

13. Gallipoli et al., *Voyages en Egypte,* 148.

14. Gallipoli et al., *Voyages en Egypte,* 82. Coffee was introduced to Europe at a later date, which is why coffee looked weird to him. The first coffee house opened in London in 1652, in Marseilles in 1671 and in Paris in 1672. See Raymond, *Artisans et commerçants,* 132.

15. *BA* 82, 1267 (1013/1604), 260.

16. It would be very interesting to know what kind of structural adjustments were made to agriculture in Yemen in order to answer increasing world demand for coffee.

17. Brouwer and Kaplanian, *Early Seventeenth-Century Yemen,* 108.

18. *BA* 85, 1220 and 2211(1014/1605), 239 and 392.

19. *BA* 98, 3506 (1025/1616), 472.

20. *Dumyat* 68, 703 (1033/1623), 331; *BA* 90, 1548 (1017/1608), 303.

21. André Raymond, "La Fabrication et le commerce du sucre au Caire au XVIIIe siècle, l'effondrement d'une 'industrie' traditionelle," in *Sucre, sucreries et douceurs en Mediterranée* (Paris: Centre national de la recherche scientifique, 1991) 213–15.

22. Nelly Hanna, *An Urban History of Bulaq in the Mamluk and Ottoman Periods* (Cairo: Institut français d'archéologie orientale, 1983), 24–25.

23. Raymond, "La Fabrication et le commerce du sucre," 215.

24. Suraiya Faroqhi, *Towns and Townsmen of Ottoman Anatolia,* (Cambridge: Cambridge Univ. Press, 1984), 86–87.

25. Braudel, *Civilization,* 3: 190–91.

26. *BA* 82, 1264 (1013/1604), 260.

27. *BA* 82, 1650 (1013/1604), 344.

28. *BA* 102, 599 (1028/1618), 138.

29. *BA* 102, 1045 (1028/1618), 243.

30. *BA* 100, 1460 (1026/1616), 220–21.

31. The debates on this matter are outlined in Kenneth Cuno, *The Pasha's Peasants: Land, Society, and Economy in Lower Egypt, 1740–1858* (Cairo: American Univ. in Cairo Press, 1994), 2–5.

32. F. Vansleb, *The Present State of Egypt* (London: J. Starkey, 1678), 67; Wild, *Voyage en Egypte*, 94.

33. Cuno, 67.

34. Shaw, *Financial and Administrative Organization*, 19, 68.

35. Shaw, *Financial and Administrative Organization*, 22, 56–57.

36. *BA* 100, 1460 (1026/1616), 220–21.

37. Charles Issawi, "The Economic Development of Egypt, 1800–1914," in *The Economic History of the Middle East 1800–1914: A Book of Readings*, ed. and with an Introduction by Charles Issawi (Chicago: Univ. of Chicago Press, 1996), 360–64.

38. *BA* 90, 651 (1017/1608), 140; *BA* 82, 1264 (1012/1604) and 2008 (1012/1604), 402; *BA* 95, 839 (1022/1613), 163.

39. *BA* 82, 1761 (1013/1604), 360 and 2008 (1012/1603), 400; *BA* 105, 2446 (1033/1623), 669–70.

40. Raymond believes that these *sukkari*s maintained their wealth throughout the seventeenth century. See, "La Fabrication et le commerce du sucre," 215–19.

41. Elyahu Ashtor, "Levantine Sugar Industry in the Late Middle Ages: A Case of Technological Decline," in *The Islamic Middle East, 700–1900: Studies in Economic and Social History*, ed. Abraham Udovitch (Princeton, N.J.: Darwin Press, 1981), 94.

42. *BA* 105, 2446 (1033/1623), 669–70.

43. *Q.Ask* 38, 106 (1034/1624), 74.

44. *BA* 82, 795 (1012/1603), 160–61.

45. *BA* 98, 3156 (1025/1616), 415.

46. Nelly Hanna, *Construction Work in Ottoman Cairo* (Cairo: Institut français d'archéologie orientale, 1983), 7–10.

47. Gabriel Baer, *Fellah and Townsmen in the Middle East* (London: Frank Cass, 1982); Pascale Ghazaleh, "The Guilds: Between Tradition and Modernity," in *The State and Its Servants: Administration in Egypt from Ottoman Times to the Present*, ed. Nelly Hanna (Cairo: American Univ. in Cairo Press, 1995), 60–74.

48. *BA* 98, 1843 (1025/1614), 230.

49. Amnon Cohen, *Economic Life in Ottoman Jerusalem* (Cambridge: Cambridge Univ. Press, 1989), 84–85.

50. *BA* 94, 896 (1021/1612), 195.

51. *Q.Ask* 38, 209 (1034/1624), 171–72; *BA* 98, 2162 (1025/1616), 275; *BA* 103, 412 (1031/1621), 134.

52. *BA* 100, 836 (1026/1617), 117; *BA* 90, 452 (1017/1608), 102.

53. *BA* 98, 3506 (1025/1616), 472; *BA* 101, 494 (1028/1618), 77.

54. *BA* 96, 1871 (1023/1613), 289; *BA* 97, 2824 (1024/1614), 380; *BA* 98, 3506 (1025/1616), 472.

55. Vansleb, *Present State of Egypt*, 118–19.

56. *BA* 102, 390 (1028/1618), 90.

57. Ashtor, "Levantine Sugar in the Late Middle Ages," 91–132.

58. Braudel, *Civilization*, 3: 142.

59. Suraiya Faroqhi, "Merchant Networks and Ottoman Craft Production (16th–17th Centuries)," in *Urbanism in Islam: The Proceedings of the International Conference on Urbanism in Islam*, vol. 1 (Tokyo: Institute of Oriental Studies, Univ. of Tokyo, 1989) 114–18.

60. 'Ali al-Jiritli, *Tarikh al-Sina'a fi Misr fil nisf al-awal min al-qarn al-tasi' 'Ashar* (Cairo: Dar al-Ma'arif, 1952), 20–21.

61. Franklin Mendels, "Proto-industrialization; The First Phase of the Industrialization Process," *Journal of Economic History* 32, no. 1 (1972): 241–61.

62. Ashtor, "Levantine Sugar in the Late Middle Ages," 99.

63. Shaw, *Financial and Administrative Organization*, 272.

64. *BA* 102, 1777 (1029/1619), 429.

65. See, for instance, Huri Islamoglu-Inan and Suraiya Faroqhi, "Crop Patterns and Agricultural Production Trends in Sixteenth-Century Anatolia," *Review* 2, no. 3 (1979): 401–36; Islamoglu-Inan and Keyder, "Agenda for Ottoman History," 31–55.

66. Faroqhi, *Towns and Townsmen*, 126–37.

67. Raymond, *Artisans et commerçants*, 180–81, 186–87.

68. Raymond, *Artisans et commerçants*, 229ff.

69. Raymond, *Artisans et commerçants*, 181.

70. Raymond, "La fabrication et le commerce du sucre," 213–25.

5. Social Structures

1. *Financial and Administrative Organization*, 1962.

2. Islamoglu-Inan and Keyder, "Agenda for Ottoman History," 31–55; Peter Gran, "Late 18th–Early 19th Century Egypt: Merchant Capitalism or Modern Capitalism," in *L'Egypte au XIXe siècle* (Paris: Centre national de la recherche scientifique, 1982), 267–81.

3. K. N. Chaudhuri discusses some of the views on this matter in his article, "Reflections on the organizing principle of premodern trade," in *The Political Economy of Merchant Empires,* ed. James Tracy (Cambridge: Cambridge Univ. Press, 1991), 424–26.

4. Subhi Labib, "Capitalism in Medieval Islam," *Journal of Economic History* 39, no. 1 (Mar. 1969): 81.

5. *Q.Ask,* 38, 184 (1034/1624), 154–55.

6. Ahmad Shalabi Ibn 'Abdul-Ghani, *Awdah al-Isharat fi-man tawalla Misr al-Qahira min al-wuzara' wa al-bashat,* ed. Abdel Rehim Abdel Rahman Abdel Rehim (Cairo: Maktabat al-Khanji, 1978), 141.

7. *BA* 18, 1266 (967/1559), 254; *BA* 31, 298 (976/1568), 57; *BA* 59, 1027 and 1028 (1001/1592), 268.

8. Hanna, *Urban History of Bulaq; BA* 35, 62 (982/1574), 287.

9. *BA* 104, 1478 (1032/1622), 445.

10. *Q.Ask* 33, 569 (1027/1617), 384.

11. *SN* 475, 330 (1005/1596), 92.

12. *Q.Ask* 38, 194 (1034/1624), 164.

13. *BA* 103, 413 (1031/1621), 134.

14. Brouwer and Kaplanian, *Early Seventeenth-Century Yemen*, tells of the losses caused by the fact that the yearly ship from Suez had not come on time (Aug. 1621), 137–38.

15. Brouwer and Kaplanian, *Early Seventeenth-Century Yemen*, 137, 166, 223.

16. *BA* 103, 413 (1031/1621), 134; *Q.Ask* 38, 115 (1034/1624), 134.

17. Wild, *Voyage en Égypte*, 31–34.

18. *BA* 82, 1266 and 1267 (1013/1604), 260.

19. *BA* 85, 923 (1014/1605), 179.

20. *BA* 96, 3506 (1025/1616), 472.

21. *BA* 42, 1755 (986/1578), 299.

22. *SN* 456, 1145 (979/1571), 279.

23. Aryeh Shmuelevitz, *The Jews of the Ottoman Empire in the Late Fifteenth and the Sixteenth Centuries* (Leiden: Brill, 1984), 128–32.

24. *BA* 96, 1870 (1023/1614), 289; *BA* 97, 2824 (1024/1615), 380.

25. Halil Inalcik, "Imtiyazat," *Encyclopedia of Islam*, 2d ed.

26. *BA* 82, 938 (1014/1605), 180.

27. Shaw, *Financial and Administrative Organization*, 193.

28. Mohsen Shuman, "The Beginnings of Urban *iltizam* in Egypt," in *The State and Its Servants: Administration in Egypt from Ottoman Times to the Present*, ed. Nelly Hanna (Cairo: American Univ. in Cairo Press, 1995), 17–31.

29. *BA* 82, 2008 (1013/1604), 402; *BA* 85, 2213 (1014/1605), 397.

30. *BA* 102, 1045 (1029/1619), 243. For other examples of large sums of money passing from Abu Taqiyya to emirs and Mamluks, see *BA* 85, 1220 (1014/1605), 239; *BA* 100, 1142 (1026/1617), 168.

31. Ahmad Shalabi Ibn ʿAbdul-Ghani, *Awdah al-Isharat*, 137–38.

32. Muhammad al-Bakri, *Kitab al-Kawakib al-Saʾira*, manuscript in the Bibliotheque Nationale, Paris, Fonds Arabe, 1852, folio 42b.

33. Holt, *Egypt and the Fertile Crescent* 79–80.

34. *BA* 126, 324 (1058/1648), 99.

35. Fatma/Stita married Muhammad b. emir Ahmad b. *al-sayyid al-sharif* Ibrahim Mutafarriqa in 1035/1625 (*BA* 107, 723 [1035/1625]), divorced him in 1042/1632 (*BA* 115, 989 [1042/1632]), and married emir Muhammad b. Kiwan (*BA* 125, 131 [1057/ 1647], 50–52). Widowed a few years later, she married emir Bashir Agha Mutafarriqa (*BA* 135, 719 [1068/1657], 187). In other words, all three husbands were emirs, and two of them belonged to the Mutafarriqa corps.

36. Abou-El-Haj, *Formation of the Modern State*, 48.

6. Shaping the Urban Geography

1. André Raymond and Gaston Wiet, *Les Marchés du Caire* (Cairo: Institut français d'archéologie orientale, 1979), maps 1–6.

2. Muhammad Sabri Yusuf, *Dur al-mutasawwifa fi tarikh Misr fi al-ʿasr al-ʿUthmani* (Belbeis: Dar al-Taqwa, 1994), 34–40.

3. See the *Index of Mohammedan Monuments*.

4. al-Muhibbi, *Khulasat al-athar*, 4: 262–63.

5. Hanna, *Habiter au Caire,* 177–78.

6. Braudel, *The Mediterranean and the Mediterranean World,* 1: 326–27; Faroqhi, *Towns and Townsmen,* 1–3.

7. André Raymond, "Le déplacement des tanneries a l'époque ottomane," in *Villes du Levant: Revue du monde musulman et de la Mediterranée* 55–56 (1990): 34–43; Masters, 38–40.

8. Charles Issawi, "Economic Change and Urbanization in the Middle East," in *Middle Eastern Cities,* ed. Ira Lapidus (Berkeley: Univ. of California Press, 1969), 102–8.

9. Roger Owen, *The Middle East in the World Economy, 1800–1914* (London: Methuen, 1987), 24–25.

10. Braudel, *Civilization,* 3: 123, 151–52.

11. Michael Heberer von Bretten, *Voyages en Egypte de Michael Heberer Von Bretten, 1585–1586* (Cairo: Institut français d'archéologie orientale, 1976), 68.

12. Wild, *Voyages en Egypte,* 91–94.

13. Van Berchem, *Matériaux pour un corpus inscriptionum Arabicarum* (Paris: Ernest Leroux, 1903), 126–27.

14. Hanna, *An Urban History of Bulaq.*

15. Ulku Bates, "Facades in Ottoman Cairo" in *The Ottoman City and Its Parts: Urban Structure and Social Order,* ed. Irene Bierman, Rifaʿat Abou el-Haj, and Donald Preziosi (New York: Aristide Caratzas, 1991), 128ff.

16. *BA* 102, 1503 (1029/1620), 355.

17. *BA* 95, 2421 (1022/1613), 388.

18. *BA* 90, 199, 44. This proportion was maintained for all further dealings relative to the construction of the two *wikala*s.

19. *BA* 97, 412 (1023/1614), 55.

20. *BA* 97, 201 (1023/1614), 25.

21. *BA* 97, 2609 (1024/1615), 351; *BA* 98, 3503 (1026/1616), 472.

22. See ʿAli Mubarak, *al-Khitat al-Tawfiqiyya,* 2d. ed (Cairo: al-Hayʾa al-ʿAmma lil-Kitab, 1969–94), 140.

23. *Q.Arab* 18, 828 (1016/1607), 527; *A.Ask* 31, 475 (1025/1616), 268–69.

24. Raymond, *Artisans et commerçants,* 403–5.

25. Her marriage contract included the condition stipulating that the clothes her husband bought for her should be in silk and velvet. See *BA* 100, 1126 (1026/1617), 163.

26. Harant, *Voyage en Egypte,* 197.

27. Muhammad al-Bakri, *"Kashf al-Kurba,"* ed. ʿAbdel Rehim Abdel Rahman Abdel Rehim, *Egyptian Historial Review* 23 (1976): 315–21.

28. Hanna, *Habiter au Caire,* 218; *Dasht* 119 (1012/1603), 504.

29. Hanna, *Habiter au Caire,* 174–78.

30. Hanna, *Habiter au Caire,* 177–78.

31. The name Ahaymar suggests a connection with the mosque called al-Jamiʿ al-Ahmar, close to the Ruwiʿi buildings.

7. Family Life at the Abu Taqiyya's Household

1. Clive Holmes, "Popular Culture? Witches, Magistrates and Divines in Early Modern England," in *Understanding Popular Culture: Europe from the Middle Ages to the Nineteenth Century,* ed. Steven Kaplan (Berlin: Mouton, 1984), 85–111.

2. *Q.Ask* 15, 141 (995/1586), 90-91; *BA* 58, 783 (1001/1592), 320–21.

3. *Dasht* 106 (1000/1591), 642.

4. *Q.Arab* 21, 253 (1025/1616), 179; *BA* 100, 126 (1026/1617), 143.

5. *BA* 97 (1023/1614), 1679, 222.

6. *BA* 82, 1412 (1013/1604), 293.

7. Robert Brunschvig, "'Abd," *Encyclopedia of Islam,* 2d ed.

8. *BA* 90, 1293 (1017/1608), 249.

9. Afaf Lutfi al-Sayyid Marsot discusses women's involvement in financial transactions nearly two centuries later, in *Women and Men in Late Eighteenth-Century Egypt* (Austin: Univ. of Texas Press, 1995).

10. In the final analysis, when Isma'il did die, she inherited a third of an eighth of his fortune, that is, the eighth was the share of the wives, and it was divided by the three who were alive at the time.

11. *BA* 100, 1077 (1026/1616), 154; see also *BA* 100, 1146 (1026/1616), 167; and *BA* 86, 1437 (1015/1606), 257.

12. Roger Thompson, *Women in Stuart England and America: A Comparative Study* (London: Routledge and Kegan Paul, 1974), 162–63.

13. Adrienne Rogers, "Women and the Law," in *French Women and the Age of Enlightenment,* ed. Samia I. Spencer (Bloomington: Indiana Univ. Press, 1984), 35.

14. al-Bakri, *al-Kawakib,* 42.

15. Edward William Lane, *An Account of the Manners and Customs of the Modern Egyptians* (The Hague, London: East-West Publications, 1978; reprint, 1989), 62 (page citation is to the reprint ed.).

16. *BA* 103, 698 (1031/1621), 210-6.

17. *BA* 103, 420, 422–28 (1031/1621), 136–38. Each of these documents was a certificate of enfranchisement.

18. *Dasht* 118 (1011/1602), 261.

19. *Q.Ask* 38, 185 (1034/1624), 154–56.

20. *Q.Ask* 38, 317 (1035/1625), 250–51.

21. *BA* 107, 723, 107.

22. *BA* 114, 92 (1041/1631), 37; *BA* 137, 306 (1070/1659), 77–78; *BA* 126, 324 (1058/1648), 99.

23. The archives indicate that Persian merchants were fewer in number in Cairo during that period than they had been earlier on during the sixteenth century, perhaps because of the wars between Ottomans and Safawis.

24. Katherine Rogers, *Feminism in Eighteenth-Century England* (Urbana: Univ. of Illinois Press, 1982), 9.

25. *BA* 114, 92 (1041/1631), 37.

26. *BA* 103, 414 (1031/1621), 135.

27. *Q.Ask* 38, 481 (1035/1625), 364; *Q.Ask* 39, 392 (1035/1625), 254; 393 (1035/1625), 254; 395 (1035/1625), 255.

28. *BA* 111, 67 and 807 (1038/1628), 19 and 243.
29. *BA* 115, 989 (1042/1632), 199.
30. The Arabic term used here is *la yatadarrar min*.
31. *BA* 121, 215 (1053/1643), 43.

8. Conclusion

1. Michael Winter, *Egyptian Society under Ottoman Rule, 1517–1798* (London: Routledge, 1992), 253.
2. Peter Gran, "Late 18th–Early 19th Century Egypt," 27–41.

Glossary

ahkam (sing. *hukm*): clauses.

amana: keeping

amin al-sukkar: state agent responsible for gathering the sugar paid as land tax to the treasury and shipping it to Istanbul.

ʿaqd shirka: partnership contract.

aqmisha misriyya (sing. *qumash*): Egyptian textiles.

ʿasal aswad: molasses.

ʿayn aʿyan al-tujjar: most notable amongst notable merchants; title used for the most prominent merchants.

bayda: lit. white; referring to Eastern European, Caucasian, or Georgian women slaves.

bey: title in the Ottoman administration in Egypt given to officers holding important administrative positions.

birka: (pl. *birak*): pond or lake.

commenda: see *mudaraba*.

dallal: broker.

dhikr: Sufi ritual performance.

dinar: golden currency worth about forty *nisf* in common use during the period.

emir: title given to high-ranking officer (ranks below *bey*).

fakhr al-tujjar: lit. the pride of merchants; title used for prominent merchants.

faqih (pl. *fuqahaʾ*): scholar in jurisprudence; teacher.

faskh ʿaqd: cancellation or annulment of a contract.

fatiha: opening chapter of the Quran.

feddan: main unit of land measurement in Egypt, 4200 square meters.

fiqh: jurisprudence of the *shariʿa*.

funduq: type of commercial establishment; in seventeenth-century Alexandria this term is often used to mean the commercial establishments where European merchants lived and carried out their businesses.

Grand Vizir: most important post in the Ottoman Sultanate after the Sultan. The

Grand Vizir headed the bureaucratic apparatus and was directly responsible to the Sultan.

habashiyya: Ethiopian woman.

hadith: compilations of the traditions of the Prophet.

hajj: pilgrimage to Mecca; used to address a person who has gone on a pilgrimage; a more general use of this form of address is for aged persons, as a sign of respect.

hammam: bath.

hanut (pl. *hawanit*): shop.

hara (pl. *hawari* or *harat*): residential quarter.

himl (pl. *ahmal*): load.

iltizam: system of tax farming. The holder of the *iltizam* (called the *multazim*) paid the treasury in Egypt a sum of money yearly, calculated, in theory at least, in relation to the amount of revenue he could expect to get. The system of *iltizam* was applied to taxation of agricultural land, as well as to other kinds of tax revenues, such as the revenues from customs or the revenues from production.

irsaliyya: yearly remittance, in cash and in kind, sent from the Ottoman authorities in Egypt to Istanbul.

kashif: position in the Ottoman administrative hierarchy. The *kashif* occupied lesser positions than the *beys*.

khan: commercial warehouse where merchants could store their goods and sell them. The most famous *khan* in Cairo was Khan al-Khalili. *Khan* is synonymous with *wikala* except that the word is also used for buildings erected along important routes for lodging travelers.

khatib: marriage intermediary.

khatt: street.

khawaja: title by which a merchant was addressed.

khawajaki: title by which a prominent merchant was addressed.

khazna nawmiyya: sleeping area.

kuttab, maktab (pl. *katatib*): elementary school.

madhhab: school of law.

al-mahkama al-kubra: main court.

maq'ad: loggia; open balcony or portico overlooking an inner courtyard in a house.

maristan: hospital.

masjid: small mosque.

matbakh: sugar refinery.

ma'tuq: enfranchised slave.

mawlana: title used for prominent religious scholars or magistrates.

min a'yan al-tujjar: merchant notable.

morjan: coral.

mu'akhar: deferred payment of bridal money. A marriage contract had to include a statement as to the amount of *mahr* or *saddaq* (bridal payment), part of which could be paid at the time of the contract while another part was deferred to a later date.

mu'allim: lit. master or teacher; title often given to the Coptic or Jewish members of the scribal profession such as secretaries or those serving in the administration.

mubashir: secretary.

mudaraba, commenda: business or commercial agreement whereby one partner provides the funds and the other provides the services; the profits are then divided in specified portions between the partners.

muhtasib: market inspector.

multazim: holder of a tax concession; a tax farmer (see *iltizam*).

muqata'a: form of tenure on the principal taxable rural and urban revenues of Egypt. The holder of the *muqata'a* was expected to administer it and to collect taxes. One of the most prevalent forms of administering *muqata'a* was through the system of *iltizam*.

mustawlida (pl. *mustawlidat*): concubine or slave woman who has borne her master a child.

naqib: holder of a position in the professional guilds. The *naqib* was under the *shaykh* in the guild hierarchy, assisting the *shaykh* to carry out his duties.

nisf: smallest unit of the silver currency commonly in use in Egypt during the Ottoman period.

qa'a: hall.

qabban: weigher of goods.

qadi (pl. *qudat*): judge; magistrate.

qard (pl. *qurud*): loan.

qasir: minor.

qibla: direction toward which Muslims turn during their prayers; the word *qibla* also means the architectural element in a mosque that indicates the direction for the prayer.

qintar: measure of weight equivalent to about 44 kg, commonly used during the Ottoman period.

qirsh: a silver unit of currency commonly used in the Ottoman period, worth about thirty *nisf*s.

quintal: measure of weight equivalent to about 50 kg.

radi': feeding child.

rahn: mortgage.

al-rajul al-kamil: person who has reached legal capacity, manhood.

ras mal: capital.

riwaq (pl. *arwiqa*): type of lodging; when used in reference to al-Azhar refers to the lodgings of the students.

sabil (pl. *asbila*): public fountain. The *sabil* in Cairo was very often surmounted by a *kuttab* (elementary school). The *sabil-kuttab* was one of the very commonplace public structures in the city, which had some three hundred of them in 1800.

sahn: plate.

salam shariʿi: advance payment for future delivery.

sarraf: money changer.

sayyid sharif: title given to people claiming descent from the Prophet.

shabb baligh: young man having reached physical maturity, puberty.

shahbandar al-tujjar: head of the guild of merchants.

shahbariyya: the position of *shahbandar*.

shahr ʿaqari: Registry department.

shariʿa: Islamic law.

shaykh al-tujjar bi-wikala al-sabun: head of the guild of merchants at the soap *wikala*.

shaykh sijada: very prestigious title given to the heads of the four or five Sufi orders, such as the Sadat al-Wafa'iyya and the Bakriyya, who claimed descent from a companion of the Prophet.

simsar (pl. *samasira*): intermediary between buyer and seller.

sufra: platter.

suftaja: letter of credit.

sukkari: sugar manufacturer; sugar merchant.

sukkar kham: dark sugar.

sukkar mukarrar: refined sugar.

suq: market.

tabiʿ (pl. *tawabiʿ*): client; follower; a *tabiʿ* was attached to a notable person, implying a degree of servitude, but did not receive wages. He was compensated with protection and with the prestige attached to his master.

taʾifa (pl. *tawaʾif*): community; professional guild.

tajir fil harir: silk merchant.

tajir fil sabun: soap merchant.

tajir khawaja: merchant; *tajir* refers to the profession and *khawaja* to one of the titles by which merchants were addressed.

tajir saffar: traveling merchant.

tariqa: (pl. *turuq*): Sufi order.

tawkil: agency; mandate.

tawkil mutlaq: mandate giving full authority to act on one's behalf in all matters.

tawqaji: bonnet-maker.

tujjar (sing. *tajir*): merchants.

ujaq (pl. *ujaqat*): Ottoman military corps in Egypt, of which there were seven. The members of these *ujaq*s filled the principal administrative and political positions.

'ulama' (sing. *'alim*): religious scholars.

'urf: usage, habits, and tradition.

wakil (pl. *wukala'*): agent.

waqf (pl *wawqaf*): religious endowment. A property was endowed or made into a *waqf* so that its revenues could be spent on a religious or charitable foundation like a mosque or school. Part of the revenue was often set apart for the founder's family. The term *waqf* is used both for the revenue-producing property and for the institution it funds. The *waqf* deeds established by the founder specified, often in great detail, the way funds were to be spent.

wikala (pl. *wikalat*): commercial warehouse where merchants could store and sell their merchandise. It was surmounted by living quarters rented either to travelers or families.

yaqut: ruby, rubies.

zawia: small mosque; also used to mean Sufi hostel.

Bibliography

Court Records

Court registers are in bound and numbered volumes. They were consulted in two locations in Cairo:

The following registers, from the various courts of Cairo, were consulted at the Registry Department (Shahr al-'Aqari). They are at present in the process of being transferred to the National Archives (Dar al-Watha'iq):

Bab 'Ali (BA): 35 (982/1574); 42 (986/1578); 54 (995/1586); 58 (1000/1591); 59 (1001/1592); 64 (1004/1595); 71 (1009/1600); 75 (1010/1602); 82 (1012/1603); 85 1014/1605; 86 (1015/1606); 87 (1016/1607); 90 (1017/1608); 94 (1021/1612); 95 (1022/1613); 96 (1023/1613); 97 (1023/1614); 98 (1025/1615); 100 (1026/1616); 101 (1028/1618); 102 (1029/1619); 103 (1031/1621); 104 (1032/1622); 105 (1033/1623); 107 (1035/1625); 111 (1038/1628); 114 (1041/1631); 118 (1046/1636); 121 (1053/1643).

Dasht (the Dasht volumes consist of loose pages from various court registers put together and organized by year. The pages are numbered, but there are no case numbers as in other volumes): 106 (1000/1591); 118 (1011/1602); 145 (1037/1627).

Qisma 'Arabiyya (Q.Arab): 12 (1005/1596); 21 (1025/1616)

Qisma 'Askariyya (Q.Ask): 15 (995/1586); 33 (1028/1618); 36 (1032/1622); 38 (1034/1624); 39 (1035/1625).

Salihiyya Najmiyya (SN): 456 (979/1571); 459 (986/1578); 470 (995/1586); 475 (1005/1596).

The court registers of Dumyat (Damietta) are housed, with other registers from provincial towns, in the National Archives in Cairo (Dar al-Watha'iq): *Dumyat* 68 (1033/1623).

Books and Articles

Abou-El-Haj, Rifaʿat. *The Formation of the Modern State: The Ottoman Empire, Sixteenth to Eighteenth Centuries.* Albany: State Univ. of New York Press, 1991.

Ashton, Thomas S. *The Industrial Revolution, 1760–1839,* New York: Oxford Univ. Press, 1964.

Ashtor, Elyahu. "Levantine Sugar Industry in the Late Middle Ages, A Case of Technological Decline." In *The Islamic Middle East 700–1900: Studies in Economic and Social History,* edited by Abraham Udovitch, 91–132. Princeton, N.J.: Darwin Press, 1981.

———. *Levant Trade in the Later Middle Ages.* Princeton, N.J.: Princeton Univ. Press, 1983.

Baer, Gabriel. *Fellah and Townsmen in the Middle East.* London: Frank Cass, 1982.

al-Bakri, Muhammad. *"Kashf al-Kurba."* Edited by Abdel Rehim Abdel Rahman Abdel Rehim. *Egyptian Historical Review* 23, (1976): 291–384.

———. *Kitab al-Kawakib al-Saʾira.* Manuscript in the Bibliotheque Nationale, Paris, Fonds Arabe, 1852.

Bates, Ulku. "Facades in Ottoman Cairo." In *The Ottoman City and Its Parts: Urban Structure and Social Order,* edited by I. Bierman, R. Abou el-Haj and D. Preziosi, 129–72. New York: Aristide Caratzas, 1991.

Bloch, Marc. *French Rural History: An Essay on Its Basic Characteristics.* Translated by Janet Sondheimer. London: Routledge and Kegan Paul, 1966.

Bois, Guy. *Crisis of Feudalism: Economy and Society in Eastern Normandy c. 1300–1500.* London: Cambridge Univ. Press, 1984.

Braude, Benjamin. "International Competition and Domestic Cloth in the Ottoman Empire, 1500–1650: A Study in Underdevelopment." *Review* 2, no. 3 (1979): 437–51.

Braudel, Fernand. *Civilization and Capitalism, 15th–18th Century,* vol. 2, *The Wheels of Commerce;* vol. 3, *The Perspectives of the World,* trans. Sian Reynolds. New York: Harper and Row, 1982–84.

———. *The Mediterranean and the Mediterranean World in the Age of Philip II.* Translated by Sian Reynolds. 2 vols. New York: Harper Colophon, 1972.

———. "The Mediterranean Economy in the Sixteenth Century." In *Essays on European Economic History, 1500-1800,* edited by Peter Earle, 1–44. Oxford: Clarendon, 1974.

Brenner, Robert. "The Agrarian Roots of European Capitalism." In *The Brenner Debate: Agrarian Class Structure and Economic Development in Pre-Industrial Europe,* edited by T. H. Aston and C. H. E. Philpin, 213–328. Cambridge: Cambridge Univ. Press, 1987.

Bretten, Michael Heberer von. *Voyages en Egypte de Michael Heberer von Bretten, 1585–1586.* Cairo: Institut français d'archéologie orientale, 1976.

Brouwer C. G. and Kaplanian, A. *Early Seventeenth-Century Yemen, Dutch Documents Relating to the Economic History of Southern Arabia (1614–1630).* Leiden: Brill, 1988.

Chabrol, M. de. "Essai sur les moeurs des habitants modernes de l'Egypte." *Description de l'Egypte, Etat Moderne,* 2, 361–524. Paris: Imprimerie Nationale, 1822.

Chaudhuri, K. N. "Reflections on the Organizing Principle of Premodern Trade." In *The Political Economy of Merchant Empires,* edited by James Tracy. Cambridge: Cambridge Univ. Press, 1991.

Chaudhuri, K. N., and Habib, Irfan. "European Trade with India." In *The Cambridge Economic History of India,* edited by Tapan Raychaudhuri and Irfan Habib, 382–407. Hyderabad: Orient Longman, 1982.

Cohen, Amnon. *Economic Life in Ottoman Jerusalem.* Cambridge: Cambridge Univ. Press, 1989.

———. "Le Rouge et le Noir, Jerusalem style." *Revue du Monde Musulman et de la Mediterranée* 55–56 (1990): 141–49.

Cuno, Kenneth. *The Pasha's Peasants: Land, Society, and Economy in Lower Egypt, 1740–1858.* Cairo: American Univ. in Cairo Press, 1994.

Darrag, Ahmad. *L'Egypte sous le regne de Barsbay.* Damascus: Institut français de Damas, 1961.

Faroqhi, Suraiya. "Merchant Networks and Ottoman Craft Production (16th–17th Centuries)." In *Urbanism in Islam: The Proceedings of the International Conference on Urbanism in Islam,* vol. 1, 85–132. Tokyo: Institute of Oriental Studies, Univ. of Tokyo, 1989.

———. *Towns and Townsmen of Ottoman Anatolia.* Cambridge: Cambridge Univ. Press, 1984.

Gallipoli, Bernardino Amico da, Aquilante Rocchetta, and Henry Castela. *Voyages en Egypte des années 1597–1601.* Cairo: Institut français d'archéologie orientale, 1974.

Gerber, Haim. "The Muslim Law of Partnership in Ottoman Court Records." *Studia Islamica* 53, (1981): 109–19.

———. "Social and Economic Position of Women in an Ottoman City, Bursa 1600–1700," *IJMES* 12 (1980): 231–44.

Ghazaleh, Pascale. "The Guilds: Between Tradition and Modernity." In *The State and Its Servants: Administration in Egypt from Ottoman Times to the Present,* edited by Nelly Hanna, 60–74. Cairo: American Univ. in Cairo Press, 1995.

al-Ghazzi, Najm al-Din. *al-Kawakib al-saʾira bi-aʿyan al-miʾa ʿashar,* edited by Jabraʾil Sulayman Jabbur. Beirut: Muhammad Amin Damaj, 1949.

Gibb, Hamilton R., and Harold Bowen. *Islamic Society and the West.* vol. 1. London: Oxford Univ. Press, 1957.

Godinho, Vitorino Magalhaes. *L'Economie de l'empire portugais aux XVe et XVIe siècles.* Paris: Centre national de la recherche scientifique, 1969.

Goitein, S. D. *A Mediterranean Society,* Vol. 1, *Economic Foundations,* Berkeley: Univ. of California Press, 1967.

Goldstone, Jack. "Trend or Cycles?" The Economic History of East-West Contact in the Early Modern World." *JESHO* 36, no. 2 (May 1993): 104–19.

Gran, Peter. *Islamic Roots of Capitalism.* Austin: Univ. of Texas Press, 1979.

———. "Late 18th–Early 19th Century Egypt: Merchant Capitalism or Modern Capitalism." In *L'Egypte au XIXe siècle,* 267–81. Paris: Centre national de la recherche scientifique, 1982.

Hanna, Nelly. "The Administration of Courts in Ottoman Cairo." In *The State and Its Servants: Administration in Egypt from Ottoman Times to the Present,* edited by Nelly Hanna, 44–59. Cairo: American Univ. in Cairo Press, 1995.

———. *Construction Work in Ottoman Cairo.* Cairo: Institut français d'archéologie orientale, 1984.

———. *Habiter au Caire: les maisons moyennes et leurs habitants aux XVIIe et XVIIIe siècles.* Cairo: Institut français d'archéologie orientale, 1991.

———. "Isma'il Abu Taqiyya et le commerce international au Caire 1585–1625." In *Les Villes dans l'Empire Ottoman: activités et societés,* edited by Daniel Panzac, vol. 1, 211–19. Paris: Centre national de la recherche scientifique, 1991.

———. "Marriage among Merchant Families in Seventeenth-Century Cairo." In *Women, the Family, and Divorce Laws in Islamic History,* edited by Amira El-Azhary Sonbol, 143–54. Syracuse: Syracuse Univ. Press, 1996.

———. *An Urban History of Bulaq in the Mamluk and Ottoman Periods.* Cairo: Institut français d'archéologie orientale, 1983.

Harant, Christophe. *Le Voyage en Egypte de Christophe Harant.* Cairo: Institut français d'archéologie orientale, 1972.

Hattox, Ralph. *Coffee and Coffeehouses: The Origins of a Social Beverage in the Medieval Near East.* Seattle: Univ. of Washington Press, 1985.

Heyd, Uriel. *Ottoman Documents on Palestine.* Oxford: Clarendon Press, 1960.

Heyd, Wilhelm von. *Histoire du commerce du Levant.* Leipzig: O. Harrassowitz, 1886.

Hobsbawm, Eric J. "The Crisis of the Seventeenth Century." *Past and Present* 5 (1954): 36–59.

Holmes, Clive. "Popular Culture? Witches, Magistrates and Divines in Early Modern England." In *Understanding Popular Culture: Europe from the Middle Ages to the Nineteenth Century,* edited by Steven Kaplan, 85–111. Berlin: Mouton, 1984.

Holt, Peter M. *Egypt and the Fertile Crescent, 1516–1922.* Ithaca: Cornell Univ. Press, 1966.

Ibn 'Abdul-Ghani, Ahmad Shalabi. *Awdah al-Isharat fi-man tawalla Misr al-Qahira min al-wuzara' wa al-bashat.* Edited by Abdel Rehim Abdel Rahman Abdel Rehim. Cairo: Maktabat al-Khanji, 1978.

Inalcik, Halil. "Capital Formation in the Ottoman Empire." *Journal of Economic History* 29, no. 1 (Mar. 1969): 97–140.

———. "The Emergence of Big Farms, *ciftliks:* State, Landlords and Peasants." In *Studies in Ottoman Social and Economic History,* edited by Halil Inalcik, 105–26. London: Valorium reprints.

———. "Imtiyazat," *Encyclopedia of Islam,* 2d ed.

———. *The Ottoman Empire: The Classical Age, 1300–1600.* London: Weidenfeld and Nicolson, 1973.

Islamoglu-Inan, Huri ed. *The Ottoman and the World Economy,* Cambridge: Cambridge Univ. Press, 1987.

Islamoglu-Inan, Huri, and Suraiya Faroqhi. "Crop Patterns and Agricultural Production Trends in Sixteenth-Century Anatolia." *Review* 2, no. 3 (1979): 401–36.

Islamoglu-Inan, Huri, and Caglar Keyder. "Agenda for Ottoman History," *Review* 1, no. 1 (1977): 33–55.

Issawi, Charles. "Economic Change and Urbanization in the Middle East." In *Middle Eastern Cities,* edited by Ira Lapidus, 102–21. Berkeley: Univ. of California Press, 1969.

———. "The Economic Development of Egypt, 1800–1914," in *The Economic History of the Middle East 1800–1914: A Book of Readings,* edited and with an Introduction by Charles Issawi, 359–74. Chicago: Univ. of Chicago Press, 1975.

Jennings, Ronald. "Loans and Credit in Early Seventeenth-Century Ottoman Judicial Records." *JESHO* 16 (1973): 168–215.

al-Jiritli, 'Ali. *Tarikh al-Sina'a fi Misr fil nisf al-awal min al-qarn al-tasi' 'Ashar.* Cairo: Dar al-Ma'arif, 1952.

Kasaba, Resat. *The Ottoman Empire and the World Economy: The Nineteenth Century,* Albany: State Univ. of New York Press, 1988.

Labib, Subhi. "Capitalism in Medieval Islam." *Journal of Economic History* 39, no. 1 (Mar. 1969): 79–98.

Lane, Edward William. *An Account of the Manners and Customs of the Modern Egyptians.* The Hague and London: East-West Publications, 1978; reprint, 1989.

———. *The Thousand and One Nights.* 1838. Reprint. Cairo: Livre de France, 1980.

Lane, Frederic C. "The Mediterranean Spice Trade: Further Evidence of Its Revival in the Sixteenth Century." *American Historical Review* 45, no. 3 (Apr. 1940): 581–90.

Lewis, Bernard. *The Emergence of Modern Turkey.* London: Oxford Univ. Press, 1968.

Marsot, Afaf Lutfi al-Sayyid. *Women and Men in Late Eighteenth-Century Egypt.* Austin: Univ. of Texas Press, 1995.

Masters, Bruce. *The Origins of Western Economic Dominance in the Middle East: Mercantilism and the Islamic Economy in Aleppo, 1600–1750.* New York: New York Univ. Press, 1988.

Mendels, Franklin. "Proto-industrialization: The First Phase of the Industrialization Process." *Journal of Economic History* 32, no. 1 (1972): 241–61.

Mubarak, ʿAli. *al-Khitat al-Tawfiqiyya.* 2d ed. Cairo: al-Hayʾa al-ʿAmma lil-Kitab, 1969–94.

al-Muhibbi, Muhammad. *Khulasat al-athar fi aʿyan al-qarn al-hadi ʿashar.* (4 vols. Cairo: al-Matbaʿa al-Wahabiyya, 1284/1867.

Murphey, Rhoads. "Conditions of Trade in the Eastern Mediterranean, An Appraisal of Eighteenth-Century Ottoman Documents from Aleppo." *JESHO* 33 (1990): 35–50.

Owen, Roger. *The Middle East in the World Economy, 1800–1914.* London: Methuen, 1987.

Pearson, M. N. "Merchants and States." In *The Political Economy of Merchant Empires,* edited by James Tracy, 41–116. Cambridge: Cambridge Univ. Press, 1991.

Phillip, Thomas, and Moshe Perlmann, eds. *ʿAbd al-Rahman al-Jabarti's History of Egypt, ʿAjaʾib al-athar fi al-tarajim waʾl-akhbar.* Stuttgart: Franz Steiner Verlag, 1994.

Raymond, André. *Artisans et commerçants au Caire au XVIIIe siècle.* Damascus: Institut français de Damas, 1973.

———. "Le Déplacement des tanneries à l'époque ottomane," in *Villes du Levant: Revue du monde musulman et de la Mediterranée* 55–56 (1990): 34–43.

———. "La Fabrication et le commerce du sucre au Caire au XVIIIe siècle, l'effondrement d'une 'industrie' traditionelle." In *Sucre, sucreries et douceurs en Mediterranée,* 213–25. Paris: Centre national de la recherche scientifique, 1991.

———. "L'Impact de la pénétration européenne sur l'économie de l'Egypte au XVIIIe siècle." *Annales Islamologiques* 18 (1982): 217–35.

Raymond, André, and Gaston Wiet. *Les Marchés du Caire.* Cairo: Institut français d'archéologie orientale, 1979.

Rogers, Adrienne. "Women and the Law." In *French Women and the Age of Enlightenment,* edited by Samia I. Spencer, 33–48. Bloomington: Indiana Univ. Press, 1984.

Rogers, Katherine. *Feminism in Eighteenth Century England.* Urbana: Univ. of Illinois Press, 1982.

Sauvaget, Jean. "Les Caravanserails syriens du hadjdj de Constantinople." *Ars Islamica* 4 (1937): 98–121.

Schacht, Joseph. *Introduction to Islamic Law.* Oxford: Clarendon Press, 1964.

Shaw, Stanford. *The Financial and Administrative Organization and Development of Ottoman Egypt, 1517–1798.* Princeton, N.J.: Princeton Univ. Press, 1962.

——. *History of the Ottoman Empire and Modern Turkey.* Cambridge: Cambridge Univ. Press, 1987.

Shmuelevitz, Aryeh. *The Jews of the Ottoman Empire in the Late Fifteenth and the Sixteenth Centuries.* Leiden: Brill, 1984.

Shuman, Mohsen. "The Beginnings of Urban *iltizam* in Egypt." In *The State and Its Servants: Administration in Egypt from Ottoman Times to the Present,* edited by Nelly Hanna, 17–31. Cairo: American Univ. in Cairo Press, 1995.

Steensgaard, Niels. *The Asian Trade Revolution of the Seventeenth Century.* Chicago: Univ. of Chicago Press, 1974.

Sunar, Ilkay. "State and Economy in the Ottoman Empire." In *The Ottoman Empire and the World-Economy,* edited by Huri Islamoglu-Inan. Cambridge: Cambridge Univ. Press, 1987.

Thompson, Roger. *Women in Stuart England and America: A Comparative Study.* London: Routledge and Kegan Paul, 1974.

Trevor-Roper, Hugh R. "The General Crisis of the Seventeenth Century." *Past and Present* 16 (1959): 44–51.

Tuscherer, Michel. "Le Pélérinage de l'émir Sulayman Gawis al-Qazdughli, *sirdar* de la caravane de la Mekke en 1739." *Annales Islamologiques* 24 (1988): 155–204.

Udovitch, Abraham. "Credit as a Means of Investment in Medieval Islamic Trade." *Journal of the American Oriental Society* 87, no. 2 (Apr.–June 1967): 260–64.

——. *Partnership and Profit in Medieval Islam.* Princeton: Princeton Univ. Press, 1970.

Van Berchem, Max. *Matériaux pour un corpus inscriptionum Arabicarum,* Paris: Ernest Leroux, 1903.

Vansleb, F. *The Present State of Egypt.* London, J. Starkey, 1678.

Wallerstein, Immanuel. "The Ottoman Empire and the Capitalist World-Economy: Some Questions for Research." *Review* 2, no. 3 (winter 1979): 389–98.

Wallerstein, Immanuel, Hale Decdeli, and Resat Kasaba. "The Incorporation of the Ottoman Empire into the World-Economy." In *The Ottoman Empire and the World Economy,* edited by Huri Islamoglu-Inan, 88–97. Cambridge: Cambridge Univ. Press, 1987.

Wallerstein, Immanuel, and Resat Kasaba. "Incorporation into the World-Economy: Change in the Structure of the Ottoman Empire, 1750–1839." In *Economie et societe dans l'empire ottoman,* edited by Jean-Louis Bacque-Grammont and Paul Dumont, 335–53. Paris: Centre national de la recherche scientifique, 1983.

Walz, Terence. *Trade Between Egypt and Bilad al-Sudan.* Cairo: Institut français d'archéologie orientale, 1978.

———. "Trading into the Sudan in the Sixteenth Century." *Annales Islamologiques* 15 (1979): 211–33.

Wiet, Gaston. "Les Marchands d'épices sous les sultans mamlouks." *Cahiers d'histoire égyptienne* 7, no. 2 (May 1955): 81–147.

Wild, Johann. *Voyage en Egypte de Johann Wild, 1606–1610.* Cairo: Institut Français d'archéologie orientale, 1973.

Winter, Michael. *Egyptian Society under Ottoman Rule, 1517–1798.* London: Routledge, 1992.

Yusuf, Muhammad Sabri. *Dur al-mutasawwifa fi tarikh Misr fi al-ʿasr al-ʿUthmani,* Belbeis: Dar al-Taqwa, 1994.

Index

Italic page number denotes map reference.

'Abdul-Raziq, Nasir al-Din Ibrahim, 28
'Abdul-Wahab, Abu Qasis, 158
Abou-El-Haj, Rifa'at 'Ali, 2–3, 7, 8, 118
Abul Tib b. Mansur, 129
Abu Taqiyya, 'Abdul-Raziq: genealogy of
    Abu Taqiyya family, 177; as merchant,
    16, 22, 28; settling in Cairo, 24
Abu Taqiyya, Ahmad (father): death of,
    31; genealogy of Abu Taqiyya family,
    177; as al-Humsi, 21; maintaining ties
    with Bilad al-Sham, 25; as merchant,
    16, 22, 28; move from Hums to
    Cairo, 21, 22, 24; pilgrimage to
    Mecca, 30; sons trained as merchants
    by, 26; as *tajir saffar*, 18, 24; trade
    route of, 22–23, 23
Abu Taqiyya, Ahmad (son of
    'Abdul-Raziq), 24, 143, 177
Abu Taqiyya, Amna: after Abu Taqiyya's
    death, 163; Ahmad Ibn 'Ariqat as
    guardian of, 161, 162; as daughter of
    Razia al-Bayda, 155, 158; genealogy
    of Abu Taqiyya family, 178; marriage
    of, 158
Abu Taqiyya, Budur, 32, 141, 143, 177
Abu Taqiyya, Fadila, 155, 161, 162, 178
Abu Taqiyya, Fardus, 152, 153, 155, 157,
    160, 177
Abu Taqiyya, Fatma, 148, 155, 178
Abu Taqiyya, Fatma (Stita). *See* Abu
    Taqiyya, Stita

Abu Taqiyya, Isma'il: ability to maintain
    relationships, 40; as absent in
    contemporary chronicles, xvi; activities
    not directly related to commerce, xi;
    adapting to changing conditions, 78,
    98; agents of, 64; Ahmad Ibn 'Ariqat
    as guardian of children of, 161–62;
    and Ahmad Ibn 'Ariqat, 160–61; in
    al-Azbakiyya development, 135–37;
    children of, 153–55, 177–78;
    coffeehouse built by, 81; in coffee
    trade, 80; concubines of, 145, 155;
    court appearances of, xiii, xvii–xviii,
    11–12, 48, 50; credit sales, 67–68;
    daily itinerary of, 48; dates lacking for,
    21; dealings with Ottoman officials,
    108–9, 169; death of, 33, 162; and
    emirs, 114; and Fadli Pasha, 59, 109;
    family legal disputes with, 31–32,
    141; family of, xx, 16, 106, 138–64;
    friendship with al-Damiri, xx, 20, 32–
    34, 161; friends of, xx; genealogy of
    Abu Taqiyya family, 177; growing up
    in Cairo, 26–28; heirs of, 41; as
    al-Humsi, 21; international trading
    network of, 34–36, 46–47; as
    khawajaki, 19; as literate, 26; local
    trade of, 36, 46; male heirs lacking,
    39–40; marriages, 142–45, 177;
    marriage to 'Atiyat al-Rahman, 144;
    marriage to Badra Ibn 'Ariqat, 32,

Abu Taqiyya, Isma'il (*continued*)
143; marriage to Hana' b. Abdalla
al-Bayda, 144–45, 148; marriage to
Rumia b. 'Abdul-Raziq, 24, 143; and
the military, 113, 114; million *nisfs*
raised by, xiv; and *multazims*, 110–
11; partnership with al-Damiri, 32–
34, 56–59; partners of, 20; religious
attitudes of, xxii; residence in Darb
al-Shabrawi, 33, *49*, 132, 141, 156,
163; residences of, 33, 132;
ruling-class life-style of, 106; as
shahbandar al-tujjar, xv, 18, 19, 36–
39, 106, 126, 137; sibling
relationships, 32–33, 141–42; social
position of, 100; in sugar trade, 81,
82–84, 86, 87, 88–89, 90, 94, 96;
and Syrian merchants, 34; *tabi*'s of,
155–56; trading independently of his
family, 31–39; training as a merchant,
27–28; Venetian trade, 64–65, 93;
waqf provision for his family, 142;
*wikala*s of, xi, 11, 33, 125–26, 128–
31, 142; working his way up merchant
hierarchy, 16
Abu Taqiyya, Jami'a: after Abu Taqiyya's
death, 164; business representative of,
152; al-Damiri representing, 33, 161;
as daughter of 'Atiyat al-Rahman, 147;
death of, 164; genealogy of Abu
Taqiyya family, 177; as married to
Ahmad Ibn 'Ariqat, 157, 160; as
surviving Abu Taqiyya, 153
Abu Taqiyya, Karima b. Zakariyya, xxii,
158, 178
Abu Taqiyya, Laila: genealogy of Abu
Taqiyya family, 177; love of silk and
velvet, 132, 188n. 25; marriages of,
24, 143; relationship with Isma'il, xx,
32, 141; residence of, 129, 142; slave
owned by, 150
Abu Taqiyya, Rumia b. 'Abdul-Raziq:
after Abu Taqiyya's death, 163;
business representatives of, 152; family
visits to, 150; genealogy of Abu

Taqiyya family, 177; marriage to
Isma'il, 24, 143, 177
Abu Taqiyya, Salha, 148, 155, 178
Abu Taqiyya, Sayidat al-Kull, 32, 132,
141, 143, 177
Abu Taqiyya, Stita (Fatma): Ahmad Ibn
'Ariqat as guardian of, 161, 162;
genealogy of Abu Taqiyya family, 178;
marriages of, 116, 145, 157–58,
187n. 35
Abu Taqiyya, Tahira, 147, 148, 161, 163,
178
Abu Taqiyya, 'Umar b. Yasin, 154, 163
Abu Taqiyya, Umm al-Hana b. Isma'il:
after Abu Taqiyya's death, 163–64;
al-Damiri representing, 33, 161; as
daughter of 'Atiyat al-Rahman, 147;
death of, 164; genealogy of Abu
Taqiyya family, 178; marriage
contracts of, xix–xx, 159–60, 163;
marriages of, 158–60; as surviving her
father, 153
Abu Taqiyya, Umm al-Hana b. Zakariyya,
164, 178
Abu Taqiyya, Yahya, 28, 177
Abu Taqiyya, Yasin: after Abu Taqiyya's
death, 162–63; court case with
Isma'il, xx, 32, 141; dealing in large
sums while a young man, 27;
genealogy of Abu Taqiyya family, 177;
growing up in Cairo, 26–28; as
al-Humsi, 21; Isma'il as agent for, 63–
64; Isma'il's *waqf* provision for, 142;
as literate, 26; as merchant, 16, 28;
pilgrimage to Mecca, 30; residence of,
129, 132, 141–42; son of, 154, 163;
wikala construction, 128
Abu Taqiyya, Zakariyya: after Abu
Taqiyya's death, 163, 164; Ahmad Ibn
'Ariqat as guardian of, 161, 162;
business ability lacking in, 40–41;
children of, 178; as emir, 116;
genealogy of Abu Taqiyya family, 178;
inheritance of, 41, 155; interest in
trade as limited, 41; male heirs

lacking, 40, 154; as merchant, 16, 28, 41; in Mutafarriqa corps, 42, 116

Abu Taqiyya, Zayn al-Tujjar, 147, 161, 162, 178

Abu Taqiyya family: after Abu Taqiyya's death, 162–64; court appearances of, xix–xx; Hums as origin of, 22, 142; inheritance law affecting, 41; marital alliances with the military, 116; in merchant community, 18–19; as merchant family, 28–31, 39–42; as merchants, 16; move to Cairo, xx–xxi, 21–26; in Red Sea trade, 29–30; social mobility of, 16; social transformation spanning three generations, 100; in Syrian community in Cairo, 17–18, 142–43, 151–52. *See also family members by name*

Abyssinia, pashas of, 107

Africa: in Abu Taqiyya's trading network, 35–36; trans-Saharan caravan trade, 67. *See also* Cano

agency: *tawkil*, 63–64; *wakils*, 64

agriculture: cash crops, 12, 171; commercialization of, 85; cotton, 13, 91; flax, 85; grain, 171; under Muhammad 'Ali, 86, 171; production for trade, 12, 13, 14, 76, 84–95, 168; rice, 46, 85; in seventeenth and eighteenth centuries, 98. *See also* coffee; sugar

al-Ahaymar, 'Ali b. Abu Bakr, 151

al-Ahaymar, 'Atiyat al-Rahman b. Abu Bakr: after Abu Taqiyya's death, 163, 164; and Ahmad Ibn 'Ariqat's guardianship, 162; children of, 147; and concubines of Abu Taqiyya, 155; court appearances of, 151; al-Damiri representing, 33, 161; death of, 164; family visits to, 150; in household hierarchy, 148; inheritance from Abu Taqiyya, 189n. 10; marriage to Abu Taqiyya, 144, 177; property of, 151; residence of, 132; as *waqf* supervisor, 150, 151

al-Ahaymar, Hijazi b. Abu Bakr, 151

al-Ahaymar, Salih, 136

Ahmad Pasha, 59, 107, 109

Aleppo: Cairene merchants from, 24; Cairo documents recognized in, 51; foreign populations in, 17; growth of, 122; merchants of, 44; trade of, 21

Alexandria: as beneficiary of Red Sea trade, 75; Eastern Mediterranean map, 3; European *funduqs* in, 46; *multazim*s in, 111; Ottoman development of, 124; pashas building *wikala*s in, 107; Red Sea merchandise in, 35, 46; sugar exports to Europe, 90–91; Venetian goods in, 65; Venetian spice purchases at, 74, 77

'Ali Pasha, 101

amana, 38

America, 79, 171

amin al-sukkar, 96

al-Amini al-Hanafi, Muhammad b. Taj al-Din, 158

'Amir, Ja'far, 132

al-'Amriti, Abil Surur, 57

Anatolia: coffee houses in, 79; demand for goods in, 166; Egyptian coffee exports to, 80; sugar trade with Egypt, 96; textile production, 91

Ancona, 65

Ankara, 91

Antwerp, 123

'aqd shirka (partnership contract), 54; Abu Taqiyya entering into, 34, 54–59; conditions on, 57; duration of, 55; *mudaraba* compared with, 55; in organizing trade, 60–63; between al-Ruwi'i's, 53; subcontracts, 57–58; termination of, 62

al-Aqmar mosque, 48, 124

Arabia. *See* Hijaz; Yemen

architecture, 119

'Ariqat family. *See under* Ibn 'Ariqat

Armenians, 17, 52

artisans' guilds, 19, 37

Ashton, Thomas S., 14

Ashtor, Elyahu, 87, 179n. 5
al-ʿAsi, ʿAbdul-Qawi: court records for, xiii; heirs of, 145; as *shahbandar al-tujjar,* 37
al-ʿAsi, ʿAbdul-Raʾuf: court records for, xiii; as heir of ʿAbdul-Qawi, 145; *wikala*s in Bulaq, 128, 131
Asian trade: Ceylon, 35; China, 46; Dutch in, 76; European penetration of, 165; Portuguese penetration of, 74; South East Asia, 35. *See also* India
ʿAsi family, xii
Atchi, 35
Atlantic trade: and Egyptian prosperity, 14; Mediterranean trade supplanted by, 2, 5, 70; Middle Eastern merchants affected by, 165
al-ʿAttar, Muhammad b. Ahmad al-Humsi, 152
Austria, 46
ʿayn aʿyan al-tujjar, 18
al-Azbakiyya, 133–37; Birka al-Azbakiyya, *134,* 135; Cairo map, *134;* coffeehouse in, 81; Darb al-Nubi quarter, 122; expansion of, 127; infrastructure in, 136
Azhar, the, 17, 120, *134*

Bab al-Futuh, 119, *134*
Bab ʿAli, court of, xvii–xviii, *49,* 50, 51, 54, 68, 109, 129, 133, 151
Bab al-Luq, *134*
Bab al-Nasr, *49,* 89, 119, *134*
Bab al-Shaʾriyya, *134*
Bab Zuwayla, 82, 119, 131, *134*
Baer, Gabriel, 89
al-Bakri, 115, 153
banking, 54
Barquq, Sultan, 124
Barsbay, Sultan, 73, 95, 104
baths (*hammam*s), 133, 136, 152
Bayazid Bey Mir Liwa, 111, 113
Bayn al-Qasrayn, *49,* 124, 129, *134*
Bayram Pasha, 107

beys, 115
Bilad al-Rum. *See* Anatolia
Bilad al-Sham: Ahmad Abu Taqiyya maintaining links with, 21, 22, *23,* 25–26; Ismaʿil Abu Taqiyya trading with, 34; links with Egypt, 24–25; partnership contracts in, 56; *riwaq* at the Azhar for, 17
Bilad al-Sudan, 35
Bilad al-Takrur, 35
bills of exchange, 61
bint al-jaria, 155
Birka al-Azbakiyya, *134,* 135
Birka al-Fil, *134,* 135
Birka al-Ratli, *134,* 135
Bloch, Marc, 11
boating, 135
Bowen, Harold, 7
Braudel, Fernand, 2, 64–65, 74, 76, 77, 83
Brenner, Robert, 12
brigandage, 56, 60
Britain, 13, 112
Brouwer, C. G., 187n. 14
building construction. *See* construction projects
Bulaq: al-ʿAsi's *wikala*s in, 128, 131; Ottoman pashas building in, 124; Sinan Pasha building *wikala* in, 107; sugar refineries in, 81, 82
al-Burdayni, Karim al-Din, 38, 107, 121
Bursa, 91

Cairo, 119–37; the Azhar, 17, 120, *134;* Bayn al-Qasrayn, *49,* 124, 129, *134;* as beneficiary of Red Sea trade, 75; coffeehouses in, 80, 81; coffee trade in, 79; court records as source for history of, xxi; as distribution center, 66; Eastern Mediterranean map, *3;* growth of, 122–23; literacy in, 26, 181n. 10; main thoroughfare of, 119; merchants and their families, 15–42; merchants in development of, 121–

27; northern section of, *49;* as religious center, 120; in 1600, 119–20; sugar trade in, 79, 81, 82, 87, 88; *suq*s, 132; Syrians in, xx–xxi, 17, 24–25, 39; trade routes through, 22, 119, 181n. 4. *See also* al-Azbakiyya

Calicut, 35

Cano: Abu Taqiyya's agent in, 35, 46, 64; Abu Taqiyya's trade with, 35, 63

capitalism: eighteenth-century merchants and, 92; Ottoman Empire incorporated into European, 4–7, 71–72, 73, 172–73; transition from feudal society to, 8

capitulations (*imtiyazat*), 112

cash: currency transformation, 125; inflation of early seventeenth century, 77; for purchases, 67; transport of, 60–61

cash crops, 12, 171

Castela, Henry, 80

Ceylon, 35

Chabrol, M. de, 26–27, 181n. 10

Chaudhari, K. N., 186n. 3

children: of Abu Taqiyya, 153–55; of concubines, 147, 155; distinctions between, 154; education of boys, 26–27; infant mortality, 153–54; obedience to parents, 154; stages of childhood, 27

China, 46

chronicles, xv–xvi, 21, 121

coffee, 79–81; demand increasing for, 79; Egyptian monopoly in trade in, 71, 79; in Europe, 81, 184n. 14; in Red Sea trade, 35–36

coffeehouses (*kahvekhans*), 79–80, 81, 130, 184n. 14

coins. *See* cash

commenda (*mudaraba*), 55

commerce. *See* trade

concubines, 147–48; of Abu Taqiyya, 145, 155; marriages of daughters of Abu Taqiyya's, 157; *mustawalidas*, 147–48

confiscations, 102–3, 115, 125–26

conspicuous consumption, 126

construction projects: of merchants, xi, 9–10, 121–33; *wikalas*, 127–33

contracts: marriage, 159–60. *See also* '*aqd shirka*

coppersmiths' market (Suq al-Nahhasin), *49,* 129, 132

Copts, 155

coral, 12

cotton, 13, 91

court records: family life in, xix–xx, 140; ordinary people in, xvi; registration of documents, 53; as source for socioeconomic history, xv–xxii; as source for this study, xiii

courts. *See* legal system

credit: debts, 61, 68; as fund-raising form, 54; sales on credit, 67–68; *suftaja* (letter of credit), 61. *See also* loans

Cuno, Kenneth, 85

customs duties, 74

customs officials. *See multazim*s

Cyprus, 83

Dabhol, 35, 77

dallal, 66

Damascus: Abu Taqiyya exports sugar to, 90; Cairo documents recognized in, 51; Eastern Mediterranean map, *3;* goods purchased at, 60

Damietta (Dumyat): coffeehouses in, 80; Eastern Mediterranean map, *3;* as major eastern Mediterranean port, 46; Red Sea merchandise in, 35, 46; rice exports, 85

al-Damiri, 'Abdul-Qadir: in coffee trade, 80; death of, 40; early business deal with Abu Taqiyya, 28; friendship with Abu Taqiyya, xx, 20, 32–34, 161; Mecca and Jedda as concern of, 36, 63; partnership with Abu Taqiyya, 32–34, 56–59; as polygamous, 145; residing in Khatt al-Amshatiyyin, 33;

al-Damiri, ʿAbdul-Qadir (*continued*)
    *wikala*s built with Abu Taqiyya,
    128–31; and Zakariyya Abu Taqiyya,
    40
al-Damiri, Abu Bakr: loans for travel, 63;
    traveling to Mecca and Jedda, 61–62,
    63; ventures with Abu Taqiyya, 32
Darb al-Shabrawi, 33, *49*, 124, 132, 141,
    156, 163
Darb al-Tahun, *49*, 120, 132, 163
Darb al-Warraqa, *49*
debts, 61, 68
Delta, the: in Abu Taqiyya's trading
    network, 35–36, 46, 64, 82;
    al-Gharbiyya, 36, 88; al-Munufiyya,
    36, 84, 86, 88
al-Dhahabi, Jamal al-Din: residence and
    wikala, 121, 128; as *shahbandar
    al-tujjar*, 37, 94; in sugar trade, 82,
    87
al-Dimishqi, 182n. 5
distribution of merchandise, 66–68
Diu, 35
divorce, 139, 159
Dumyat. *See* Damietta
Dutch East India Company, 76, 93, 109

Egypt: commercial ties with Syria, 25–26;
    and European capitalism, 4–7;
    expansion of cultivable land in, 85;
    international trade as transit trade, 97;
    Ismaʿil, 172; new trading trends in, 8–
    14; peripheralization of, 92, 166;
    political crisis in, 70; raw materials
    exported from, 6, 170; Saʿid, 172;
    sugar trade in, 12, 13, 82–83, 166,
    167. *See also* Alexandria; Bulaq; Cairo;
    Damietta; Delta, the; Mamluks;
    Muhammad ʿAli; Rashid
elementary schools, 26–27, 121, 136,
    181n. 10
emirs, 13, 114, 145, 169
endowments. *See waqf*
England, 13, 112

epidemic of 1028/1618, 153–54
Europe: Alexandrian sugar exports to,
    90–91; Antwerp, 123; in Asian trade,
    165; Austria, 46; Britain, 13, 112;
    coffee in, 81, 184n. 14; competing for
    Mediterranean trade, 77, 93;
    competition with Egyptian textiles, 6,
    171; Dutch East India Company, 76,
    93, 109; Fuggers and Welsers, 9;
    *funduq*s in Alexandria, 46; Hara
    al-Afranj for, 26; *imtiyazat* for, 112;
    linen exports, 98; mercantile relations
    with Ottoman Empire, 165; Muslim
    merchants in, 64–65; Ottoman
    Empire incorporated into European
    capitalism, 4–7, 71–72, 73, 172–73;
    Salonica, 35, 46. *See also* France; Italy;
    Portuguese
exchange of merchandise, 66–68

Fadli Pasha, 59, 109
fakhr al-tujjar, 18
families: in court records, xix–xx; family
    life, 138–64; household hierarchy,
    145–53; marriages within, 17;
    patriarchy, xx, 139–40; professions
    transmitted by, 16. *See also* children;
    marriage
famine, 123
Farah (wife of Abu Bakr al-Ahaymar),
    151
Faroqhi, Suraiya, 91
al-Farra, ʿAli, 136
fiqh, xix, 48–49
flax, 85
Florence, 46
followers (*tabiʿs*), 106, 150, 155–56
*fondaco*s, 65
fountains, 121, 126, 130, 136
France: *funduq* in Alexandria, 46; grain
    demand in, 171; *imtiyazat* for, 112;
    linen imports, 98
friendship, xx, 33–34
Fuggers, 9

fund raising, 53–59. *See also* credit;
   pooling of capital
funduqs, 46

Gaza, *3*
Geniza documents, xxi, 68–69
Geniza merchants, 46, 52
Genoa, 46, 79
Gerber, Haim, 49–50, 91
al-Ghamri, 120
al-Gharbiyya, 36, 88
Ghayt al-Hamzawi, 135
Ghayt al-Ja'bari, 108
Ghazaleh, Pascale, 89
Ghubrial, 155
al-Ghuri, Sultan, 82, 95
Ghuriyya, 28, *49, 134*
Gibb, Hamilton R., 7
Goa, 77
Goitein, S. D., xxi, 52, 61, 68–
   69
gold. *See* cash
government. *See* state, the
governors. *See* pashas
grain, 171
Gran, Peter, 13, 14, 170, 171
guilds: artisans' and tradesmen's
   guilds, 19, 37; in Cairo, 19; in
   production, 89–90. *See also*
   merchants' guild

Hajir al-Bayda, 155
hajj (pilgrimage), 30–31, 67
hall (*qa'a*), 146, 156
Hama, *3*
al-Hamawi, Rajab, 64
Hamdun b. 'Abdalla al-Habashi, 65
Hammam al-Sultan Inal, 133
hammams (baths), 133, 136, 152
Hana' b. Abdalla al-Bayda, 144–45, 148,
   177
Hanafi legal school, 51
Hanbali legal school, 51, 57

hara (residential quarter): in Cairo, 26;
   merchants in development of, 121,
   122; as social group, 15
Hara al-Afranj, 26
Hara al-Maghariba, 26
Harant, Christophe, 46, 132, 181n. 3
harim, 149
Hasan Pasha, 108
hasils (storerooms), 130
Herat, 46
Heyd, Wilhelm, 179n. 5
Hijaz: in Abu Taqiyya's trading network,
   46; Cairo documents recognized in,
   63; Jewish *multazims* trading with,
   111. *See also* Jedda; Mecca
al-Hinnawi, Muhammad, 68
Holt, P. M., 102
household, hierarchies in, 145–53
houses, 145–46
Hovhannes, 44
Hums: Eastern Mediterranean map, *3;*
   families in Cairo, 25–26; as origin of
   Abu Taqiyya family, 22, 142
al-Humsi, Ahmad Ibn Siddiq, 152

Ibn 'Abdul-Ghani, Ahmad Shalabi,
   107
ibn al-jaria, 155
Ibn al-Muhalhal al-Jizi, Qadi Shams
   al-Din Muhammad, 158, 159
Ibn 'Ariqat, 'Abdul-Mu'ti, 152
Ibn 'Ariqat, 'Abdul-Nabi b. Zayn al-Din,
   143, 177
Ibn 'Ariqat, Abu Bakr, 143, 177
Ibn 'Ariqat, Ahmad: in Abu Taqiyya
   family business, 34, 40–41, 59; after
   Abu Taqiyya's death, 163, 164; Abu
   Taqiyya's relationship with, 160–61;
   Abu Taqiyya's *waqf* provision for, 142,
   160; death of, 164; as guardian of
   Abu Taqiyya's minor children, 160–
   61; as married to Jami'a, 157, 160;
   Rumia Abu Taqiyya represented by,
   152

Ibn ʿAriqat, Badra b. ʿAbdul-Rahman:
after Abu Taqiyya's death, 163;
brother ʿUthman as representative of,
151–52; family visits to, 150; in
household hierarchy, 148–49;
marriage to Ismaʿil Abu Taqiyya, 32,
143, 177; as *waqf* supervisor, 150
Ibn ʿAriqat, ʿUthman ʿAly al-Din, 151–52
Ibn ʿAriqat family: marriages with Abu
Taqiyyas, 143, 157; migration to
Cairo, 25; Syrian origin of, 24. *See also*
family members by name
Ibn Kuwayk family, 39
Ibn Yaghmur, Muhammad: in
al-Azbakiyya development, 135; court
records for, xiii; as monogamous, 145;
as *tajir saffar,* 24
Ibn Yaghmur, ʿUthman: in al-Azbakiyya
development, 135; court records for,
xiii; as *shahbandar al-tujjar,* 24, 37
Ibn Yaghmur family: archival records of,
xii; inheritance in, 41; Syrian origin of,
24–25, 30. *See also family members by*
name
Ibrahim (Mutafarriqa), Muhammad b.
Ahmad b. *al-sayyid al-sharif,* 158,
178, 187n. 35
Ibrahim Afandi b. Diaʾ al-Din
Muhammad, 157–58
Ibrahim Pasha, 107, 125
*iltizam*s (tax farms): loans for purchasing,
84; military groups controlling, 101,
104, 113, 114. *See also multazims*
imtiyazat (capitulations), 112
Inalcik, Halil, 72
India: in Abu Taqiyya's trade network,
34–35, 58, 77; demand for textiles
from, 165; Goa, 77; Portuguese in,
34, 74
indigo, 36
industrialization, 13–14, 91–92
infant mortality, 153–54
inflation, 77
infrastructure, 121, 126, 128, 136–37
inheritance, 41, 51

international trade: Abu Taqiyya's trading
network, 34–36, 46–47; in
agricultural products, 13; and Cairo's
expansion, 123; difficulties of, 22–23;
economic change affected by, 97; links
to other aspects of the economy, 168;
routes through Cairo, 22, 119; state
intervention in, 72, 169;
trans-Saharan caravan trade, 67;
vitality of, 9. *See also* Asian trade;
Atlantic trade; Mediterranean trade;
Red Sea trade
investment: in agriculture, 86; in sugar,
83–84, 169; trade and industry, 169;
in urban development, 121–27
Iran (Persia), 21, 52, 132, 189n. 123
Iskandar Pasha, 107
Islamic law. *See shariʿa*
Islamoglu-Inan, Huri, 4, 6, 7
Ismaʿil (Khedive), 172
Istanbul: in Abu Taqiyya's trading
network, 35, 46, 78; Cairo documents
recognized in, 51; coffeehouses in, 80;
as religious center, 120; sugar imports,
96
Italy: *funduq*s in Alexandria, 46; Muslim
merchants trading with, 65. *See also*
Venice
Iznik ware, 106, 138, 156

al-Jabalawi, Abu Bakr, 64
al-Jabarti, xv–xvi, 37–38
Jamiʿ al-Nubi, 136
Janissaries, 96
Jedda: in Abu Taqiyya's trade network,
34–35; Cairo documents recognized
in, 51; coffee trade, 80; commerce
with Cairo, 61, 63, 93; as entrepôt for
Indian goods, 29; merchants'
representatives in, 47
Jennings, Ronald, 49–50
Jerusalem, 17, 51, 90
jewelry, 132
Jews, 109

al-Jiritli, ʿAli, 91
justice. *See* legal system

kahvekhans (coffeehouses), 79–80, 81, 130, 184n. 14
Kaplanian, A., 187n. 14
Karimis: Cairo merchants compared with, 46; disappearance of, 75; family enterprises among, 39; geographical extension of trade, 77; and the ruling class, 104; spice trade monopoly, 29, 73
Kasaba, Resat, 4, 6, 7
kashif, 114
Katkhuda, Mustafa, 136
Khan Abu Taqiyya Street, 33, 121
Khan al-Hamzawi, *49*, 124
Khan al-Khalili, *49*, 132, *134*
Kharrubi family, 39
khatib (marriage intermediary), 157
al-Khatib, Ahmad, 131
Khatt al-Amshatiyyin, 33, *49*, 88, 124
Khatt al-Khurunfish (Khatt al-Khurushtuf), *49*
Khatt al-Khurushtuf (Khatt al-Khurunfish), *49*, 129, 132, 141–142
Khatt Sirr al-Maristan, 128–29, 130, 131
khawajaki, 18–19
khazna nawmiyya (sleeping area), 146
kuttabs (elementary schools), 27, 121, 136, 181n. 10

land acquisition, 129–30
landowning classes, 118
land tenure, 84–85
Lane, Edward, 154
Lane, Frederic C., 74
Laval, Pyrard de, 77
legal system: debt collection, 68; economic influence on, 8; extensive use of, xvii; family disputes, xix–xx;

merchants' use of, 10–12; *shahbandar al-tujjar* in court cases, 38; for trade, 48–53. *See also* court records; *madhhabs*; *shariʿa*
letter of credit (*suftaja*), 61
Lewis, Bernard, 1
linen, 85, 98, 167
literacy, 26, 181n. 10
loans: from merchants to pashas, 107; from merchants to the military, 114; from merchants to those in power, 169; Ottoman fund raising, 54; for sugar production, 84
loggia (*maqʿad*), 146, 156
long-distance trade. *See* international trade
luxury goods, 12, 35, 132

madhhabs: in business cases, 51; in Cairo courts, xvii; Hanafi legal school, 51; Hanbali legal school, 51, 57; Maliki legal school, 51, 182n. 23; Shafiʿi legal school, 51
Mahmud Pasha, 108
al-Mahruqi, Sayyid Muhammad, 37
Mahruqi family, 37
maktabs (elementary schools), 27, 121, 136, 181n. 10
Malabar, 35
Maliki legal school, 51, 182n. 23
Mamluks: Barsbay, 73, 95, 104; beys, 115; in Cairo's development, 119, 124; centralized state of, 72; in commercial agriculture, 13; court system of, 10; Egypt and Syria as unified under, 25; al-Ghuri, 82, 95; and the Karimis, 104; loans from merchants, 114; monuments of, 126; reemergence of, 101; sugar monopoly, 95, 97
al-Mansuri, Ibrahim, 121
maqʿad (loggia), 146, 156
market inspector (*muhtasib*), 89
markets. *See suqs*

marriage: of Abu Taqiyya's children, 157–
60; within families, 17; merchants'
patterns of, 10, 20; polygamy, 139,
145, 159; within Syrian community,
18; termination of, 139, 159. *See also*
wives
marriage contracts, 159–60
marriage intermediary (*khatib*), 157
Marseilles, 171
Marsot, Afaf Lutfi al-Sayyid, 189n. 9
maskans (lodgings), 146
Masters, Bruce, 21, 44
Matbakh al-Qawwas, 88–89, 142
Mecca: Cairo documents recognized in,
51; Cairo trade, 56, 63; as entrepôt
for Indian goods, 29, 34; *hajj,* 30, 67
Mediterranean trade: Abu Taqiyya's
trading network, 34–35, 46; and
Atlantic trade, 2, 4–5, 70; decline
alleged in, 70; European nations
competing for, 77, 93
merchandise, exchange and distribution
of, 66–68
merchants, 15–42; activities not directly
related to commerce, xi, 9–10;
adapting to changing conditions, 78;
in agricultural production, 84–95;
associations of, 8; confiscations from,
102–3, 115, 125–26; corporate entity
not created by, 104; al-Dimishqi's
classification of, 182n. 5; diversity of,
45; emerging from anonymity, xii, 9–
10, 71, 73–76, 102; European impact
on, 4–5, 8; families of, 28, 39, 47;
frameworks of action of, 168–69;
investments by, 86, 169; legal system
used by, 10–12; marriage patterns of,
10, 20; obituaries of, xv; and the
pashas, 107–8, 115; in political
transformation, xii–xiii, 167; and the
power structure, 104–16, 167; raw
materials exported by, 4, 6; roles in
Ottoman Empire, 102–4; ruling-class
life-style of, 106; specialized skills
lacking in, 44; and the state, 102–3;

sukkaris, 87, 89, 185n. 40; ties
between, 20; titles of, 18–19;
transformations in condition of, 71,
100, 116–18; in urban development,
121–27; *wikala* construction, 127–
33. *See also* Karimis; trade
merchants' guild, 19–20; and
transformation of merchants' condition,
117. *See also shahbandar al-tujjar*
military, the: Janissaries, 96; merchants'
relations with, 112–16; and the
pashas, 114–15; power structure
dominated by, 167; troop revolt of
1586, 133–34. *See also ujaqs*
min a'yan al-tujjar, 18
modernization, 170–72
molasses, 88
money. *See* cash
money changer (*sarraf*), 66
monogamy, 145
monopolies: of Barsbay, 73, 95, 104; of
coffee by Cairo merchants, 79;
discontinuation of state, 73; of spice
trade by Karimi, 29, 73
monuments, public, 119–20, 124
mosques, 121, 124–25, 130, 136
mubashir (secretary), 155
mudaraba (*commenda*), 55
Muhammad Afandi, 108
Muhammad 'Ali: agriculture put under state
supervision by, 171; industrialization
under, 14, 91–92, 171; and mercantile
investment in agriculture, 86;
Muhammad al-Mahruqi and, 37;
state-run system of, 7, 171, 172
Muhammad 'Izz al-Din Badir, 64
Muharram, Mahmud, xv
muhtasib (market inspector), 89
Mukha: in Abu Taqiyya's trading network,
34–35, 64; Cairo documents recognized
in, 51; yearly ship to, 61, 109
multazims (customs officials; tax farmers):
in agricultural production, 84, 86;
Jewish customs officials in Venetian
trade, 65, 83, 93; Jews as, 109;

merchants' relations with, 107, 109–12; payments by, 113. *See also iltizams*
al-Munufiyya, 36, 84, 86, 88
Musa b. Khalafa, 111, 113
Musa Pasha, 115
Mustafa Pasha, 115, 125
mustawalidas, 147–48
Mutafarriqa corps, 42, 113, 116, 158, 187n. 35

Naharun b. Da'ud b. Salamon, 112
naqib, 39
al-Nasiriyya, *134*
al-Nasir Muhammad b. Qalawun, 124
al-Nubi, Ahmad, 122, 136
Nusuh b. 'Abdalla, 114

obituaries, xv
Ottoman Empire: core-periphery changes in, 100–102; court system in, xvii; diversity within regions of, 72–73, 167; the Eastern Mediterranean, *3;* economic stagnation in, 2–3; incorporation into European capitalism, 4–7, 71–72, 73, 172–73; peripheralization of, 4, 75–76; political crisis in, 70–71, 112–13; political transformation in, xii–xiii; raw materials exported from, 4, 6, 9, 170; between sixteenth and eighteenth centuries, 1–14; social similarity of different regions, 25; social structure of, 100–118; as static, 7; Sulayman, 23, 100; Venetian trade, 92–93. *See also* Anatolia; Egypt; Istanbul; state, the; Syria

partnership contract. *See 'aqd shirka*
pashas, 101; conflicts with the military, 114–15; merchants' relations with, 107–8, 115; monuments of, 126; in urban development, 124–25

patriarchy, xx, 139–40
Pearson, M. N., 72
pepper, 21, 73, 76, 104
Persia (Iran), 21, 52, 132, 189n. 123
pilgrimage (*hajj*), 30–31, 67
polygamy, 139, 145, 159
ponds. *See under* Birka
pooling of capital: as fund-raising form, 54, 60. *See also 'aqd shirka*
Portuguese: in Asian spice trade, 34, 74; Dutch competing with, 76
prices: for coffee, 80; fluctuation of, 67; for spices, 77, 80; for sugar, 84, 96
private sphere, 149–50
profits, division of, 62
property rights of wives, 150–51, 153
"Protestant ethic," 106–7
public sphere, 149–50

qa'a (hall), 146, 156
qabban (weigher of goods), 66
Qadi al-Qudat, xviii, 50, 107, 109, 133
Qalawun complex, 48, *49*, 124, *134*
al-Qarafi, Badr, 122
Qisma 'Arabiyya, court of, *49*, 129
Qisma 'Askariyya, court of, *49*, 129
Qitas Bey, 115
quarters, residential. *See hara*
Qusun, Emir, 119

Radwan Bey, 115, 131
al-rajul al-kamil, 27
Ramadan, 50
Rashid (Rosetta): Eastern Mediterranean map, *3;* Ottoman development of, 124; pashas building *wikalas* in, 107; Red Sea merchandise in, 35, 46
al-Rashidi, Muhammad, 30
raw materials: export from Ottoman Empire, 4, 6, 9, 170; guild control over, 89, 90; military control over, 113

Raymond, André, 29, 37, 61, 82, 87, 98–99, 122, 132, 171

Razia al-Bayda, 155, 158

Red Sea trade, 29–30; Cairo on route, 22; coffee, 36; dangers of, 56; Indian trade, 34–35; Karimi spice trade monopoly, 29, 73; in merchant hierarchy, 19; before nineteenth century, 12–13; pepper, 21; seasonal winds hampering, 29, 61; spice trade after Portuguese penetration, 74

registration of documents, 53

residential quarters. See hara

rice, 46, 85

Roccheta, Aquilante, 46

Rosetta. See Rashid

al-Rukn al-Mukhallaq, 128, 134

al-Ruwi'i, Ahmad: in al-Azbakiyya development, 136; coffeehouse built by, 81; court records for, xiii; as head of family enterprise, 30; partnership contract with 'Ali, 53

al-Ruwi'i, 'Ali: court records for, xiii; as head of family enterprise, 30; partnership contract with Ahmad, 53; as shahbandar al-tujjar, 30, 36–37; in sugar trade, 94

al-Ruwi'i, 'Isa, 30

al-Ruwi'i, Muhammad, 30

Ruwi'i family: court records for, xii; as merchant family, 30, 39; and al-Sawwaf, 52, 64; in sugar trade, 82, 87, 88. See also family members by name

al-Ruwi'i quarter, 121, 127

Sadat al-Wafa'iyya order, xxii, 120, 158

al-Safadi, Mustafa, 61, 80

Sa'id (pasha), 172

Salamon b. Da'ud b. Salamon, 65

salam shari'i, 83–84, 86–87

sales on credit, 67–68

Salihiyya Najmiyya, court of, 49, 50, 129

Salonica, 35, 46

Samarqand, 46

sarraf (money changer), 66

al-Sawwaf, Ahmad, 52, 64

Sayma al-Bayda, 147, 148, 153, 155, 163

scholars. See 'ulama'

schools, elementary, 27, 121, 136, 181n. 10

servants, 149

Shafi'i legal school, 51

shahbandar al-tujjar, 36–39; Abu Taqiyya as, xv, 18, 19, 36–39, 106, 126, 137; in merchant hierarchy, 19; prestige of, 9, 19, 117; responsibilities of, 37–38; social position of, 38–39; in sugar trade, 94; in urban development, 122

Shalum b. Murdukhay, 111

Shams al-Din Muhammad b. Salama, 129

al-Shanawani, Muhammad, 84, 86

Shara' Khan Abu Taqiyya, 33, 121

Shara'ibi family, 37

al-Sha'rani, 'Abdul-Wahab, xvi, 120

al-Sharaybi, Qasim, xv

shari'a: business law in accord with, 69; fiqh, xix, 48–49; in Ottoman courts, xvii, 11

Shaul, 35

Shaw, Stanford, 1, 85, 96, 101, 102, 113

Shaykh al-Turi, 136

shaykhs, 18, 19, 36, 89, 120

shipwreck, 56

Shu'a b. Da'ud b. Salamon, 112

al-Shuja'i, Nur al-Din: court records for, xiii; loan from his children, 53; residence of, 132; and son's concubines, 149; two million nisfs raised by, xiv

al-Shuja'i, Sulayman, 135

Shuja'i family, xii, 39

silk: Aleppo trade in, 21; Armenian merchants in, 52; Bursa trade in, 91; Suq al-Harir, 28, 32, 49, 120, 132; Syrians in industry, 17, 26

simsar, 66

property owners, 150–51, 153; receiving visitors, 150; slaves owned by, 150; status of, 147

women: multiple roles of, 139; private sphere associated with, 149–50. *See also* concubines; wives

Yaghmur family. *See under* Ibn Yaghmur

Yemen: in Abu Taqiyya's trading network, 46; agricultural production for trade, 168; coffee production, 79, 184n. 16; pashas of, 107, 109; Sinan Pasha's expedition to, 101. *See also* Mukha

Yusuf b. Husayn Jawish, 114

*zawiya*s, 120